MANIFEST

MANIFEST
Our Call to Faithful Creativity

Edited by Nathan Brown and Joanna Darby

SIGNS PUBLISHING®
Established 1885

Proudly published and printed in Australia by

SIGNS PUBLISHING®
Established 1885

Signs Publishing Company
Warburton, Victoria

This Book Was
Edited by Nathan Brown and Joanna Darby
Proofread by Lindy Schneider and Kerry Arbuckle
Designed by Shane Winfield
Cover designed by Shane Winfield
Cover illustration "After the Flood" by Joanna Darby
Typeset in Myriad Pro Light 11/13

ISBN 978 1 921292 85 9

"Everything was created through Him and for Him."

—Colossians 1:16

DEDICATIONS

Nathan dedicates this book . . .

To my mum on her retirement after more than 23 years as the exhibitions coordinator for a major regional art gallery. Growing up in her home introduced me to artistic creativity as a normal, important, worthwhile, wonderful and faithful thing.

Joanna dedicates this book . . .

To Dr Wayne French—a man whom I have watched empower and give wing to countless individuals to explore their creativity within various ministry contexts, with encouragement, impossible trust, and incredible freedom—including myself.

COVER IMAGE

"After the Flood" **Joanna Darby** acrylic and enamel on board, 160cm x 180cm, 2007

There's something extraordinary and mesmerising about the scene after the flood (see Genesis 6) . . .

A world ravaged and devastated.

Completely destroyed.

Laid waste.

A landscape that was hopeless and despairing.

But even in that rubble He saw potential! And so the dullest places start to sprout colour. The grim fades. The grey is rubbed out. Life is re-awakened. The bland buds with beauty. Every tint and hue is re-applied.

And the earth breathes again. So different from a first breath.

This—a sensational rejuvenation!

It's unlike the day flowers were first flung over the fields.

This—a second chance!

It's more than making something from nothing—it's making lovely from awful, beauty from ugly.

This—a resurrection of sorts.

It's a resuscitation on the grandest scale. It's life from death!

This—a picture of grace!

He saw beauty in that which seemed ruined—hope for every "stumped" artist, every poet facing "writers block," and every musician struggling to salvage a melody.

He saw beauty in that which seemed ruined—hope for every sinner.

This—is re-Creation.

OUR CALL TO FAITHFUL CREATIVITY
Foreword

It's a message Christian artists, entertainers and record companies needed to hear. At a time when they were developing what the late Bob Briner called a dangerously entrenched posture, he asked in his book *Roaring Lambs*: "In light of Christ's call to be salt and light in the culture around us, why do we want to keep all this talent huddled behind church walls?"[1]

Too often, faithful creativity has been missing from our culture—at the same time, it has only had limited or narrow acceptance within the church itself. At times, it seems the choice has been to be faithful (in the church) or to be creative (in the world). In many respects, we have not done well at embracing and encouraging faithful creativity . . . anywhere.

One reason for this is we are not sure what to do with culture. Christians typically appropriate, condemn or consume culture, says William Romanowski, author of *Pop Culture Wars*.[2] Our true calling, he says: to *transform* culture. And I'll add: from the inside—inside our churches *and* inside our broader culture. The influence of the mass media on popular culture means artists are best placed to meet this challenge.

Manifest Creative Arts Festival explores, encourages and celebrates faithful creativity, particularly through the arts. It began with the first of what is now an annual arts festival in 2011 after Avondale College of Higher Education and Signs Publishing Company had collaborated over six years on book launches and writing seminars. Inspiration for the festival also came in part from the Adventist Church-sponsored SONscreen Film Festival. Manifest is also a producer (of creative worship services) and a publisher (of a blog, an e-newsletter and a Facebook page—and now a book). The Seventh-day Adventist Church in the South Pacific coordinates Manifest through Adventist Media Network and Avondale.

Most importantly, Manifest seeks to create a community of artists. *Manifest: Our Call to Faithful Creativity* is an example of this community—a number of the writers are Manifest alumni. It is an expression of a common belief: churches need to foster creativity and become centres for creativity and creative influence in our communities.

We recognise a common belief is meaningless, though, unless it influences behaviour. In *Flickering Pixels*, Shane Hipps writes about how technology shapes your faith. He also asks: "How does your faith actually manifest in this world to bring about justice, altruism, compassion, and peace?"[3]

So *Manifest: Our Call to Faithful Creativity* is also an acknowledgment of the fallenness of our world and the brokenness of our lives. Wisdom calls us to seek redemption, to act justly and to love mercy. Faithfulness calls us to share these truths in partnership with our Creator and Re-Creator.

This book will help you better appreciate creativity and perhaps challenge some of your perceptions and attitudes. It will inspire you, but it will not act for you. Our call to faithful creativity is also your call and we must each respond faithfully.

Manifest welcomes you to our community. Join us in print, in person or online.

Brenton Stacey

Co-convenor
Manifest Creative Arts Festival

1. Bob Briner, *Roaring Lambs: A Gentle Plan to Radically Change Your World*, Zondervan, 1993.

2. William Romanowski, *Pop Culture Wars: Religion and the Role of Entertainment in American Life*, Wipf & Stock Publishers, 2006.

3. Shane Hipps, *Flickering Pixels: How Technology Shapes Your Faith*, Zondervan, 2009.

CONTENTS

A STORY OF A CONVERSATION THAT BECAME A BOOK WITH A PAINTING ON ITS COVER

Introduction

Of course, like many good stories, it is hard to pinpoint where this really began. Many conversations had led to this one.

It was a sunny autumnal morning. The kind that you see pictured on a child's seasons chart—blue skies, trees dappled with the warmest hues, and just a friendly dancing breeze. It's also the kind that generates confused ensembles of scarves and sandals, cardigans and shorts.

Seated on stools in the corner of Café Rejuve, on the campus of Avondale College, were two writers nursing warm drinks and thumbing last week's edition of the student newspaper. The gentle sounds and aromas of the cafe eddied around us.

The first conversations—more than 18 months earlier—had looked similar to this one and had occurred in this same place, sparked by mutual friends suggesting we should talk to each other about making books. Except, rather than sitting in the warmth of spring, we were now inside, looking out across the lawn at students coming and going in their confused autumnal attire.

We paused for a few moments after a meeting reviewing the recent Manifest Creative Arts Festival. It was a moment of relief, celebration and more planning for the next festival. After catching our breaths, hands wrapped around warm paper cups, we reported on the respective church camps we had contributed to over the Easter weekend just passed, and a few upcoming speaking and writing opportunities.

We continued to sip our cooling drinks and watch the various scarf and sandal combos walking past. Then the conversation turned to "Other Projects." Since that first conversation, we had found ourselves with a growing list of collaborative projects. Our friends' suggestion to work together turned out to be a good one, albeit a suggestion that has made us both much busier.

Some items on the "Other Projects" list had real deadlines, like a fascinatingly creative youth rally about transformation entitled "tragic/beauty/true" and a joint workshop for an upcoming youth congress on the topic of "Living Justice." But other items were more of the "dreaming about changing the world" kind, like a common burden to do more with our opportunities to speak and write to the church about "re-creativity"—a term that was becoming our shorthand for talking about how justice, beauty and faithful creativity were inherent in our understanding of the gospel and the mission of the church in the world today. Let's be honest, if two writers are going to sit in a cafe sipping hot drinks and talking about books and ideas, the picture wouldn't be complete unless it included some philosophical discussion about God and changing the world.

We continued the conversation over the sounds of the ever-clinking café and the rowdy arrival of some exuberant students who had just finished a presentation and had "totally smashed it, man!" So now with empty cups in hand, we focused on a number of potential book projects, ideas we had talked about before and new ones that turned up only that morning and haven't been heard from since. Our ideas were running in many different directions. Tangents abounded. That's how good conversations go. The best kinds are rambling but energetic creations with pieces flying off along the way—sometimes forgotten, sometimes collected later—but usually circling back to the things that seem most important or engaging or imaginative.

From those initial conversations and many more that have followed, there is a collection of projects still percolating (that "Other Projects" list isn't getting any shorter!) but this is the one that got our attention that day, perhaps for two primary reasons. First, it gave us the opportunity to invite others to join this conversation and to broaden the conversation in our church. Second, Nathan suggested that Jo's painting "After the Flood" would make a wonderful cover for such a book, both artistically and philosophically. And, well, when you've already got a cover, you've already started. The book had begun.

Many conversations had led to that conversation in the cafe. And even more led to this conversation, the book you now hold. We formulated an initial list of people we had worked with in various ways or who otherwise might be interested in such a project. We personally invited them to write on an aspect of creativity that seemed to fit with their expertise, experience and passion. Some of the contributions to this book came from presentations at the Manifest Creative Arts Festival in past years.

But then there were more conversations as we worked on some of those "Other Projects" along the way. The book was growing. Conversations at a speaking appointment on the Gold Coast led to another contribution; a conversation while walking in downtown Chattanooga, Tennessee, sparked an additional chapter; a conversation at a staff Christmas party prompted a Christmas-holiday writing assignment and yet another chapter. And we soon had a collection of articles, essays and stories from 30 other writers, artists, academics, pastors, church leaders and friends.

We were inspired by many of these chapters and awed by the years of creative practice, education and life experience that has created such a breadth of thought and insight. As the contributions rolled in, we were humbled to realise that many of these might not have been written without the prompting of our invitation or conversations. This book did not have to exist but somehow we have been given the opportunity to create it. This is a privilege and one that we have been honoured to share with so many others.

This volume still has many of the hallmarks of conversation—incompleteness, obvious gaps, worthwhile disagreements between some participants, overlapping ideas and some general messiness. And of course, there are other ways to arrange these contributions and other ways to present them. But creativity requires choices and to experiment with all available possibilities is often less useful than getting on and making something, as deficient and incomplete as it might be. In addition to careful planning, the organic, fluid and surprising dynamics of community have significantly shaped the final collection. We have been reminded that none of us creates alone—and that creativity requires flexibility.

Shaping these disparate pieces into what we hope is a coherent collection has been the subject of many more conversations. Almost as valuable as the conversations themselves are the countless wonderful "conversational diversions"—often adding even more items to the "Other Projects" list and occasionally drawing in our spouses when they could not help but overhear our enthusiastically shared ideas or frustrated questions.

So thank you to the many conversation partners who have contributed to this book in unpublished ways, especially to our families who listened to our talking about it and helped us create it in so many ways.

Of course, we are also grateful to all our conversation partners who are published contributors to this book. Thank you for sharing so much of yourselves, your creative experiences and passion, your faith-focused thinking about creativity, your time in just sitting down to write it out and your patience with our editorial vagaries. Thanks also to Brenton Stacey and his support of this project as an outgrowth of the Manifest Creative Arts Festival. Thanks to Daniel Reynaud for reading over the draft pages of the book and to Signs Publishing and Adventist Media Network for their support of the project.

And now we extend the invitation to you to join these conversations. While we acknowledge the incompleteness of this collection, it becomes more complete as soon as you engage with it. We believe this is an important conversation for the good of the church, for the better understanding of the gospel and what it means to live as members of the kingdom of God today. It is crucial for the spiritual health of so many people who have not felt that their passionate and faithful creativity has a place within the church, and for the good of the world and the opportunities we have to be agents of beauty and justice in a world that needs both. Sadly, we have not often been good at this conversation—or practice. That's why we need you, your faithfulness and your creativity.

This is our call to faithful creativity. Please join the conversation.

Nathan Brown and Joanna Darby

BELIEVING

A CHRISTIAN AESTHETIC FOR THE ARTS

Creativity and Theology

Daniel Reynaud

The Christian legacy in the arts is unrivalled. The soaring architecture of the medieval cathedrals, most of whose designers and builders are anonymous, are testaments to the highest levels of artistic taste devoted to the glory of God. It is Western society, mostly in the context of the church, that developed polyphony and created the richest musical tradition in the world. Christianity patronised painters, who developed perspective and realist representation, both of which were significant advances in visual representation. Sculpture, drama, poetry and prose literature, though in some cases inherited and revived from Greek and Roman traditions, have been cultivated by Christianity. In a largely illiterate medieval society, church mystery and morality plays, festivals, paintings and stained glass windows communicated the stories of the Bible.

However, in the modern era, artistic innovation has been taken over by secular culture, and many Christians ignore or even fear the arts. We are often suspicious of them and critical of their pernicious influence. Adventists inherited from their spiritual forebears—particularly the Methodists—a prejudice against novels and other forms of fiction, stage drama, movies (especially when shown in theatres), television (which we roundly condemn while we regularly watch), pop and rock music (also roundly condemned but widely listened to), modern art (which often strikes us as bizarre and incomprehensible), and even of architecture (reflected in the lack of taste in the design of so many of our churches). While there is plenty to complain about in the arts, a poverty not only of aesthetic value but also of moral worth, to discard all arts on the basis that much of it is valueless and corrupt is a mistake: let us aim to retain the baby even as we drain out the bathwater.

The sad history of this began with the Protestant Reformation in the 1500s and continued through the increasingly strict Puritan tradition, which has left its mark on many modern Protestant denominations, especially those with their roots in the non-Conformist faiths, such as Seventh-day Adventism. It began with some

Reformers who rejected everything that smacked of Catholicism, even throwing out church organs and singing in harmony as being evil practices. As champions of the Word, Protestants struggled to understand the role of non-verbal arts and destroyed images in churches as distracting idols, holding up the simple word of God. It didn't help that England's King Charles I combined outstanding artistic taste with a Catholic-leaning religious inclination. His Puritan opponents came to associate the arts with his Catholic outlook—and condemned both. The English Civil War hardened opinion and ensured that English non-conformist Protestants would carry a deep suspicion of the arts as being spiritually dangerous. They argued that only the plain and unadorned represented pure and untarnished religion, and enforced it in all matters from the decoration of churches to personal dress codes. There are elements of truth in this, but at an extreme it becomes its own form of idolatry, and it robs faith of the God-given gift of the creative arts. Christianity needs to reclaim this gift that speaks richly of God's character.

Part of the difficulty that Adventism has had in dealing with the arts has been a lack of understanding where art fits into the overall scheme of things. Perhaps the only art form welcomed by early Adventists was music, again as a legacy of their Methodist forebears, where the hymn-writing Wesley brothers raised music in the artistic repertoire of Evangelical Christianity. But early Adventism's passion for theology was all-consuming, leaving little room for anything else. The Seventh-day Adventist Church began as a movement compelled by the imperative of an imminent Second Coming. In the light of that and the exciting discovery of new truth such as the Sabbath and the investigative judgment, it seemed a waste of time and energy—a mere distraction at best and an evil at worst—to encourage what was seen as "frivolous" creativity. Why paint beautiful pictures if they were all soon to be destroyed in an apocalyptic conflagration? Instead, Adventist energies were devoted to discovering truth and saving souls.

Consequently, "The Truth" is something close to the Adventist heart. The branch of philosophical activity that studies truth is called epistemology. The major discipline devoted to epistemology is theology. As Christians, we note that the ultimate Truth is not a set of doctrines, but a Person. Yet Jesus proclaimed Himself to be more than just Truth. He said He was also the Way and the Life (see **John 14:6**). Metaphysics—the study of reality (the domain of the sciences)—might well be equated to the Way, and axiology—the study of value—might be equated to the Life.

Axiology has two parts: ethics, the study of right and wrong, and aesthetics, the study of what is beautiful. Adventists have a well-developed biblical theology, and take a strongly biblical approach to the sciences and to ethics. However, when it comes to aesthetics, we tend to respond to the arts not from a biblical aesthetic but rather from a biblical epistemology.

However, while theology, the sciences and even ethics deal largely with binary opposites—right and wrong, black and white—aesthetics does not follow the same process. We need to approach each discipline according to its own principles. For example, neither the existence of God nor His character can be proved—or disproved—by science. Not because believing in God is unscientific, but because He is bigger than the scientific method. The scientific method is based on testing evidence by subjecting it to standardised tests. For something to be strictly scientific, it must be a repeatable event, producing the same results when tested under the

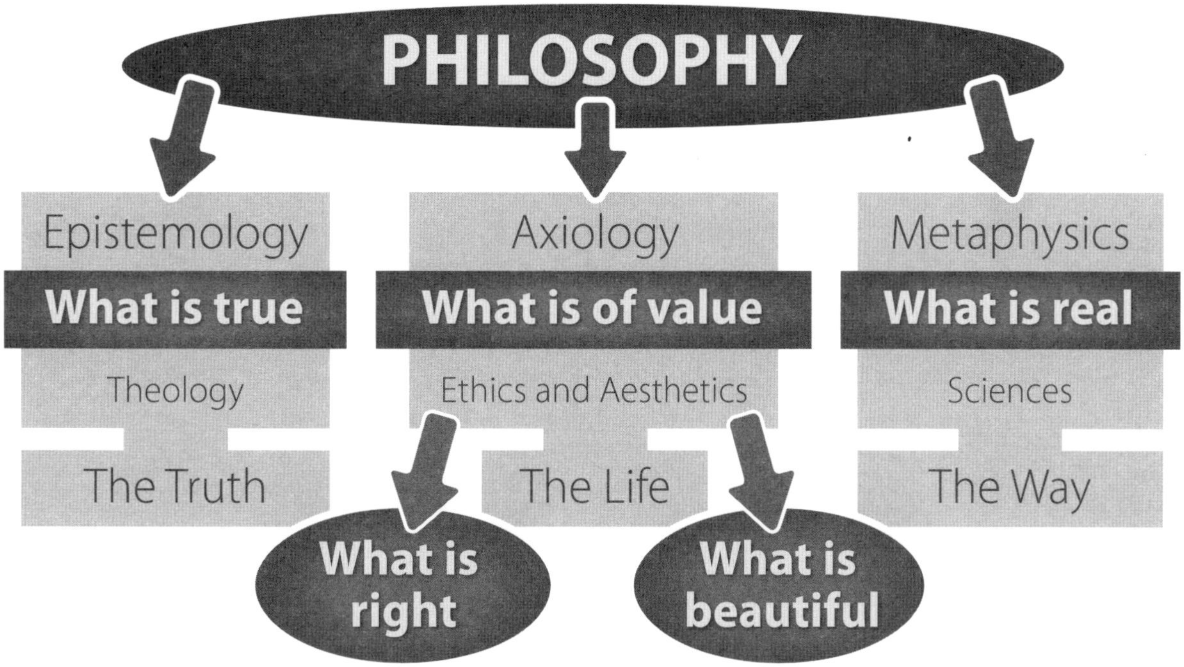

same conditions. However, "science" is often used quite loosely, often meaning that there is evidence rather than proof. There is scientific *evidence* for evolution—and for creation, for that matter—and even for God, but none of these can be *proven* by the scientific method. When working on a larger canvas in the sciences, scholars look for weight of evidence, rather than absolute proof. But the strictly rational methods of science are imperfect tools for exploring truth. Christian author and apologist G K Chesterton noted that, "You can only find truth with logic if you have already found truth without it."[1]

To find the truth about God, we must use the methods of theology. To find reality, we use the scientific method. If we want to know about gravity, we ask a scientific rather than a theological question. Medieval theologians made the mistake of applying misinterpreted scripture to the scientific realm, insisting that the world was flat with corners (repeating a mistake of their scientific colleagues, it might be added). Modern Christians have no trouble with the science of a round Earth, because we recognise that the shape of the Earth is a scientific rather than a theological issue. We must avoid making the same mistake by applying the rules of theology to the study of beauty. We cannot judge beauty by the rules for determining truth. We must use aesthetic principles to judge aesthetic concerns.

C S Kilby writes, "Our excuse for our aesthetic failure has often been that we must be about the Lord's business, the assumption being that the Lord's business is never aesthetic."[2] By contrast, as has been noted by a number of commentators,[3] the first biblical mention of the gift of the Holy Spirit is in endowing Bezalel with artistic skill (see **Exodus 31:2, 3**). Creation is also linked to the Holy Spirit (see **Genesis 1:2**). It seems creativity is an inherently spiritual activity.

The first biblical principle of aesthetics is that **to be creative is to reflect the image of God**. When God said "Let us make human beings in our own image" (Genesis 1:26), He was Himself undertaking His most creative task that we know of. To be in His image must therefore mean that we too are creative. John Oswalt writes, "We are most fully human, most fully experiencing our uniqueness, when we are being most creative."[4] To be creative is to make a statement about the character of God, one that is different from those that theology or science make about Him.

The second biblical principle is the **wholeness of humanity—mind, body and soul**. One of Adventism's great strengths is the health message—that God wishes to restore our whole being, not just the "spiritual" parts. Creativity is also a God-given quality that needs restoring.

The Bible also promotes a **variety of art forms**. While the First Commandment forbids images, the tabernacle and temple were full of them, from cherubim and carvings to oxen holding up the laver. In 2 Chronicles 3:6, we read, "And [Solomon] garnished the house with precious stones for beauty" (KJV). Jesus used parables, including the fictional story of Lazarus and Abraham (see Luke 16:19–31). Poetry, dance and music are all recorded in the Bible, used both positively and negatively, showing that art forms and instruments are not inherently moral, but it is how they are used that matters.

Biblical art suggests that **art should have an artistic end**, not just an epistemological one. Some psalms for example describe God as uncaring, sentiments that are theologically inaccurate. Psalm 137 blesses those who in vengeance dash Babylonian babies against the rocks. Psalm 88 is a lament that offers no hope of rescue or salvation. The function of these psalms isn't to hold up a pure theology but to accurately represent our limited human perspectives. God so approves of this kind of honesty that He inspired their composition and then preserved them in His divine songbook.

Similarly, the sensual language of Song of Songs is an artistic celebration of Love. It does not describe love theologically, as perhaps 1 Corinthians 13 or 1 John might, or scientifically (say in terms of hormonal activities), but its artistic description reveals love experientially and emotionally, which are such vital dimensions of Love. By allowing its aesthetic to speak, we are led back to truth as we enter the beauty of Love, and therefore of God.

Of course, there may be cross-over: 1 Corinthians 13 is a masterpiece of language and a profound theological statement, and much of the Bible is literary art. The best art often carries powerful statements on truth and reality—but it doesn't have to. Solomon placed precious stones on the temple walls, not for their religious symbolism but for their beauty. That made its own statement about a beautiful God.

Approaching art from a theological perspective leads to confusion. Should Christian artists only make religious art? What of other professions: should Christian builders only build churches or Christian mechanics only repair the pastor's car?

Our confusion stems from seeing Christian art as purely evangelistic—that is, epistemologically, for spreading truth. But it is the task of preachers to preach truth; artists testify to the wonder and beauty of God. However, art often leads us to truth and reality. In doing so, they may in fact "preach" as powerfully as any evangelist, but through a different avenue. As Ellen White notes about music, artistic expression "is one of the most effective means of impressing the heart with spiritual truth."[5]

Because art involves taste, it creates a problem for binary theological or scientific thinking. We should learn to *appreciate* art as much as possible, that is to understand and value the quality of form and content, but we need only *like* what we like. Liking or not liking is not a matter of good and bad: it is entirely acceptable not to like a piece of good art, but we should learn as best we can to appreciate. For example, I don't particularly like Charles Dickens' books, but I can appreciate the qualities that made him a good writer.

Perhaps one of the key reasons for a Christian suspicion of the arts is that they have all-too-often been used for evil. For example, popular entertainment often contains values that contradict Christian truth, as does some classical literature, art and music. How do we respond to this? How do we respond to the depiction of evil in art? Firstly, we recognise that not every representation of evil is morally deficient. The point is whether the art speaks truthfully about evil. For example, popular film often presents situations where law-breaking violence by the hero is justifiable and casual sexual relationships have no repercussions. Neither of these represents the truth.

> Liking or not liking is not a matter of good and bad: it is entirely acceptable not to like a piece of good art, but we should learn as best we can to appreciate.

But take a biblical example of the representation of evil: the concluding three chapters of **Judges**. They document in cold-blooded tones crimes such as rape, murder, betrayal, genocide and mass abduction. But they do so in the context of the moral judgment: "In those days Israel had no king; all the people did whatever seemed right in their own eyes" (**Judges 21:25**). In other words, Judges documents carefully that evil behaviour has evil consequences. Thus, while the emphasis is on evil, its true results are clearly demonstrated. This is the context in which the portrayal of evil should be judged in art: does it tell the truth about good and evil?

Art that does not tell the truth can be interesting at an aesthetic level. However, by turning to other aspects of philosophy, we can engage it at an ethical and theological level and draw conclusions about its worth, deciding that while it is aesthetically valuable, it is morally defective, and therefore not appropriate for the Christian.

The best way to illustrate the difference between an aesthetic approach and that of theology or science is by example. So let's take Joanna Darby's painting "After the Flood"—reproduced on the cover of this book. When I first saw it, I did not know its title, so I had no clues as to its subject. It was merely a piece of abstract art to me.

So, if I was to approach it theologically, I would ask, "What truth does it tell me?" And the answer would be: "Not much." I can see a white bird in the top left, which could be a dove, and there appears to be the outline of a twig in the centre. I might connect these to biblical symbols of the Holy Spirit, and perhaps an olive branch, symbolising peace—but the rest of the painting is pretty confusing.

So let's take a reality approach. It is rather much the same: one somewhat-stylised bird and one outline of a twig. There is not really much else that looks real. My conclusion could be now that this is a "useless" painting.

But let me approach it aesthetically. First, I look at its composition: lines, colours, textures, shapes. I see three main features: the brilliant "sky," the pinkish hill, and the busy rectangle below the horizontal line. That rectangle is full of shapes—mostly round or oval—and colours. A tip I have learned to help access art that appears difficult at first is to ask: "How does it make me feel or how do sections of it make me feel?" Then ask: "What elements in the work make me feel that way?" The rectangle is very busy, noisy even. Emotionally, it feels a bit like my week, chock-full of "things" crammed together and apparently trapped under a ruled line. The line is the only rigidly straight thing in the painting. It feels forced, man-made, while all the other shapes have more natural lines. It feels like a human world, busy, rigid, perhaps even repetitive.

Above the line is what appears to be a hill. It has a number of the shapes from below the line repeated, but much less densely. However, it also has a strong suggestion of "bleeding" with red, pink and brown paint allowed to run down the canvas. The feeling is of a costly effort, as if these shapes have escaped the ruled line and climbed the mountain, but have had to bleed to do so.

Then there is the sky. To the right, it has pinkish hues, but that is eclipsed by the left and centre, with their luminous gold tones. In these, I can distinguish the bird and the twig. It looks like a brilliant dawn, the bird a well-recognised symbol of peace, as is an olive branch. (By the way, did you notice that the tone of my language changed when I shifted from the truth and reality approaches—which are more cognitive and less personal—to the aesthetic which uses highly subjective, emotional language?)

Put it all together and my initial decoding comes up with this: out of the busyness and trapped life that I live, there is the possibility of escape. But escape to the top of the mountain requires sacrifice, but then a golden dawn breaks, promising peace.

Now, interesting things happen from here. Taking the aesthetic approach from the start actually opens up the worlds of truth and reality. I have found truth and reality in the painting, which I couldn't find when I used truth and reality as my primary approach. But someone might argue that Joanna might have meant something quite different in the painting—and, seeing her title, that is probably true.

Nevertheless, I would argue that part of the beauty of creativity is that it isn't a one-answer-is-right-therefore-all-others-are-wrong system. My interpretation of the painting is valid, because it rests on the actual features of the painting. Someone might offer a *better* interpretation, drawing conclusions that make richer and more unified use of the painting's features, but that wouldn't entirely negate my understanding. And, after all of this, I don't relate strongly to this painting. Visually it doesn't appeal to me. But I do appreciate it, because I can see a value in it. On the other hand, other Darby paintings really appeal, so much so that I have purchased two of them that now hang on my wall at home.

Jesus is the Way (reality), the Truth (doctrine) and the Life (beauty). As we respect each of these avenues to understanding God, our love and knowledge of Him will grow. Theology testifies to His truth, science to the realities He made, and aesthetics to His awe, beauty and wonder.

—Daniel Reynaud grew up in a home where both faith and art were deeply valued. Painting, sculpture, music, literature, photography and film were discussed and appreciated, all within an Adventist Christian context. For all of his professional life, first as a secondary school teacher in New Zealand, then as a lecturer at Avondale College of Higher Education, he has been involved in creative practice, particularly in music, drama and writing for film and television.

1. G K Chesterton, "The Maxims of Maxim," *Daily News*, February 25, 1905.
2. C S Kilby, in L Ryken (editor), *The Christian Imagination*, page 44.
3. Among them, Joanna Darby, Gabe Reynaud Awards speech, Manifest Creative Arts Festival, March 31, 2012, Avondale College of Higher Education.
4. John Oswalt, *The Leisure Crisis*, Scripture Press Publications. 1987, page 89.
5. Ellen White, *Education*, page 167.

OF TRUTH AND GOOD STORIES

Creativity and the Bible

Trudy J Morgan-Cole

It is not hard to see evidence of God's creativity in the Bible. On the very first page, God bursts onto the scene with creative power, calling light from darkness, shaping a man from the earth. From the opening creation story to the earth-made-new in Revelation, the Bible reminds us over and over that we serve a Creator-God, one who has not only the power to make something out of nothing, but also the desire and the ability to make things beautiful.

But does the Bible celebrate human creativity as well as God's creativity? Christians over time have produced different answers to that question (as they have to almost every other question). This has led to some branches of Christianity producing sublime works of art, music and literature, while other Christians have emphasised uniformity and strongly discouraged creative expression.

The first creative artist mentioned in the Bible is Jubal, "the first of all who play the harp and flute" (**Genesis 4:21**). No more information is given about Jubal, not even a set list of his favourite tunes, but he's sandwiched in between his brother Jabal, father of all those who live in tents and raise livestock, and his half-brother Tubal-Cain, forger of bronze and iron tools. These briefly-mentioned sons of Lamech are given archetypal professions, as if they are meant to represent major categories of human activity at the time. It's intriguing that the musician is given an equal position of honour alongside the herdsman and the metalworker, perhaps suggesting that making music may be just as important as making food and tools.

After the mysterious Jubal, musicians and singers keep turning up in the story. Women compose and perform songs at crucial moments in the Old Testament narrative: Miriam, Deborah, Hannah (see **Exodus 15, Judges 5, 1 Samuel 2**). God demonstrates His power by having the Temple choir and band go into battle ahead of the army (see **2 Chronicles 20**).

Then the Psalms explode in the middle of the Bible, full of hymn tunes and choir directions. (Have you ever wondered what the tune of "Do Not Destroy" was? It must have been popular, with at least four psalms being set to that tune.) Perhaps more to the point, it's equally full of human emotion: joy, praise, rage, despair. One hundred and fifty songs with lyrics celebrating everything from the sublime love of God to the all-too-human desire to crush our enemies into dust—that these made it into the Scriptures seems to me the clearest possible indication that God wants to hear His people expressing themselves.

In fact, I'd argue that not only does the Bible show us God as a creative genius, not only does the Bible give numerous examples of humans expressing themselves creatively with God's approval, the Bible itself is the highest possible testimonial to the value God places on human creativity.

> God could have given us a much simpler sacred text. If He'd simply dictated what He wanted to say—word for word—to a single author over a short period of time, we could have gotten the basics.

Let's face it: God could have given us a much simpler sacred text. If He'd simply dictated what He wanted to say—word for word—to a single author over a short period of time, we could have gotten the basics. The Ten Commandments, certainly. A few key bits of history? **Micah 6:8** and Jesus' two great commandments to summarise the moral code? *One* gospel with a clear and coherent storyline, and some edited bits of Paul's letters . . . ?

Well, I'm sure every Christian could make their own shortlist of what they think the "essential" bits of Scripture would be, but the point is that it's possible to imagine a much shorter, tidier, more coherent document than the current sprawling collection of 66 books by a diverse group of authors, written and compiled over a period of centuries in a variety of places and cultures.

Why, then? Why the Bible we have? Why this complex, sometimes difficult collection of books, instead of a single, tidy, easy-to-understand document? Because God chose to inspire human authors: not to dictate to them, but to impress His thoughts on their minds, knowing those thoughts would be filtered through the language, experience and worldview of those human writers. Let's face it, it is not the most efficient system for getting your message across. But it's the one God chose to use.

After a lifetime of reading and struggling to understand the Bible, I've concluded that at least part of the reason God chose to communicate with us the way He did is that He values our creativity. It seems He was willing to sacrifice simplicity and efficiency in favour of allowing His people to express His message in their own language.

When you think about it, this is pretty breathtaking. God wants us to speak—and to sing and to paint and to sculpt—even though by doing so we flavour His message with our own personalities, our own culture, our own perceptions. God values the creativity of His people even more than He values the clarity and consistency of His own message.

At least, that's how it strikes me when reading the Bible. We might not struggle so much with the character of God—whether He really is wrathful and vengeful—if He hadn't given a bunch of violent ancient tribespeople the job of telling His stories. We might not argue about faith and works if God had simply sat Paul and James down and said, "OK, only one of you gets to tell people how to be saved, and you're going to follow the script I give you, all right?" Wouldn't everyone agree with the Adventist interpretation of Revelation if only John had written in a more straightforward fashion, without all that imagery, symbolism and poetic language (and maybe a few maps and timelines added to clarify prophecy)?

Why four gospels? Wouldn't one well-edited account work better? Then no-one would have to wonder whether Jesus cast demons out of one madman or two (see **Matthew 8, Mark 5, Luke 8**). We wouldn't have to reconcile Mark's Jesus, who warns everyone *not* to say He's the Messiah, with John's Jesus, who boldly stands up in the Temple court and announces, "The Father and I are one!" (see **Mark 8:30, John 10:30**). We would lose the richness, the beauty of these four different portraits of the same God-Man, but aren't simplicity and ease of understanding more important in founding a religion than variety and creativity?

Apparently not, according to God. John's story was as valuable as Mark's, as Matthew's, as Luke's, because each one had something unique to add. Each of them told recognisably the same story—but in a different way. In his own way, each showed us how he saw Jesus.

Of course, Jesus Himself was also a storyteller. In fact—particularly if you look at the synoptic gospels—He was a storyteller more than anything else. His parables are small masterpieces of creative truth-telling: wisdom wrapped in short scenes so unforgettable that just to say "the good Samaritan" or "the prodigal son" unfolds entire layers of theology for those who know the stories.

When I think about the role of creativity in the life of faith, one of my favourite stories is the story of the rich man and Lazarus in **Luke 16**. In this parable, Jesus describes Lazarus the beggar after death, nestled in Abraham's bosom, while the rich man suffers the flames of hell and longs for the comfort he once denied Lazarus.

Why do I love this story? Because it's a difficult one—at least for Seventh-day Adventists. The plot of this story clearly doesn't fit with the rest of the Bible's teaching on the afterlife and with Jesus' own many references to death as a sleep. Instead, it draws on imagery from popular cultural beliefs of the time, to make a point that has nothing to do with life after death, and everything to do with how we're supposed to treat others in *this* life.

In other words, Jesus didn't let the doctrinal truth get in the way of a good story. He told a story that was creative, that was memorable, that drew upon familiar cultural images and sketched unforgettable characters. He brought the story to life and didn't seem to care that future Adventist pastors would have a difficult time explaining it in Bible studies on the state of the dead. Here, as in the rest of the Bible, one kind of truth—the kind embodied in story, in song, in art—sometimes trumps the purely factual, doctrinal, rational kind of truth.

Maybe it's more important, the Bible suggests, to tell a good story than to get all the facts straight. Was there one demoniac or were there two? Matthew remembered seeing two; Mark and Luke only heard about one. What matters is that all three writers knew that the power of Jesus defeats the power of Satan, and that people who are broken and cast off by society can be healed and made whole.

Do rich men who ignore the poor actually writhe in the flames of hell and long for beggars to bring them cool drinks? Not according to the rest of the Bible—but what matters is that you don't forget the story the next time someone less fortunate asks you for help.

Does the litany of curses poured out by the writer of **Psalm 109** really square with the command to love our enemies? Of course not, but what matters is that a man who was suffering pain and injustice expressed how he felt—and God valued his prayer enough to enshrine it in Scripture, to remind us that our cries of pain and anguish, just as much as our shouts of joy and praise, matter to Him.

Sing your song. Tell your story. Howl out your pain if you have to. Or paint your prayer. The result might not always be simple or clear—but it will be real. And it will be true. Just like the Bible.

—Trudy J Morgan-Cole is a writer and teacher in St John's, Newfoundland, Canada. Her recent books include James: The Brother of Jesus*;* Lydia: A Story of Philippi*; and* That Forgetful Shore*. Trudy blogs and vlogs about writing, reading and faith at <www.trudymorgancole.com>.*

YESTERDAY, TODAY AND FOREVER

Creativity and Jesus

Matthew W Gamble

From the very beginning, Jesus creatively created. It's always been a part of His nature. The gospel writer John accurately described this creative Jesus as the Word:

> In the beginning the Word already existed. The Word was with God, and the Word was God. He existed in the beginning with God. God created everything through him, and nothing was created except through him. The Word gave life to everything that was created, and his life brought light to everyone. The light shines in the darkness, and the darkness can never extinguish it. . . . So the Word became human and made his home among us. He was full of unfailing love and faithfulness. And we have seen his glory, the glory of the Fathers one and only Son (**John 1:1–5,14**).

Note the "In the beginning . . ." parallels between the language of **Genesis 1** and the introduction of Jesus in **John 1**. Here we discover that all things were created through Jesus and without Him nothing was created (see **John 1:3**). This means the God we read about in the Creation account is one with Jesus, so all the genius of Creation can also be attributed to the person of Jesus. This tells us that while we recognise God as Creator who is therefore by nature creative, we must also recognise Jesus as Creator who is therefore by nature creative.

In other words, it's the same Jesus in Genesis who—several millennia later—came to the very planet that He created and lived among His creation.

Not only does this passage tell us that He was God and that all things were created through Him, but it emphasises that He continues to be the source of life for all humanity—"his life brought light to everyone." And here's the most phenomenal part: Jesus became what He created—flesh—and "moved into the neighbourhood" (**John 1:14**, MSG). The revelation of God in a man, an incredibly unexpected and creative solution to the problem of sin.

Jesus was creative

By the time Jesus was 12, He was in the temple creatively teaching with such a level of authority and insight that the hearers "were amazed at his understanding and his answers" (**Luke 2:47**). Then, at the age of 30, Jesus' public ministry kicks off. From the beginning, this Rabbi marches to the beat of a new drum. He doesn't go to the temple or rabbinical schools to find His disciples. Instead, Jesus opts to call a rag-tag crew of men who have little to no theological prowess and would appear to be the least likely bunch of guys that the King of kings and Lord of lords (see **Revelation 17:14**) would choose to work with—or even be seen with. But Jesus is creative. And he sees potential where others do not. Isn't that the entire story of creation, re-creation and redemption?

The gospels are full of examples of the creative approach Jesus took during His short three-and-a-half years of ministry. When we think of Jesus' creativity in His ministry, we most often think of His storytelling and parables. While incredibly profound, His teaching style is also often quite simple. His ability to creatively weave sayings and quotes from the Torah is unexpected and stirring. His use of everyday scenarios, situations and objects is not only a creative way to teach truths, but teaches us to look at the scenarios, situations and objects in our daily lives with new eyes, looking for truths and revelations of God around us.

Everything about His ministry is surprising and creative. For three-and-a-half years, Jesus remains homeless—like a true artist!—and He shatters the cultural norms of His day—like a true artist! He has a high level of disregard for self-righteous religious people and He's not afraid to show it. His response when His authority is questioned is not even framed in words but is drawn in dust. When His followers are doubtful, we don't find Jesus explaining Himself, instead the Creator walks on water and calms the storm.

He doesn't just drive the demons out into the void but into pigs. Truly. Into pigs!? Jesus' response to a request for healing is not to pray but to spit in the dust. He continues in the fashion of the Genesis account and creates something from nothing when he feeds the multitudes and when the empty-handed fishermen suddenly draw a net full of fish. And perhaps the ultimate example of Christ's creativity is when He breathes life where there is none—Jairus' daughter, the son of the widow in Nain and Lazarus.

Again and again we find Jesus demonstrating principles of the kingdom of God in creative and unforgettable ways. When looking at the life of Jesus, we should be reminded of **Isaiah 55:8**: "'My thoughts are nothing like your thoughts,' says the Lord. 'And my ways are far beyond anything you could imagine.'"

I was recently asked by an agnostic friend, "What do you think was the most important thing Jesus taught?" I had never thought of this before but, after a few moments, I came up with Jesus' statement in **John 14:9**: "Anyone who has seen me has seen the Father!" Could it be that the primary reason the Son of God became flesh was to set the record straight? In other words, could it be that because Israel—God's chosen people—had tarnished the image of God that Jesus came to creatively—in an entirely new and revolutionary way—reveal the reality of God?

• A life-changing, re-creating conversation

A stand-out example is found in the story of the nameless but infamous "woman at the well" (see **John 4:3–42**), which provides incredible insight into Jesus' creative approach. For starters, Jews had no dealings with Samaritans. But that didn't stop Jesus. Always thinking of the alternative, He goes where traditional Jews wouldn't. Furthermore, a Jewish man would never speak to a woman in public, much less a rabbi, and more so when it become clear Jesus knew this woman's story. But again, Jesus wasn't bound by the cultural norms of His day.

I can imagine, as Jesus prayed that morning, the Father telling Him, "So today, around noon, You've got a divine appointment with a lady who'll be coming out to that well that Jacob built back in the day. As You know, she's a pearl of infinite value and I want You to give her the gift of the Holy Spirit to abide in her deeply. Today is her day of breakthrough!"

So Jesus took the direct route through the heart of Samaria that day. And, right on time, as the Father said, the woman showed up. Jesus could've taken any number of approaches, but He simply asked for something to drink, mentions that He can give her living water, piques her interest and curiosity, and suddenly turns this woman's world upside down.

He took a creative approach and it paid off. This woman ends up going back into town and based on her encounter with God, ends up converting the entire town of Sychar.

• A meal to remember

Another noteworthy example of the creativity of Jesus' ministry is the extraordinary gift of communion. As human beings made in the image of God, we are sensory beings. Knowing this, Jesus left us a gift that taps into our senses, that can be experienced and felt and understood more deeply than words alone. As N T Wright has put it, "When Jesus wanted to explain to His followers the meaning of his death, He didn't give them a theory; He gave them a meal."[1]

On the night He was betrayed, Jesus took the disciples into an upper room in Jerusalem at Passover. He introduced a new Passover experience—one that would become a powerful teaching and worship tradition for millions of Christians. The act of Jesus humbling Himself as a servant and washing the feet of the disciples was not just a poignant teaching moment for the twelve. It is one of the most sensory-rich teaching experiences we still use regularly in our churches today (see **John 13:1–20**).

Then Jesus took the bread and the cup on the table and offered it to them—but this was not just any bread and drink:

> Then he took a cup of wine and gave thanks to God for it. Then he said, "Take this and share it among yourselves. For I will not drink wine again until the Kingdom of God has come." He took some bread and gave thanks to God for it. Then he broke it in pieces and gave it to the disciples, saying, "This is my body, which is given for you. Do this to remember me."
> After supper he took another cup of wine and said, "This cup is the new covenant between

> God and his people—an agreement confirmed with my blood, which is poured out as a sacrifice for you" (**Luke 22:17–20**).

These forms of daily nourishment, symbols of the Passover that had become weary, were now resurrected and given new life to represent the body and blood of Jesus. For the believer, Jesus left a creative gift that provides a tangible experience and reminder of what He has done for each one of us.

Jesus is creative: a personal experience

In my own life, I have found Jesus to be extremely creative. For more than half my life, I didn't know Jesus. When I was a teenager, I didn't have a lot of value for life, so was trying almost anything on offer to fill me. One day I had an eye-opening experience that lead me to believe that there had to be a Creator somewhere who was actually at work in my life. It was a divine experience.

As time went on, I found myself increasingly drawn to the things of nature. In the first line of *Steps to Christ*, Ellen White writes, "Nature and revelation alike testify of God's love"[2]—and I found this to be true.

I started spending long periods of time in God's first book of revelation: nature. I would spend hours in solitude at the beach. During this time, Jesus—the creative Creator—started to reveal Himself to me through the incredible details of the natural creation all around me. In short order, my prayer life began to take off as my desire to know this Creator grew.

Amid this growing experience, I ended up at a wedding in a Seventh-day Adventist Church. At the age of 20, I had never heard of "SDAs" but I had a great conversation with the officiating pastor that lead to him handing me my first Bible. From that day forward, I started reading the Bible and was introduced to the God of the Bible as seen in Jesus.

Returning home, I contacted the closest Adventist church to my home. Unknown to me, it was an all-black church family and when I arrived it became apparent that I was the only white guy there. Yet this church family loved me in, like I was one of their own.

After a couple of months of attending the church, I enrolled at Andrews University studying Business Management and Aviation. However, within weeks of being at Andrews, I shared my testimony publicly and received a strong affirmation from the church body—and God—that I was being called into full-time preaching ministry. I switched my major to theology the following week. Since that time, Jesus has opened the door for me to travel on six continents sharing the good news that is the gospel of Jesus Christ.

I believe Jesus took a creative approach in my life. His power is transformative and creative. With great vision, He called me out of the life I was living and into a new life of which He is Lord. He continues to minister creatively to me and through me to this day! While this is exciting on its own, it is magnified when I consider that the work He has done and is doing in me is the same thing He has done and is doing in countless other individuals—including you.

Jesus will be creative

Yet the creativity of Jesus Christ is eternal, extending beyond His earthly ministry and even beyond the transformation of my own life. Because it is His nature, He never stops creating and re-creating.

While some of us have a picture of heaven in which everything is perfect and complete, I don't think heaven is a nirvana-like experience where we stop growing and expanding. Take a look at these verses from the Book of Revelation:

> Then I saw a new heaven and a new earth, for the old heaven and the old earth had disappeared. And the sea was also gone. And I saw the holy city, the new Jerusalem, coming down from God out of heaven like a bride beautifully dressed for her husband. . . . And the one sitting on the throne said, "Look, I am making everything new!" And then he said to me, "Write this down, for what I tell you is trustworthy and true" (**Revelation 21:1–5**).

We are made new. The earth is made new. The making never ceases. For all of eternity, Jesus—our creative Creator—will be helping us grow and develop, ever more and more.

From the beginning of time, the Word—Jesus—spoke into existence what was not yet. Throughout His earthly ministry, we see Jesus creatively ministering to a myriad of people in ways that radically turned this world upside down. In my own life, Jesus has proved Himself a creative Creator, creating in me a new heart (see **Ezekiel 36:26**), giving me new eyes to see with. Chances are, He is doing the same with you. And God will continue His creative process as He makes all things new and continues to create new opportunities for us to grow.

The Word was. And the Word is. And the Word will be.

—Matthew W Gamble, DMin, is the lead pastor at Elmshaven SDA Church (aka The Haven), located on the campus of St Helena Hospital in California, USA. He's ecstatically married to his wife Susan and together they have a daughter Julia. Matthew is also the author of Reboot Your Spiritual Life. *He loves God, church, people and culture. Titus 2:11, 12 is taped on his bathroom mirror.*

1. N T Wright, *How God Became King*, HarperOne, page 238.
2. Ellen White, *Steps to Christ*, page 9.

WHEN IT DOESN'T MAKE SENSE

Creativity and Grace

Bruce Manners

I was standing before Jackson Pollock's *Blue Poles*. Its story had made me seek it out. *Blue Poles* is a large abstract piece (about 2 metres x 5 metres) painted by Pollock in 1952. It originally had the rather catchy title: *Number 11, 1952*.

When bought by the Australian government in 1973, it caused a public furore. They paid about $US2 million dollars for it, a world record for a contemporary American painting at the time. The media called it a scandal. There was even a suggestion that it had been painted by a couple of barefoot drunks—Pollock and a friend. That proved to not be true, but the story lingers.

There was no-one else in that part of the National Gallery of Australia when I was there, which meant I could check it out up close and from a distance without the view being interrupted. I was looking for the attraction of the work, something that would make me "get it" and understand what the fuss was about.

Someone who apparently does get it wrote:

> *Blue Poles* seduces by its vibrant and energetic colours and its sheer size, drawing the viewer in to marvel at the chaotic skeins of paint that show no signs of traditional brush marks. . . . One can see that most of the swirling rhythms of the dripping, twirling and thrown paint were made while the canvas was on the floor. . . . After those bouts with chance the artist took firm corrective action (probably by putting a length of wood in paint and slapping it down) to produce the march of eight swaying poles across its full length. It is that kind of daring balance of powerful opposites that established Jackson Pollock as the most famous artist of his generation in the United States.[1]

I wasn't seduced. I wasn't drawn in. The poles didn't sway for me. I was underwhelmed. I could appreciate the size, the mix of colours and how they fit together, and the story around it—but I didn't understand it. Of course, that may label me as ignorant, as one without artistic sensibility or even a philistine of some kind. But I had the impression that I could have had a go at it and come up with something similar—I can do swirling paint and plank slapping—and would have been happy to sell it to the Australian government for half the price.

We have a similar problem when God paints His pictures of grace as we attempt to explain it. He's used a creativity that is difficult for us to "get." It's like nothing else because it steps outside our expectations. *The Macquarie Dictionary* says this: "**creative** / kri'eitiv /, *adj.* **1.** Having the quality or power of creating. **2.** Resulting from originality of thought or expression." You would expect that God, the ultimate creative being in the universe, would show originality in the pictures He paints.

Reward for effort

We live in a reward-for-effort world. It starts when as a child you're promised that if you have three more mouthfuls you won't have to eat any more. Or you'll get dessert. It's "do this, get that." This makes sense to us. So much sense that it becomes a natural way of life. Go to school, do the work, get the grades. Get a job, do the work, get the pay. Get a mortgage, give the pay, keep the house. That's reward for effort.

Even relationships, including love and romance, have elements of reward for effort. In fact, a good relationship doesn't happen without effort. A good marriage is no accident. A family that's together has spent time making that happen: camping trips, ferrying kids to events, planning times together. This can be hard work. Enjoyable? Mostly—but it's still a huge amount of effort.

Most religions—perhaps all except Christianity—have obedience for salvation at their core. Even those with *nothingness* as the goal teach you how to achieve nothingness. Do this, get that. Nothingness is the reward for effort.

Christianity, though, is based on grace. Back to *The Macquarie Dictionary*: "**grace** /greis/, *n Theol.* **a.** the free, unmerited favour and love of God." That's the free, unmerited *favour* of God. It's also the free, unmerited *love* of God. Both are undeserved. It's like nothing we would naturally imagine. It's like no picture we could paint.

Imagine if Christianity was a 12-step, self-help process like Alcoholics Anonymous. We'd meet regularly and I'd say, "My name is Bruce and I'm a sinner." And the others would all say, "Hi, Bruce." Then it would be the turn of the person next to me. Then the next, and the next, and so on. Then we'd talk about our week and what had happened. Where we had success. Where we had failure.

This may be great for alcoholics because it focuses on one weakness, one sin. I'm still left with this multifaceted sin problem in my life. Overcome one and there's another, and the ones I thought I'd overcome still make an appearance every now and again. Self-help doesn't help because the sin problem is bigger than I can handle. That means I'd keep turning up to my 12-step program to say, "My name is Bruce and I'm still a sinner" without ever really touching the big problem. I'm a natural-born sinner.

Fortunately, God knows that reward for effort doesn't work for salvation. When I tell Him, "My name is Bruce and I'm a sinner."

He says, "I know."

"Oh."

"I can fix that."

"Oh?"

"Here, put this on," He says as He hands me a robe. He explains it's a robe of righteousness. In comparison to my clothes of, well, unrighteousness I understand the difference. He says that it's a robe of blood-bought righteousness and tells me the story of Jesus.

"My Son died for your sins. Put this on and you put on His righteousness. You are no longer a sinner because you're covered by His righteousness."

I want that, but the reward-for-effort mantra is ingrained in my being: "So, what do I have to do?"

I want that, but the reward-for-effort mantra is ingrained in my being: "So, what do I have to do?" "Accept it."

"Accept it."

"Is that all?"

"Nothing more. Nothing less."

That's grace. It's undeserved. It's free. It's a gift of love.

I put the robe on. Such a perfect fit.

"Wait a minute!" I don't want to complain, but something doesn't feel quite right.

"What's the problem?"

"It's still me in this robe?"

"Well, that's true. Do you want me to give it to someone else?"

"No, what I mean is that when I look at myself I still see that I have many of the same problems to deal with in my life. I'm sure others will notice them as well."

"What's more important? How you see yourself, how others see you or how I see you?"

"You, of course, but . . ."

"As long as you wear the robe of righteousness, I don't see you as a sinner. I see you as part of My family, and as whole and as pure as My Son. You are covered by Him."

Simul justus et peccator, that's how Martin Luther described this dilemma—"simultaneously justified and sinful." Saved but still sinful. Sinful but saved. That's grace.

One more question: "But what do I do about the sins I still see in my life?"

"Ah, I can help you with those, too. Let's begin with your . . ."

More grace.

God's creative grace

The first chapter of Genesis demonstrates both God's creativity and His grace in dramatic fashion. God takes chaos and transforms it into an inhabitable planet. This is creativity in extreme: first, to be able to conceive of a universe with a dot called Earth a part of it; second, to speak it into being with no construction cranes in sight. This is definitely—to use the dictionary definition—"originality of thought or expression."

Actually, it's originality of thought *and* expression.

God takes the soil of earth and hand-crafts the shape of a human—Adam ("the man" is the literal translation of the Hebrew). Not willing to merely speak him into life, He does something more intimate and bends over this form to breathe into his nostrils. Adam comes alive, thanks to the free, unmerited favour and love of God.

To this point, Adam was merely a dirt shape on the ground. No heart, no brain, no bones, no sinews, no muscles, no intestines, no skin—merely a mound of dirt. There was nothing he could do to create himself. The doing was all God's. Adam had done nothing, could do nothing to deserve it.

So God helps Adam to his feet and shows him around. He sees the vegetation, he feels the grass beneath his feet, he watches birds fly from tree to tree, he touches a giraffe, he smells a rose, he bathes in a river. Sensations of life. And God says this life I give you, this place I created is all yours. That's grace.

The Bible repeats the grace theme again and again. God says He had chosen Israel to be "His own special treasure" not because they were a great people, but because they weren't. "Rather it was simply that the Lord loves you." That's why He had saved them from slavery under the Pharaoh (**Deuteronomy 7:6–8**). That's grace.

The call of Abraham demonstrates grace—but there's more. Every time God provides a judge. Every time He sends a prophet. Every time He raises up a king. Every time He rescues His people. That's grace.

Bethlehem. God wrapped in baby flesh and a swaddling cloth and placed in a manger. The Almighty Lord God and Creator of all condescends to not only be human, but to go through the stages of growth from foetus to adult. This is definitely originality of thought *and* expression. And what a demonstration of grace!

The greatness of God and the love of God is demonstrated best at Calvary. Unfortunately, because our age "teaches us both how great we are and how small we seem," Harold Kushner says, "we have largely lost the capacity for reverence, the sense of awe that comes from realising how much greater God is than we are."[2]

Paradoxically, His greatness is seen best not in his power, but in His grace.

Max Lucado explains it this way: "By His perfect life, Jesus fulfilled the commands of the law. By His death, He satisfied the demands of sin. Jesus suffered not like a sinner, but as a sinner. . . . God's holiness is honoured. Our sin is punished. And we are redeemed. God is still God."[3]

God is also love. And it shows.

Storytelling Saviour

Matthew tells us that Jesus never spoke to the crowds without using stories (see **Matthew 13:34, 35**). He told stories of the kingdom (the wheat and the weeds growing together, one of them); a story of hearing God's word (the farmer scattering seed on various soils); a story about identifying your neighbour (the Good Samaritan). The story of the lost sheep (see **Luke 15**) is about grace, demonstrating the lengths to which our Shepherd will go to restore us to His flock. There are at least four grace points in the story.

In that day, a shepherd with 100 sheep would be considered well off. Losing one would not be too much of a financial problem because, come next breeding season, there'd be plenty more. So, the intelligent thing to do is cut your losses and wait. But this is not any shepherd—this is the Shepherd. He is different.

Some suggest that back then farm animals were like pets and while there's some truth to that, when you have 100 it's difficult to treat them like pets. If you have a dog or a cat, it's easy. But if you have 101 Dalmatians, it's impossible.

If it was once a prize sheep, there's no indication of it now. But the Shepherd always looks beyond such externals to the value that's within.

Grace point 1: Every person has significance in God's eyes. Numbers don't count.

"Won't he leave the ninety-nine others in the wilderness and go search for the one that is lost?" (**Luke 15:4**). Well, no, not really. This is the *wilderness*—Greek: *eremos*—meaning desolate place, isolated place and lonely place. It makes no sense to leave the 99 unprotected. They're not in a pen; they're not in a cave; they're not protected in any way. The head decision is to stay with the 99. The heart says, don't let any be lost. The Shepherd goes with His heart of unmerited love.

Grace point 2: God is willing to risk all for the one lost. Always.

Sheep prefer to be a flock—they flock together. In all probability the lost sheep is fearful, it has been running in various directions looking for its flock. Its wool is matted and filled with rubbish from the ground and wilderness bushes. Its feet are bloodied as it has scrambled from place to place. Its face is bloodied from a fall on to rocks.

If it was once a prize sheep, there's no indication of it now. But the Shepherd always looks beyond such externals to the value that's within.

Grace point 3: God doesn't care what condition the lost one is in. Ever.

The romantic picture has the Shepherd pick up the gentle sheep and place it neatly on His shoulders to carry it back to the other sheep. Often it's pictured as a lamb sitting like a fur collar on his neck.

Reality check. This was a fully-grown sheep—lambs tend to stay with their mothers. A heavy sheep. A heavy sheep probably using its last strength kicking and bellowing in protest at being picked up. The Shepherd has to protect Himself until the sheep settles down, then carry it back several kilometres through the wilderness to the other sheep. This is hard work, but the Shepherd is up for it because He has a love for His sheep.

Grace point 4: God is there, whether there is a desire to be rescued or not. He knows when the time is right for the rescue. He's always there.

The Shepherd we follow is one who risks all for us. It doesn't matter what the danger. No matter our condition. Or our desire to be rescued. He's there with His free unmerited favour and love.

Blue Poles and grace. Neither of them makes sense, not really. Abstract art isn't meant to depict reality—that's its definition—but it is real. Grace is so outside human thinking that it is hard to believe. But it also is real. And it's where our hope lies. Nothing else works.

Timothy Keller writes: "The founders of every other major religion came as teachers, not as saviours. They came to say, 'Do this and you will find the divine.'" But, he continues, "Jesus came essentially as a saviour rather than a teacher (though He was that as well). Jesus says: 'I am the divine come to you, to do what you could not do for yourselves.'"[4]

That's grace.

—Bruce Manners is lead pastor of Lilydale Seventh-day Adventist Church in suburban Melbourne, Australia. He is a former editor of church magazines and author of two books, most recently Reckless Love.

1. < https://www.americanaustralian.org/benefitdinner2010/bluepoles/>
2. Harold Kushner, *Who Needs God?* Touchstone, 2002, page 45.
3. Max Lucado, *In the Grip of Grace*, Thomas Nelson, 1999, pages 94-5.
4. Timothy Keller, *The Reason for God: Belief in an Age of Skepticism*, Dutton, 2008, page 185.

BEING

THE THING OF IT IS

Creativity and Purpose

Terry Benedict

> In the Beginning . . . there was Creativity
> emanating from the Creator . . . as constant today as in the Beginning.

More than a theory

[Fade in: Interior—Christian Hospital Delivery Room]

A baby's first cry pierces the air. A cheer rises from the family and medical staff.

The doctor confirms, "Yep, he's got all his toes and fingers. Congratulations, you're the proud parents of a healthy boy. Don't break him now." Laughs all around.

The proud father decries, "I can't wait to teach him to be the next Michael Jordan."

The mother says, "No, he's going to become the President."

The father, more realistic: "No, I'll make him a partner in the business. He'll love it". And so it begins.

> You made all the delicate, inner parts of my body and knit me together in my mother's womb (**Psalms 139:13**).
>
> But even before I was born, God chose me and called me by his marvellous grace (**Galatians 1:15**).
>
> In his grace, God has given us different gifts for doing certain things well (**Romans 12:6**).

Do we really believe these precepts? Or do we think they just make for great poetic prose? Are they a salient part of the Master Plan or is the Master Plan just about finality at the end of time? How important are these precepts in the big scheme of life? Does this have anything to do with our purpose?

When starting the Shae Foundation, I explained our philosophy—*that giftedness implies purpose*—to a woman who told me the story of her son who loved to draw. She showed me some of his artwork from his toddler years to first grade. It was obvious he was gifted, not just technically, but expressively. There was an inspiring insight from his perspective on life. When I asked to see more, her emotions percolated to the surface. There was no more. Turns out, her son was told by his father that all boys who grow up to be artists are gay. The young boy put down the pencil and didn't draw again.

Our first reaction is, "I would never say that." And perhaps you wouldn't. But perhaps you've heard it—in one form or another:

> "You can't make a living doing that."
>
> "You need to follow in your father's footsteps."
>
> "But we planned on you going to this school."
>
> "It was good enough for your parents . . ."
>
> "You're really talented—but at some point you'll have to get a *real* job."

How many of us are actually living a life where our giftedness is being utilised? Do you know your area of giftedness? Did your dream get nurtured or squashed by parents, church family or the education system?

We've unknowingly caused an epidemic. "How To" books hit the *New York Times* bestseller list by the dozens every year, most recommending sure-fire ways of finding your path to happiness. This seems to indicate an insatiable desire to quench the thirst of a large sector of society who have not found purpose and meaning and lead unfulfilled lives.

Recently, I gave a series of seminars about discovering your giftedness and purpose. I'm always amazed that the line of people waiting to talk with me can usually be divided into two groups: the happy people who are thankful that someone finally validated that being creative is a Divine gift; and the conflicted group who want a "How to" recipe to discover their giftedness, passion and purpose.

In today's digital and information age, we think we should be able to find the answer to questions about purpose, happiness and our gifting by Googling or reading it in Wikipedia, through intellectual and analytical processes. But the reality is it's the shortest recipe arguably ever written. Any sporting coach worth his or her salt after seeing their team fall into a pattern of mistakes will say, "We've got to get back to the basic fundamentals of the game." In the spiritual context, this doesn't mean looking back to the good "ol' time religion" of 150 years ago. We need to go back further—to **Genesis 1**.

The very first thing God asked Adam to do required creativity:

> So the Lord God formed from the ground all the wild animals and all the birds of the sky. He brought them to the man to see what he would call them, and the man chose a name for each one (**Genesis 2:19**).

God's creativity didn't end with the creation of the world, or even with the creation of humanity. When God created us in His image, He genetically infused us with His own creativity. That one phrase—"to see what he would call them"—tells us much about the nature of God and the nature of human beings created in His image. Of course, Adam could only complete the task because of the creativity God had initially given him. Nevertheless, he was also given incredible freedom. It seems God is more interested in partnering with us and seeing His creativity flow through humanity than controlling it to a perfect result.

Our Creator has endowed each of us with different facets of His creative spirit for a specific purpose. Like a prism, His white light passes through us giving each of us a unique colour. A dimension of His creative spirit is given to us "to devise artistic designs" (see **Exodus 31:2–4**), whether they be with paint on canvas, through the lens of a camera, sounds, words or ideas. And He presents opportunities to see how we will use our creative spirit to honour Him and serve others. Our purpose is not hidden in some dark shrouded mystery. The Creator expects us to create using His divine spirit, taking the leap from knowledge and ability to devising artistic designs that serve others and bring honour to Him.

This genetic infusion of God's creative spirit is the foundation of the enigmatic miracle that happens every time we create using the unique skill set the Creator provides. At that *inspired* moment, the Spirit of God enables our creative spirit to take the idea, a concept without form, create an original and unique path from within, then manifest it outwardly. The Creator must take great pleasure watching creatures He made in His image creatively express themselves through the gifts He placed in each one of them. He delights "to see what" we will create through this collaborative process.

This genetic infusion of God's creative spirit is the foundation of the enigmatic miracle that happens every time we create using the unique skill set the Creator provides.

Unfortunately, many of us have succumbed to societal influences and neither discovered nor experienced this most salient dimension of our lives—a dimension that our Creator intended for our fulfilment and happiness. Too often, we've heard young and old alike share how they were told to be "realistic." Self-choosing our purpose in life—or worse, choosing for our children—leads down a path of discontentment. But when a person is in sync with God, he or she can realise and fulfil their creative purpose.

Seventeenth-century philosopher, John Locke, proposed the well-known theory known as *tabula rasa*. Essentially, he believed we are all born as blank slates, waiting for the world to make its indelible mark on us. In other words, we're strictly a product of our environment. This idea flies in the face of the fundamental biblical principle that we are "fearfully and wonderfully made" (see **Psalms 139:14**).

While Locke clearly did not subscribe to the divine principle that we all were born *hardwired* with a certain giftedness to fulfil a specific purpose, he does point out an all-too-painful truth still visible today: "Parents wonder why the streams are bitter, when they themselves have poisoned the fountain."[1] Imagine if, rather than fighting the will of the Creator, we accepted that God already has it figured out! It makes sense that as parents, teachers and society, it is our obligation to help a child discover their gifts and nurture them so they may take their rightful place in the Master Plan, as contributors to the global community.

An imperfect world doesn't change this core divine principle—that we were given a creative spirit driven by love. If it did change this sacred principle, it would make the Master Plan a fraud. And would nullify what King David, the Apostle Paul and Jesus Christ talked about regarding the essential role we have to play on this world stage—the revelation of the heart of God to this world and the restoration of human beings in His image. Certainly, being onstage can be intimidating—especially if you don't know your role. An actor who doesn't understand his or her part has a hard time fulfilling the character's purpose in the story. As a result, a chain of dysfunction occurs—starting with a poor performance that communicates a weak message, leading to an unresponsive audience.

The what if

Not long ago, the faith community was conflicted. The realisation was that we long ago gave away the birthright of creativity to a secular scientific mindset. We had forgotten from whence we came—in the beginning. Today, many still find themselves trying to reconcile what to do with the creative spirit. Outside forces try to contain and control it when it is meant to be free, without form inside us, then purely released as a unique expression in the context of a relationship with the Creator, in a way that honours Him and blesses others. The more we exemplify our creative spirit in positive, accountable ways, the more we manifest the Creator's intention in our lives.

The traditional assumptions by many suggest that the arts are suspect and can lead to spiritual or moral denigration. They assume the answer is *No* to the following misapplied questions frequently asked: Can the arts lead to spiritual transformation? Can they provoke people to ask the right questions, do the right things? Can they make a positive difference?

But more and more of us are coming to believe that our Creator intended that the answer to these questions is *Yes*. Expressing our creative spirit is the natural way the Creator intended us to glorify Him and serve one another. Inspiring through the arts is the key to planting seeds that change, enrich and save lives.

Our mission—not just for the Shae Foundation, but for all Christians—is to lead by example, making a positive impact in the lives of artists, encouraging, inspiring, and guiding them in using their Creator-centred gifts in service to their local and global community. It is to that end that we believe it essential to nurture the creative spirit in all of us.

The thing of it is

Simply put: If you want the answer to your questions about purpose, giftedness and happiness, ask your Creator. He's the only one who actually knows. More than your parents, more than the church, more than society, He knows precisely why you came out of the womb the way you did.

The Apostle Paul points out the fact that we can only see "imperfectly, like puzzling reflections in a mirror" (1 Corinthians 13:12), but our Creator sees the purpose-picture perfectly clearly. Reconciliation and continual communion with Him makes evident the giftedness in each of us and illuminates the path of purpose. That's the beauty of the Master Plan that includes a unique design for every snowflake reflecting God's creativity.

We are all His prisms, bending His white light into infinite unique hues, colouring this world in beautiful ways that all point back to their source—our Creator.

—Terry Benedict is a filmmaker, mentor, husband and father. He has worked on major movies (including The Terminator*) and made TV commercials for major brands. These days, he works more often with documentaries and has founded the Shae Foundation <www.ShaeFoundation.org> to inspire artists and creativity.*

1. John Locke, *Some Thoughts Concerning Education*, 1693.

CARRIED ON HIS BREATH

Creativity and Calling

Joanna Darby

It was a week before the opening of my latest solo exhibition in Newcastle. My mind was a flood of questions and my heart was awash with emotions. I was drowning. It felt as if all the good intention of the paintings, as well as hours of effort, might get swept away in a torrent of doubt.

I had mistakenly assumed that because I had presented several exhibitions before, I was past the insecurities that I was now swimming in: *Why am I doing this? Am I really an artist? Is this just a dumb idea? Is this going to send me broke? What if people don't like it? Is this all just a waste of time?*

While almost choking on these quandaries, I recalled attending a lecture presentation by a significant Australian artist, where he admitted still questioning himself in much the same way. Though I took momentary comfort from a highly successful and well-recognised figure in contemporary art still circling around those same doubts, it did little to relieve my reality . . .

I was uncertain of my calling. And I wanted to be certain of it. Desperately.

There had long been an ominous grey cloud of uncertainty and doubt hovering over my pursuit of the arts and the legitimacy of my *calling* to the arts. *Could I even label it a "calling"?* Throughout college, I had wrestled with this idea while I studied chaplaincy and art alongside each other, treating them as if they were two disconnected practices that might overlap in a merely token way but were essentially competing with each other. I could articulate great arguments about the relevance of one to the other, but deep down, I felt that one was about service to others, while the other was about self. One was clearly a ministry calling, and the other, well, I guess it could be sometimes, maybe, used in ministry, sort of . . .

So here I was—one week before the exhibition—floundering in the waters of confusion and skepticism.

Is this really how God wants me to spend my time and money, setting up a costly exhibition? Am I truly honouring God? Maybe I should just go back to the chaplaincy idea . . .

All this and more raced through my head as I sat at the Gabe Reynaud Awards—part of the Manifest Creative Arts Festival run by our church, celebrating the significance of arts in ministry and in our lives. The irony was almost too much.

But the floodwaters began to recede as I listened to speeches and presentations re-affirming the place of arts in expressing hope and love and the extraordinary God–human connection. I was reminded of the unique ability of the arts to give voice to the gospel in completely new and different ways. I was reminded that images have an unmatched power to explore the deep and mysterious things of God, that some truths must be seen or felt or heard or sung. I was convinced again that there are discoveries about the heart of Grace that simply fall short without the support and expression of a creative.

The waves subsided and confidence and purpose started coursing through me again. It was like a commissioning! I felt empowered and supported by my church. I no longer had to justify the value of my creative pursuits but could step into confidence that I was ordained for this. What an incredible about-face we are making in our churches! We are gradually moving toward a deeper understanding of the source of creativity and the value that God Himself places on creativity, allowing Christian artists to overcome insecurities regarding their gifting and calling.

And increasingly, our church is recognising and affirming this calling in the lives of many artists. This is more than just the freedom to include dance or a video clip in our worship services—in many places we've been doing that for years anyway. What I'm talking about is a profound shift in attitude and philosophy that embraces the arts and sends out the artist—just as we send out the teacher and preacher—as those *ordained* by God for this purpose. *Ordained by God!*

So why are so many artists (musicians, writers, actors, filmmakers . . .) still so unsure of their *calling*? Why are we hesitant to apply the concept and label of "calling" to an artistic life? And what do we mean by an "artistic life" anyway?

For many of us, the only *calling* we seem to be certain of is the giant slice of cake in the refrigerator that is begging to be eaten and the pillow that beckons at the end of a long day. I think I could be certain of both of these callings without dilemma or discussion. A calling to ministry, however, often seems to come with greater difficulty. And a calling to the pursuit of arts seems particularly shrouded and troublesome.

Yet many artists—both the secular and the Jesus-following kind—will refer to their creativity as something that burns in them or fills them. Perhaps they will mention a desire or passion or impulse that drives their practice and need to create. The Jesus-following kind certainly have a sense that this is more than just a desire to make stuff and there is something more significant going on than just a set of talents or skills being dumped in their lap. They may articulate being drawn by something beyond themselves to do something with their creativity. Some may even identify this as coming from the Holy Spirit but may still be reluctant to refer to it as a calling, because the phrase is usually reserved for those who study theology to work in formal pastoral ministry.

So they become troubled. Or at least, I did.

If I am passionate about my art, recognise the source of the inspiration, feel called by the Holy Spirit, and am increasingly being affirmed in my calling by my church, then that should be enough, right? "Go! Be an artist!"

Nope. Still unsure of my purpose. Mission. Calling. Whatever it is.

While calling may be difficult to define and can seem ambiguous at times, we do know it to be something affirmed in us and conferred on us by someone or something outside ourselves, namely, the Holy Spirit and the church as the body of Christ. Perhaps the problem emerges when we admit a disregard for the next step—that this *therefore implies a sense of responsibility to someone or something outside of ourselves.*

Responsibility? Really? I believe one of the most significant reasons artists are hesitant to refer to themselves as "called" is that we—the artists—have separated art-making from responsibility.

Maybe the obstruction to "certainty of calling" is no longer the church (though it has been fun blaming someone else for stifling our creativity all these years, hasn't it?). Maybe it's *us*, the artists. Perhaps the danger is that the church will be ready to embrace our creative contributions before we are willing to accept the responsibility of our calling.

In the past, artists were appointed as the speaker for their clan, the storyteller of the tribe, the artist for the sanctuary. Elders or the church or some other authority conferred their role, and they responded by creating for their community. Outside of themselves. Beyond their own studios. The sense of responsibility to pass on history or culture or faith to their community was deeply felt and the purpose of their art to educate, uplift or serve others was widely known and understood—with a responsibility to something outside themselves. The purpose was clear.

This is not the case for many modern artists and creatives. As a result of our individualistic and humanist society, artists have not only claimed that creativity is entirely birthed within themselves, they have also proposed that their creative expression only needs to have significance to themselves to have worth. There is no sense of responsibility or accountability to anyone or anything else.

Occasionally I get a chance to teach art students and I'm surprised at how many young artists matter-of-factly verbalise this phenomena when talking about their art practice:

> "I don't need to explain it. It only matters to me anyway."
>
> "I only make art for myself."
>
> "I don't care if it impacts anyone else. That's not the point."

Unfortunately many Christian artists have also adopted this mentality, often for no other reason than protection against rejection or judgment from their church. It's a good defence: "My art doesn't need to be valued by you, as long as it is valued by me." And this is true—but only to a point.

I fear that, in our self-preservation, we have created unhealthy perceptions of the purpose of art and we run the risk of using "significance to me" as an excuse for not contributing to a wider community. Subsequently, we not only rob our communities of the opportunity to feel, explore and know something by engaging with our art, but we rob ourselves. When we completely internalise the purpose of art and creativity, and we make personal development the primary concern, we separate it from any responsibility to anything and anyone outside ourselves.

Undoubtedly, I can—and should—find meaning for myself in making art. And, yes, it is undeniably important for my own relationship with God and the development of my own ideas. But on it's own, this is simply expression—valuable expression—but not a faithful response to calling.

This does not mean that unless your paintings are exhibited they don't matter. Or that unless your poetry is published, it doesn't matter. It still matters. But we must not continue to hide behind the "significance to me" shield. As Christian artists we do have a responsibility—through our expression—to raise questions, start discussion, share experiences and continue the dialogue about how we interact with God and others and this world. An artist is given a responsibility much like a prophet—to awaken, to stir, to shake, and rouse people from numbness, giving breath to the wonder and beauty of God. Both the artist and the prophet have the unique responsibility and ability to knock on the doors of people's souls.

For those artists who have already been sharing their gift outside their sketchbooks and lounge-room recording studios, this discussion may seem obvious. Even redundant. But it is still possible to exhibit and publish your work believing that it only has value to yourself, or mistakenly believing that the response of the viewer or community determines the value. However, the viewer will not always announce the value. The messages of the prophets were not always welcomed with open arms—or even understood, at times—but this did not diminish the value of their message. To reunite calling with responsibility to our communities, we must reflect on the value that our creativity has to others—the value of presenting an idea, presenting hope, no matter what the response.

To reunite calling with responsibility to our communities, we must reflect on the value that our creativity has to others.

The role of the artist is not always to paint the beautiful things or write the pretty poems. Like the prophets, artists are often called to challenge the norms of society, to question politics and trends, and to point out the ugliest realities of our world. Both the artist and the prophet offer symbols and metaphors, for the most beautiful as well as the most awful. They are the ones given the responsibility to raise their voices for truth, especially the kinds of truths that are hard to face. Ultimately, a Christian artist is called and graced with the same responsibility and capacity as the prophet—"to spark the imagination of [the] people"[1]—giving expression to hope, and offering an alternative to the ugliness.

Of course, the risk of reuniting calling with responsibility is that we are likely to be overwhelmed by the magnitude of the thing. (Especially when we start using words like artist and prophet in the same sentence.) Responsibility is scary. And most of us prefer to run from it, rather than embrace it. (Fleeing to Joppa doesn't seem so silly now, does it?) This is where a proper understanding of the source of our creativity and the role of the Holy Spirit in inspiration is indispensable. There are several biblical examples that make it clear that without direction from and connection to the Holy Spirit, our creative endeavours will end up severely misguided. Consider Joseph's brothers, who creatively concocted a cunning story about their little brother and a wild animal, or Nebuchadnezzar, who decided a giant sculpture in his front yard would be a good idea. We may be holding the tools, but, apart from Jesus we can do nothing (see **John 15:4, 5**). Developing our creativity and faithfully using it is a spiritual discipline and, like any other discipline, we are useless on our own. If we recognise Him as the source of our creativity, we must also recognise Him as the sustainer of it.

In C S Lewis's Narnian story *The Silver Chair*, Jill Pole and Eustace Scrubb find themselves unexpectedly whisked away to a strange and magnificent land. While exploring the unknown landscape, the friends are separated by a terrible accident and, alone and afraid, Jill finds herself face to face with Aslan himself. Jill is alarmed to discover she was not brought to Narnia to escape the schoolyard bullies but rather because Aslan has appointed her to an important and dangerous task—to find the lost Prince. The quest seems far beyond what Jill could ever imagine or possibly achieve. After some time, Jill summons the courage to ask Aslan how she could begin such a daunting quest. And he explained that she would be carried on his breath. Together they walk to the cliff's edge:

> She had been setting her teeth and clenching her fists for a terrible blast of the lion's breath; but the breath had been so gentle that she had not even noticed the moment at which she left the earth. . . . She felt frightened for only a second . . . floating on the breath of the Lion was so extremely comfortable. . . . If Jill had ever been in a balloon, she might have thought it like that, only better."[2]

This description has significant parallels to my calling to pursue an artistic life and my overwhelming fear of that responsibility. As Jesus sent out His disciples on their daunting mission, He said "'Peace be with you. As the Father has sent me, so I am sending you.' Then he breathed on them and said, 'Receive the Holy Spirit'" (**John 20:21, 22**).

The only way to avoid being overwhelmed by the responsibility of our calling is to become dependent on His Breath, the Holy Spirit. The same Breath that first created. The same Breath that was breathed over the darkness and the void and made something from nothing. The same Breath that re-creates us into His likeness. The Breath of Creativity Himself. Recognising that the calling and gifting for a creative life has come from the Holy Spirit is one thing, but surrendering yourself to be carried by the Holy Spirit, trusting that you will be equipped with wisdom, knowledge and understanding is another—and is essential to a faithful response.

How this "carried on His Breath" actually works is no less ambiguous than the idea of calling, but it is a clear-cut promise nonetheless. A promise that we can be certain of and a promise we can trust: Jesus gives you something to do, and He promises to carry you.

What that looks like is up to you to discover and experience. So may you remain connected to the Vine, giving voice and shape to the wonder and beauty of God in ways that no-one else can, with wisdom, knowledge and understanding that only the Spirit can give.

—Joanna Darby is a co-convener of Manifest Creative Arts Festival and co-editor of this book. She is a mother, artist, teacher and preacher from Newcastle, Australia.

1. Walter Brueggemann, *The Prophetic Imagination*, Fortress Press, 2001, page 77.
2. C S Lewis, *The Complete Chronicles of Narnia*, Harper Collins, 2005, page 560.

IN JUST SIX WORDS

Creativity and Identity

Becky De Oliveira

The worksheet said to "Colour the Bear's Ball Red." I had a comprehensive box of Crayolas in every hue, complete with a built-in sharpener, and my greatest irritation at the age of six or seven was the way some crayons were quickly reduced to stubs, while others—less applicable to most situations—remained ever sharp. I wanted some semblance of equality and even more than that I wanted my work to be colourful. So I looked for a red that wasn't seeing much in the way of action. My box had no shortage of reds. Red—obviously. Watermelon red. Brick red. Maybe Tomato red. Sports-car-owned-by-older-man-with-self-esteem-issues red. (Now I'm just making up names).

I have no idea how many reds there were, only that I settled finally on a colour I recall as "Indian red," observing that it was more of a rusty brown, presumably—this being a less enlightened time—to simulate the hue of a First American person's skin. I coloured the bear's ball—vigilantly applying the wax in thin layers for a smooth and flawless look.

My teacher—a painfully thin proponent of natural foods who often urged the first grade to sample homemade cashew nut milk and sprouts with the dirt still hanging off the roots—paced up and down the perpendicular aisles, observing over our shoulders. She paused to my right and waited. I waited, too, expecting a hearty congratulations, maybe some extra reward tokens to put in my empty brown plastic bottle (still smelling of vitamin E). Combined with many others—each representing a job well done—these tokens would possibly earn me a box of watercolours or a single random volume (something like "N") of the encyclopedia as a reward at the end of term. Instead I felt the sharp rebuke of her nails digging into my shoulder as she squeezed me to signal her disapproval.

"That's not red," she said, her voice tinged with mild disgust. "Didn't you read the instructions?"

"It's *Indian* red!" I said proudly, certain this bit of verbal gymnastics would provide the clarity necessary to earn me my accolades. I couldn't conceive of anyone not being impressed with a child choosing an *underused variation* of the colour red. I have no idea what happened next—my sense is that it was underwhelming. She didn't beat me with her paddle or stand me in front of the class to be publicly humiliated the way children unfortunate enough to wear earrings to school or be African American were often treated. But I remember clearly the dismay and confusion I felt at the realisation that my creativity had gone unappreciated.

There really should have been a thunderous voice at this point—or at least a skywriter—someone to really thump it to me: "Wake up to reality, Beck. This is your world and you better get used to it."

If you want to be *appreciated*, creativity is not the shortest and most direct route. Probably there is no route. If you want to be appreciated, you should, well, you should quickly—don't spare the horses!—get another goal.

Creativity crazy

Us creative people like to do crazy stuff, like spike our hair and get tattoos. We dress in outlandish fashion, casually modelling clothes that other people claim they'd "never have the nerve" to wear. People like me waste vast amounts of time—the hours other people spend on productive and meaningful activities that add value to their communities—playing silly games. For instance, we like to "Write Our Life Story Using Just Six Words." Why six? Who knows? I'm convinced it probably has something "beastly" about it.

> Should have really been something else.
>
> Wanted everyone to like her lots.
>
> Had potential; squandered most of it.

About 90 per cent of my problem (the other 10 per cent is my hair) is that I've had significant difficulty throughout my life accepting myself. I have always wanted to be something else—often going to great lengths to whip myself into submission. What I'm really good at is words and images. I am visual and verbal. And I enjoy using these strengths to create the world around me whether that involves writing a chapter like this one—which I'll have written and rewritten several times before anyone else reads it, anxious to get the words just right, focusing on the meaning, the rhythm, the music of it all—or framing and hanging my children's artwork or rearranging my furniture to make a living space that is unique and beautiful. I draw and paint—not as much as I used to, but more than most people.

These are useful talents and I've managed to make a living from them to some degree—but it has bothered me much more than it should that no-one *takes me seriously*. Why do I care about this? I'm really not sure. It's been an enormous waste of energy over what is coming up to something like a lifetime.

My sense is that although they try hard to pretend otherwise, almost everyone fears and loathes the creative. Take, for instance, the backhanded way in which we are routinely complimented. If only I had a curly twig for every time someone has called me "artsy" or "quirky"—why, I could fashion a bird's nest-style house shaped like a castle with turrets and macramé chandeliers. Or take, for instance, my earlier observation about comments regarding clothing that other people would never have "the nerve" to wear. This feels like a code—as so much of the dialogue between creatives and non-creatives does. What I suspect it *really* means—reading between the lines—is "You should not have chosen those trousers. No sane person would wear those crazy fancy trousers with the sequinned toucan stitched just above the knee." That's what it means to "not have the nerve" to wear a particular item. It really means to not demonstrate the lack of judgment about what's appropriate. A result of this code, for me, is that I'm never quite sure whether I'm being complimented or gently chastised, but being unusually paranoid, I generally suspect the latter.

Of the adjectives commonly used to describe me, "artsy" and "quirky" come up most frequently and neither of these is particularly how I want anyone to see me. But there's nothing I can really do about this, so I just fume and stew in a rather infantile and unproductive way. And sketch angry faces and poisoned arrows in my Moleskin notebook, obviously.

Those creative types

Malcolm Gladwell observes that Americans, when surveyed, claim to want a "bold, strong" coffee. In fact, this is not what they want at all. They want weak, milky sweet coffee. But they don't want to *say that* because it sounds, well, kind of lame. Similarly, everyone claims to *want* creativity—in employees, in friends, in volunteers—but few people are serious about this. Creativity is as much an acquired taste as dark, bitter coffee. It's unpalatable to many. The idea is attractive—seems impressive, intellectual, daring—but the reality maybe starts you on the path toward an ulcer.

Of the adjectives commonly used to describe me, "artsy" and "quirky" come up most frequently and neither of these is particularly how I want anyone to see me.

People like their people *milky*—easy to swallow, palatable, not too offensive, too strong or too specific. This makes it hard to be creative in the sense that you continually get mixed messages. People are always telling you how wonderful you are—the affirmation is endless—while at the same time finding ways to subtly communicate that you need to really consider becoming someone entirely different.

Before I start to sound too whiney (perhaps a bit late to be worrying about that?), it's important for me to point out that I've had a huge amount of support in my life from people who have loved me—as well as people who have sometimes merely tolerated me—and I'm convinced that has ultimately given me the strength to allow myself to be, even if it has taken me the better part of 40 years to get to this place. I owe a huge debt to the teachers who complimented my work, to church members who gave me gifts like easels to use for my painting and offered me jobs creating murals for Sabbath school, and to my parents who kept an uncanny likeness of Adolf Hitler that I had sculpted for eighth-grade history class displayed on their fireplace mantle piece for years, in spite of all the disapproving eyebrows it brought from visitors. This toast is to my parents—saintly beyond reason.

As with many words and terms that people casually toss about, the very definition of "creativity" is in doubt for me—by which I mean that I'm not entirely sure we all mean the same thing when we use it. When people call me "creative," it's most often in reaction to some outward manifestation of nonconformity; when I call myself *creative*, it's most often in reaction to something I have made. *Ex nihilo*. Out of nothing. The way God created the world—not to sound overly egotistical or anything—but that's how it feels. That's where the creative process gets its addictive power.

Right here, on this page, at one point there was *nothing*. I came along and covered it with something. I can't even tell you how good and powerful this feels—and how this feeling mostly even squashes any fears I have about whether what I've created is any good. *Good* is almost beside the point. Where there was nothing, I have made something. If I sense that it might also be good, well, that's pretty sweet and infinitely more satisfying: *And God saw that it was good. And the evening and the morning were the first day.*

Creative people aren't creative because they spike their hair or wear nose rings or exhibit signs of nonconformity. In fact, many of us—here I'm mostly talking about myself—look much like suburban soccer moms, dressed in athletic gear for virtually all occasions (creativity requires a high level of physical comfort). And rather than seeking out thrills and new experiences, I'm very much a person who favours routine and repetition. I wake up at precisely the same time every day and either walk or run outdoors before much of anyone else is up.

My favourite food is oatmeal. My favourite activities are reading, visiting cafés, browsing farmers' markets, antique shops and art galleries, and hiking in the woods. I don't have a favourite colour—and flatly refuse to name one because I like colours only in relation to the specific context in which they appear. This, I'm told, is an obvious sign of my obnoxious and contrarian creative personality—and who am I to argue?

I also like staring at fire and water and looking out the window of any sort of moving vehicle. I'm prone to depression at times and deep melancholy. I can be a drama queen, although I find this trait inexcusable and am working hard to eradicate it. I'm creative because my impulse—given all the options in the world—is to stamp something that is uniquely mine on the world, whether that's through writing or visual art or simply the way I arrange the books on my shelves or the frames on my walls.

I go back and forth on the question of whether every single person is creative and those who manifest no obvious signs are simply repressed in some way and need unlocking. Isn't it possible that not everyone needs to create their world the way creative people do? That some may have other needs—no less essential or urgently felt?

Uncreative writing?

Regular people always seemed better and safer to me. I wanted to be one of them. Raised in a Seattle suburb, I grew up surrounded by doctors, engineers, nurses, lawyers—and later, computer programmers who do some kind of work that might be creative but that I cannot, for the life of me, visualise in concrete terms. (Even now, visiting my parents, I walk past the offices of Google and I can't stop wondering what all these people do at Google. What would it even be?). Over and over I buried my creative impulses, trying to fit in a bit better and feel safer.

When it came time for college, I ditched art and majored in history, planning to go to law school where I would become a criminal prosecutor. Later I moved to England and did my first master's degree—in education because it seemed useful (it isn't particularly). I finally branched out into my real area of passion just as I reached 30, doing another master's—this time in creative writing. This led me, oddly, to the least creative job I've ever held—one I only gave up after four years—as an instructor of academic writing in the School of Education at Andrews University.

During my tenure there, I was told repeatedly that "academic writing is not creative"—this issued, it would seem, as a warning. I should by no means try to attempt to teach my students to add any interest or flair to their description and analysis. Mostly people seemed keen that I make sure students knew the appropriate levels of headings (bold centred, roman centred, bold left align, italics left align) and that they master the reference style used by the American Psychological Association (APA).

"But none of that is *writing*," I'd say, baffled at this bizarre emphasis. Also, not to be a contrarian, but I tend to believe that *all writing* is creative. Where there was nothing, you have created something. *Ex nihilo*. Creativity doesn't have to come with sequins. The fervent rejection of creativity in academic writing is interesting because it seems to indicate a belief that what is creative is somehow soft or intellectually inferior. I allowed myself to be bullied by these sorts of ideas for a long time—often feeling that I, too, was soft and intellectually inferior as a result of my creative impulses. Maybe I am. But so what?

Alternative six words

Let's get back to my parents for a minute—and allow this to sink in. They displayed—*publicly*—a sculpture of Adolf Hitler in their home, simply *because I had made it* and they wanted to show that they were proud of me. This is significant to me, probably because I know how I would struggle if one of my children were to, say, draw an uncanny portrait of contemporary politicians I didn't agree with or disliked. There is simply no way I could hang that up—I'd be embarrassed and probably berate them for their choice of subject. But what if the church could be more like my parents—what if we could simply celebrate without censure? Perhaps we'd have whole generations of people whose lives summed up in six words could go something like:

> Was able to be fully myself.
>
> Felt like what I did mattered.
>
> Valued by God and other people.

—Becky De Oliveira is the author of a collection of essays titled Keeping it Real in the Real World *and two children's books*—Your Angel *and* What Shall I Dream About?*—and is editor of the Christian lifestyle magazine* LIFE.info*, published in the United Kingdom. Becky is originally from Seattle but lives in Michigan where she is a full-time doctoral student in English Education at Western Michigan University. She currently teaches Methods for Teaching Writing in Secondary Schools at WMU and Creative Writing at Andrews University.*

AWAKENING THE CREATIVE SPIRIT

Creativity and the Everyday

Graeme B Frauenfelder

We have fun in my university classes. I have been known to lecture in my clown costume! For "Learning and Creativity," the semester begins with a game called "Big Wind Blows." The students sit in a circle and I stand in the centre. Then the action begins.

"Big wind blows for anyone who loves the beach," I call out, and most of the class race around trying to find a different seat.

Soon there is a new person in the middle. There is much hilarity as each centre person finds something to say that gets as many people as possible out of their chairs and creating a whirlwind of bodies around the room. Students can hardly believe this is a university class!

Finally, I dawdle to make sure I'm the one left in the middle. "Big wind blows for everyone who is creative," I say.

Mostly there is silence, as only one or two race for a new seat. I purposely stay in the middle. "Big wind blows for anyone who is creative and knows it—but is not sure about telling everyone." A few more race across the circle.

". . . anyone who is a little bit creative" and ". . . anyone who doesn't think they are creative" are the final calls. The majority of the class respond to one or the other. When I ask about their responses, many say something like "I'm not creative, but I wish I was."

These university students study "Learning and Creativity" because they hope that over the semester they'll be given something like "The Top 10 Ways to be a Creative Teacher." We don't do that. Instead we awaken their creative spirit and they unleash it and find their own authentic ways of being creative educators as well as teachers of creativity.

Join the class

"On the count of three, clap your hands. One. Two. Three." A loud sound of hands slapping together fills the air. I remind them that thousands of cells just died—and right now their bodies are making brand new cells to replace them. In some organs of the body, the cells are replaced every six weeks. Haemoglobin cells are renewed every 90 days. It is said we have a different "new" body every few years.

"Do you realise you are creative, without even trying to be? Have you ever tried something new, figured out a different way to go somewhere, solved a problem, made an excuse or told a story? Of course, we are all creative!" I encourage my students to awaken to a realisation of who they are, what they already manifest and their potential yet to be realised.

One student says she doesn't have an imagination, so I ask about her last holiday. A vivid description of the place, the people she was with and what she experienced on the tropical island enthrals us, almost as if we were there.

"Is this holiday happening now?" I ask.

"No," she exclaims with a roll of her eyes as if to say, "Dumb question!"

"When you told us, were you seeing it as if you were there?"

"Of course!" she replies, wondering where I am going with this bizarre, but friendly, interrogation.

The questioning continues. "What are you planning to do on the weekend?"

Her eyes light up as she talks of going out to eat at a favourite restaurant with her friends and a night of dancing and music in the city. I remind her that neither the holiday she recalled, nor this weekend's entertainment are happening right now. They are all in her imagination. I take a vote on whether the class thinks she has a great imagination. It's unanimous—and she can't argue!

"You are quite a storyteller, as well," I reflect. "I noticed how you had the attention of the whole class as if they were right there experiencing it all with you. Storytelling is a form of creativity."

I ask my students if they have ever made up excuses for why they haven't done something. They all have. We chuckle as they realise they have all been creative at that kind of storytelling!

Over the next hour, we explore everyone's lives to discover their many manifestations of creativity. Many think that creative means being an artist—so cooking, dancing, coming up with ideas to entertain kids, being a handyman or problem solving aren't on their creativity radar. I recall a student who constantly drew beautiful detailed pencil sketches of flowers on the cover of her notebook, but considered herself not to be highly creative because she only draws for herself, doesn't exhibit her work and has never sold a drawing. A practical guy doesn't do art, so thinks he isn't creative. Someone who loves to sing declares, "I am not creative because I'm not professional." I tell my students that professionalism, perfection, publicity, popularity, profit or recognition aren't the criteria of whether a person is creative. Those qualities come with choosing to pursue and polish a form of creativity and marketing it.

"Who can sing?" is another of my questions. One or two hands are raised if I'm lucky. Then I start singing "Twinkle, twinkle little star" and soon the whole class joins in. Then I ask, "Who can't sing?"—and not a hand goes up!

As the class ends, almost everyone can stand and say with confidence, "I am creative and proud to be creative." For those who can't, I get them to stand and say the words just to humour me. They usually do, and I reflect that they have just acted and recited some lines—which is another form of creativity! We laugh, and for the rest of the semester experiment with a variety of forms of creative expression in a safe and encouraging environment.

We don't focus primarily on teaching creative techniques, but rather on awakening the spirit of creativity that for many has been dormant or unrecognised and often unvalued. When the major projects for the semester are presented in our "Marketplace of Learning and Creativity," the students amaze themselves—and often I'm surprised as well, even though I see dramatic transformations every semester.

Arts Anonymous

Our human creativity is a tiny part of Creation in everyday life. Often Creation is spoken of as an event in the distant past, forgetting that it is an all-the-time amazing phenomenon. New life is constantly being generated. New galaxies, stars and other cosmic bodies are being born right now. Atoms and molecules are continually being recombined into different animate and inanimate forms. Soil, sun and rain become grain that is turned into bread, which becomes energy to propel my muscles and glucose in my blood to fuel my brain. Grass becomes milk. Yesterday's worms become today's eggs and become part of our human organisms during and after dinner. Now that is highly creative! Love creates babies, the miracle of new life. Our work creates an income that turns into food, shelter, pleasure, generosity and future security. Life, existence, the universe: without creativity, they would neither begin nor continue.

Imagine if there was one type of animal, one type of bird, one type of fish, one type of flower, one type of tree, one type of food, and there was only one colour. If every sunset looked the same and every person was identical, how mundane and boring would that be? Diversity, variety and creativity are abundantly displayed throughout all of Creation. They are inherent in the nature of the Creator in whose image the writer of **Genesis 1** says we are created. All of life radiates variety and diversity and creativity. How can we awaken our senses and aesthetic capabilities to enhance our awareness of the creativity, to share it, to celebrate it, to open to the potential of its beauty and power? To have it is integral to the quality of our lives, relationships and worship.

I recall a time when my creative expression seemed to have dried up and inspiration was lacking. A time of major physical health struggles and deep wrestling with the fog and burden of long-term depression. As I scanned the local newspaper ads, there was a surprising tiny advertisement that captured my curiosity:

> Arts Anon. A 12-step program for recovering your creativity. 6 pm Wednesday at Katoomba Community Centre.

I had learned from people in recovery about the value of the Alcoholics Anonymous principles for people's addictions, co-dependence, debt and other life struggles. But for art? All the other 12-step groups were about getting rid of something in their lives. Surely Arts Anonymous wasn't about getting over an addiction to creative expression?! My curiosity led me to a small weekly group of fellow artistically creative people on a journey of healing, honesty and rediscovering their abilities in creative expression.

"Hi! I'm Annabel and I'm an opera singer."

"G'day! I'm Steve and I'm a jazz guitarist."

"Hello, My name is Jen and I'm a book illustrator."

As we introduced ourselves and our form of creativity, I realised that each person was identifying with the way they used their creativity as a profession. I felt small and inadequate, a phoney who shouldn't be there. I had never made a living from a particular form of music, art or writing—but it was my turn to speak:

"I'm Graeme. An actor, storyteller, clown, singer, poet, dancer, songwriter, painter, guitarist and more—and I'm scared you'll ask me to prove myself with them all, but I can't. It's not what I once did for a living that counts, but that all of these are inside me. Some I've done, others are in me waiting to get out. You all seem so professional and I feel like I don't belong because I'm not as competent as you."

> The question "How have I been creative this week?" opened a space of consciousness that soon became a daily one.

There was no commenting as people identified themselves, so I sat in my feelings of inadequacy for a little while. As the group moved into a time of sharing thoughts, feelings and experiences, I relaxed as I was validated, valued and welcomed "just as I am." The following week, I noticed how everyone included all the other forms of artistic expression that lived within them—not just the ones they used, or once used, professionally for earning money.

Each week, there was time for each person to say what they had done "for their art" in the past week. To start with, there was little for me to say. As I climbed the hill, walked through the bush, and wandered through the streets to Arts Anon each week, I would wrack my brain to recall how I had expressed creativity since the previous meeting. The question "How have I been creative this week?" opened a space of consciousness that soon became a daily one. Without even trying, my dried-up creative expression began to awaken and often surprise me. I now kept looking for creativity in my life to recognise and value, and for creativity I could express.

My daily life became more interesting. University assignments became innovative and often turned into artistic projects with deep meaning and enjoyment. Sometimes I would be offered creative opportunities with payment—what a bonus in a time of poverty! One of my year-long major research projects on wellness documented my ongoing journey of healing and recovery that included creativity, playfulness and healthy pleasure. The title—"Dead Bones Dancing!"—came from the story in Ezekiel of a valley of desolation coming to life (see **Ezekiel 37**). The research was about the resurrection of the spirit of life from times of dryness and brokenness.

These are stories from my life. What are your stories of creativity and the ongoing process of creation in your everyday moments? How would you like to experience your creativity blossoming and flourishing and enriching your life, family, work, church and community? Creation is taking place in you, in me and in our world right now. Watch what the Creator will do with all that potential when we value it and get out of the way!

Let's play

I hope you are recognising that you—and everyone else—is creative without even trying, just by being human, as well as in many activities of our everyday lives. I encourage you to value what you already have within you and let go of any mind games of comparing your proficiency and competence with others. Be daring and experiment and give things a go in an environment of encouragement and non-judgment.

Stretch yourself sometimes—no, do it often—that's the best way to develop creative abilities. The seeds of creativity are in you. Nurture and fertilise them in a supportive environment and there is no limit to what will blossom and the joy you and others will experience from the fruits of your own personal styles of creativity.

The easiest way to take your creativity to a new level: Do something different. It's that easy. Then keep doing that again and again—and make sure you're enjoying it!

Better still, play with kids, loosen up and lose yourself in the moment and their creativity. Life can be an experimental adventure of great joy and fulfilment. I know. You don't know where you will end up—and that's half the fun. Come play with me!

Creativity is the awakening and expression of the Spirit of Life.

—Graeme B Frauenfelder is a global adventurer of love, kindness, playfulness and creativity. As an entertaining storyteller, inspirational professional speaker and creative facilitator of experiential learning, he awakens people of all ages to the Spirit of Life. During each Olympic Games and soccer World Cup, you will find him in the host country as a clown and clown trainer at community-building festivals. His nieces and nephews have good reason to call him "The Fun Uncle!"

WITHOUT TWEED COAT, BUFFALO HORNS OR PIPE

Creativity and Criticism

Jotham Kingston

"Hey, I read your book," he said.

"Oh, really," I said, suddenly feeling quite modest.

"Yes," he continued. "In fact, I was wondering whether you'd like to come over some time this week and discuss it."

Grand visions flashed through my mind. A large lacquered table, presided over by a large set of buffalo horns; he, leaning forward intently, almost whispering, "*How did you do it? How did you write such genius*?"

Me, dressed in a tweed coat, chewing the stem of a bakelite pipe nodding sagely, *knowing*.

"Thursday is good for me," I said.

"Thursday it is, then," he replied.

Thursday arrived. There was a large table but no buffalo horns, tweed coat or pipe. His wife served us each an ice-cold lemonade, then retreated from the room.

My book sat on the table in front of him, well thumbed.

"I read your book," he repeated, by way of introduction, but before I could respond modestly, as before, he said, "I didn't *like* it."

He looked at me and nodded a few times for punctuation.

"Oh," was all I could manage. I reached for my ice-cold lemonade and took a swift sip. "Why is that?"

"I didn't get it," he said, with a shrug. He took the book, opened it and thumbed through from the beginning, a pained expression on his face. "See, you didn't really *say* anything until page 32." A strong finger stabbed down onto the book, squashing the words onto the paper like he was destroying a bug. Then he rifled through the earlier pages. "See, all this stuff . . . it's nothing."

He shrugged, closed the book, turned it and slid it across the table.

And there it sat, marooned, in no-man's land.

So much for the tweed coat, the buffalo horns and bakelite pipe.

My head swam and my vision blurred. He just sat, waiting for an explanation, as if I had set out to do him personal wrong by writing my book.

I wanted to twist his nose and tell him he was an idiot. I wanted to remind him of the cold, early mornings I had dragged myself from sweet repose to sit, shivering at my keyboard. I wanted to explain the sacrifices I had made to my career as a pastor to write, and how God had clearly opened doors for me and wanted me to pursue a career in writing.

I wanted to say, "Hold on, buster. I graduated at the top of my class in Theology. *Theology!*" The stuff I was writing was gold—and he didn't *get* it? How he could sum up all my work with a simple, dumb "I didn't get it" was beyond me. I was astonished, to say the least.

When I finally found my vocal cords, what I said was a lot more diplomatic than what I thought. "So what you're telling me is that this book wasn't for you."

"No," he said. "And I don't think it was for anyone." He leaned forward, lifted his hands and brought the tips of his fingers and thumb together to articulate his point. "You've got to *connect* with your audience," he said. "There's no point writing if you're never on the same page as the people you're writing to."

As he explained, he shared stories from his hard-won experience as a real-estate developer, about how *connection* with clients was crucial to the success of his business. To tell you the truth, I remember more of the flavour of his words rather than the words themselves. Then, with the flourish of a magician, he extracted a book from behind his back and also slid it across the table. "Here," he said. "Read this."

The underlying message was clear: he had read *my* book and I owed him. Now it was time for me to read one of *his*. Of course he had not written it himself. That would be too symmetrical. But he recommended it heavily. The book was by a "Successful Author," he said—Harry Beckwith and its title was *What Clients Love*.

While he gave me a detailed summary of the book, I clutched onto my glass. The condensation oozed between my fingers. My heart remained heavy, yet a hard resolve built within me: to write, to write again, and to write better than I had ever written before.

I took the book and promised to read it.

To my own credit, I took the pounding like a man. None of the hurt, disappointment or offense I felt was conveyed in the meeting. In fact, a few weeks later I heard from a third party that he had been impressed by the way I had taken the criticism. He had fully expected me to get offended, to not listen to what he had to say.

So why do we write or create?

I heard an author say once that the reason he had taken up writing was so that he could fulfil his daydream of sitting at a coffee shop with his writer friends, sipping a black coffee, and complaining expansively about how this or that writing project was or was not getting on.

To a certain degree, we write for ourselves. As creatives, we like the sound of our own voices. We like showing other people our stuff. We like being the Writer, rather than the Reader. The minority, and not the masses. The silk cravat, so to speak, and not the Windsor tie. But I suggest that as good writers—and good Christian writers in particular—there comes a point in our writing journey where we come face-to-face with our ego, and we must put our ego to death.

To a certain degree, we write for ourselves. As creatives, we like the sound of our own voices.

I am drawn to the Bible story of Joseph. Many times, when my life has felt like a dead-end, when my dreams have felt like they're slipping away, or there is a glaring lack of buffalo horns and I am face-to-face with a blunt critic, I have sought out the comfort of its wider perspective. In Joseph, I have seen reflections of myself.

When he was just a teenager, something crucial happened to Joseph. These days, we would say he "caught a vision." He literally had a dream about his future. Joseph, it seems, did not understand the social and political implications of his dream. He was just excited that he *had* one. Joseph was not arrogant for having the dream, it had been given to him as a gift.

But God gave the dream to Joseph long before he had the skill, experience and maturity to carry it out. Not only that, but the dream confounded Joseph's life and turned it upside-down. In many ways, the dream functioned like a curse. Had Joseph not had the dream, he would have doubtlessly come of age, married a local girl like his brothers, settled down and contributed in equal measure to the dysfunction of his extended family.

Throughout the story, we see Joseph's ego fighting for supremacy, preventing him from finding his true voice as a man of God. A slave in Potiphar's house, Joseph's rise to prominence caught the attention of his master's wife. While Joseph rejected her sexual advances, it was clear from his words (see **Genesis 39:8, 9**) that he believed that his success in Potiphar's house was due solely to his own skill, ability and personal magnetism. His ego was a stumbling-block to what God wanted to do in his life.

He was then thrown into prison and this same ego continued to struggle for survival. We are told that "God blessed Joseph and everything he did"—and again Joseph rose to the top of the heap. When he met Pharaoh's butler and baker and interpreted their dreams, Joseph's battle with his ego was evident in his words. He was bitterly preoccupied with the injustice of his own plight (see **Genesis 40:15**). You can almost hear him grinding out the "If Only . . ." song over and over again on his little violin.

At several points throughout this story, I see Joseph as being torn, stretched in two directions, between the dream that burns like a fire and the reality of his current circumstance—in a foreign prison, no hope of release, wrongly accused, a world away from where he felt he was meant to be. Yet this Joseph—torn between two opposite poles—is not the Joseph we see just a few verses later when he is taken as a dream-interpreting specialist before the Pharaoh of Egypt.

The Bible is silent about exactly how, when and where Joseph's ego was killed but, in the words of his response to Pharaoh, we see a 180-degree turnaround. To Pharaoh's question, "Can you interpret my dream?" Joseph's immediate response was a simple, "No. I can't." Then he added, "But God will give the Pharaoh the answer he desires" (see **Genesis 41:15, 16**).

Joseph heard the dream and explained its meaning. He could have used the opportunity before Pharaoh to push his own agenda, to seek justice for himself and realise his own dream. But it was a different Joseph who stood before Pharaoh. His concern was not in fulfilling his own dream, but in helping Pharaoh with his. There was not an ounce of ego in his advice as to how Pharaoh should respond to the predictions from his dreams. Somehow, Joseph had emerged the victor from the death struggle against himself—quietly confident, thoughtful and wise.

What does all this have to do with taking criticism as a writer? Note carefully that it is not until Joseph sacrifices his own dream in favour of helping Pharaoh with his dream that God sees Joseph is fit for fulfilment of his own destiny. I believe that in order to be truly powerful, to write for God, every good Christian author or artist must come to the point where they sacrifice their own ego.

All creativity is autobiographical. All writing is autobiographical. All speaking is autobiographical. Create, write or talk long enough, and you won't be able to stop your own story from leaking through the cracks. It is impossible to write or create something that is not your own story.

Herein is the problem.

What if, like young Joseph, my story is full of my own ego and my own striving to survive? What if, in my intent to be a good, Christian writer, I never get beyond using a Christian audience of readers and thinkers as a platform for my own ambition? My creativity will be impotent.

That meeting I had at the dining room table with my critic who shall remain nameless was a nail in the coffin of my ego. It was by no means the last.

As good Christian writers, why do we write? There is no denying we write for the sheer joy of creativity, to fit words and ideas together that flow, to express and explore our God-given unique perspective on the world. There is no denying the satisfaction that comes from having one's work read and appreciated. May I suggest that for a "good writer" this *might* be the end of it. But for a Christian writer, our purpose to write, I think, is much deeper.

We write and create for no less purpose than to change the world.

Around me is the world. It's home to seven-odd billion people, has a total land mass of around 150 billion square kilometres, and is filled with all sorts of societal and political problems. Many of its inhabitants do not know Jesus and are ignorant of their inheritance rights to the universe as sons and daughters of the Most High God. *This* is why we write. *This* is why we create.

Taking criticism is hard. Death of the ego is painful. But, like me, you have a God-given dream to give people a message that will set them free. Now, it's kind of surreal, but the tools in front of *you* have the power to change the world—if we would get ourselves out of the way and let our ego die in favour of confidence in the providence of God.

—Jotham Kingston is some guy who teaches Science and Technology at an Adventist school in Mildura in regional Victoria, Australia, where it hardly ever rains. He has written a few books—including Brinn: War in Her Veins *and* The Door Between Worlds*—that he keeps parked in his garage near his Fiat 125 Special.*

GIVE UP YOUR DREAMS

Creativity and Sacrifice

Andy Nash

Recently I spoke to a group of high-school seniors, and gave them some advice that they probably didn't expect. I told them that, at age 18, they were at a time of life when they were probably getting a lot of advice that went something like this:

> Follow your heart.
>
> Sacrifice everything for your dreams.
>
> Never, ever, ever, ever, ever, ever, ever, ever, ever give up. (Ever, ever.)

I told them that, since they were already getting plenty of advice for age 18, I was just going to skip that step and tell them what advice I'd give them when they were 28 or 38.

> The advice would be this: *Give up your dreams*.

Huh?

I acknowledged that my advice was a little unusual for high-school graduates—perhaps a little uninspiring. How often do you see "Give up your dreams" as a senior class vision statement? How often do you find it on a Hallmark card? "Dear Graduate: Give up your dreams. Love, Grandma."

But I absolutely believe this is one of the most important things we can ever do—give up our dreams.

When I say to give up your dreams, I told the students, I don't mean that you shouldn't still have dreams and desires in your heart. You should. And as you move forward into college or university study and a career, you should work hard at whatever you do.

But you also have to be careful not to clutch too tightly onto your own plans and dreams because they can end up becoming too important to you. They can become a god.

I have a friend who was a gifted writer coming out of university. In fact, all he wanted to do was write a bestselling novel. Writing a novel was his dream. He woke up thinking about it and he went to bed thinking about it. He travelled throughout Europe doing research for his novel, then lived on a kibbutz in Israel. He was a Jew—a very secular Jew. As he continued working on his novel, he fell in with some Christian friends and began to learn about Yeshua, Jesus, the Messiah. After an incredible series of events, he was baptised in the Jordan River.

But my friend's story wasn't yet complete. In fact, he wasn't truly converted, even after being baptised in the Jordan. He returned to the United States and continued working on his novel. One night he was walking the streets of Gainesville, Florida. He kept hearing this voice over and over in his head: *If you want Me, you've got to burn the book. If you want Me, you've got to burn the book.*

This was asking a lot. This book was my friend's most cherished dream, his deepest desire. There was nothing he wanted to clutch onto more. *If you want Me, you've got to burn the book.*

It was as though my friend had known it all along. There wasn't room in his life for two masters. He went back to his apartment and using a hot plate his mum had given him to cook with, he set his manuscript on fire. He literally watched his dream go up in smoke.

> This is one of the most spiritual experiences you can ever have—letting go of what you most want to clutch onto.

"I want your best"

This is one of the most spiritual experiences you can ever have—letting go of what you most want to clutch onto. Because it means you're deciding to obey the first commandment: "You must not have any other god but me" (Exodus 20:3).

I invited the students to go back to their rooms that night and read Malachi 1, a chapter all about giving up what you most want to hold onto. The Jews were supposed to bring their best animals for sacrifice. Instead they were bringing their worst. God says to them: "When you bring injured, crippled or diseased animals and offer them as sacrifices, should I accept them from your hands?" (see Malachi 1:8, 9).

Why did it matter to God what kind of animals were brought for sacrifice? Because by giving Him our best, we're putting the most faith in Him. A sacrifice, by definition, is supposed to feel painful to us. It isn't painful to give up our worst. Ask a child to give up a toy they don't play with anymore. But then ask a child to give up their best toy—their favourite doll or car. It's no different as we get older. What do we value most in our life? Are we willing to put that on the altar?

God asks us to release what we want to clutch onto—a sacrifice without defect. Here's the interesting part: When an animal sacrifice was cooked in the fire, a portion of it was typically given back to the priest to be eaten.

So what the worshipper offered, the worshipper also ate. If you offer what's pure, you eat what's pure. If you offer what's tainted, you eat what's tainted.

The emotions in Malachi weren't all that different from the emotions expressed when a bright young man wants to follow Christ—but isn't willing to give up what matters most to him. Jesus says, "There is still one thing you haven't done. Sell all your possessions and give the money to the poor, and you will have treasure in heaven. Then come, follow me" (**Luke 18:22**).

Jesus didn't give this same counsel to every wealthy person He met. But to this young man, money had become too important. It had become a god and was keeping him from the fullness of life in Christ. The man walked away sad; he wasn't willing to give up his best.

It isn't just the bad things that keep our relationship with God from soaring. It can also be the good things: the things that become too important to us, the things we wake up and go to bed thinking about. This can include careers, dreams, possessions, relationships, and even some of the most honourable things on earth, including service and ministry. All these can become too important to us.

In my memoir *Paper God*, I shared my own experience with this: a personal dream years ago of publishing my own magazine. I took such a massive risk that I was, in effect, sacrificing other areas of my life to pursue this one. Though my dream itself was a good dream, it became too important to me. I grew to despise it and so did my family.

Stepping in faith isn't supposed to be exciting; it's supposed to be painful. It means walking *away* from what matters most to us, leaving it on the altar to be refined by the fire of God.

After my friend burned his book, he experienced great peace in his life. Incidentally, God didn't take away his gift for writing. He transformed it. Clifford Goldstein went on to be one of the leading writers in the Adventist Church. But first, his gift needed to be refined in the fire: the fat burned up and the blood drained.

Give up your dreams. Entrust to God what you most want to clutch onto. Then watch what happens.

—Andy Nash is professor of journalism at Southern Adventist University, based in Collegedale, Tennessee, USA. This essay is adapted from his new book: The Haystacks Church *(Review and Herald).*

SERVING

THUNDERBIRDS, LEGO® AND WORKING WITH GOD

Creativity and Ministry

Tony Knight

Tiptoeing down the stairs in an effort not to wake the rest of the house, I furtively crept toward my goal. The massive "ON" switch made a deafening "CLICK", followed closely by a loud humming as our huge black-and-white TV began its laborious warm up. I literally trembled with anticipation as the congealed mass on the monochrome screen gradually resolved itself into a test pattern. For a kid growing up in the 1960s, school holidays were the best time of year, especially since at least two of the four TV stations started broadcasting an hour earlier.

Finally, the awaited moment came—"10, 9, 8, 7, 6, 5, 4, 3, 2, and 1 . . . THUNDERBIRDS ARE GO!" As the mighty strains of the *Thunderbirds* anthem shook the house, I was now oblivious to the noise, being swept into a captivating world of adventure, resourcefulness, heroism and wondrous machines seemingly designed for every contingency.

For those unfamiliar with the world of *Thunderbirds*, the show uses a vast array of beautifully constructed models, miniature sets and puppet characters to tell the story of International Rescue, a service dedicated to saving human lives. Spawned in the fertile mind of creative genius Gerry Anderson, the scenes are complex and elaborate. You don't just board your rescue craft, you stand with your back to a life-sized panel with your picture on it. The panel revolves, then tilts, shooting you headfirst down a chute where your slide is arrested, you again rotate, the panel reshapes into a chair while an articulated arm carries you to your rocket and places you in the cockpit. Fantastic stuff—and the real adventure hasn't even begun yet . . .

The next 50 minutes would inevitably pass by all too quickly. As the final scenes were replaced by a dying white blip on the screen and the call to breakfast would come—dragging me from my reverie—my mind would be filled with an unquenchable creative spark. The rest of the day would be spent with cardboard and sticky tape, felt-tip colours and glue, re-creating the scenarios that had been played out before my receptive eyes and absorbed by my fertile mind. The scenes I re-created were just as elaborate, the models just as detailed, no part of the house was spared—stairways, landings, every square inch was covered with my own carefully constructed miniatures. The panels rotated, the chute shot, the turntables turned, even the palm trees leaned over at the appropriate time (if you've watched the show, you'll know what I'm talking about), as all the while I hummed along to the theme running around in my head.

Then someone gave me Lego! It's no exaggeration to say that my life changed that day. Through those little coloured blocks, I was swept into a love affair with the three dimensions that has never entirely left me. The cardboard and sticky tape were replaced with a more sophisticated set of building materials, but the underlying principle remained: whatever it is, you can make it. If you can picture it in your minds-eye, you can create it! In many ways, this has been my mantra throughout life and, now, long into my ministry.

The God of Creation

Not long after this, I experienced another one of those life-changing "light-bulb" moments that many of us experience from time to time. The difference here was that I was still a child, constructing some bizarre new Lego creation, and the thought was philosophically profound, at least more than normally profound given my early years. The thought was this: "The world only works because things can't go through other things!"

You might chuckle at the naiveté of this but to me as a five year old, this was a watershed moment. Holding the two Lego pieces and putting them together and apart again, considering gravity and the fact that we don't sink through the earth but stand on it, that our clothes hang from our shoulders rather than passing through our bodies, and our stomachs hold in our hurriedly eaten breakfast, all this was a new way of looking at the world.

But where did the thought come from? How did a five year old come to this conclusion by himself? And how does he know how to fold the paper like this, cut it like that and place the sticky tape here, and arrange the blocks in that fashion according to those colours in that scale to create the replica of the things he has seen only once on a flickering screen a few moments before? Or perhaps not at all—things he has conceived all by himself? And where did the creative spark come from that inspired the scriptwriter, director, artist or author of whatever TV show, painting, poem, photograph, play or story it was the child had just seen or heard or read?

I have no doubt in my mind. With the same clarity and certainty that allowed me to "know" and "understand" how certain physical laws operate, I also "know" and "understand" that the creative impulse originates with the Creator God. This too has become my mantra: "I am creative because He is creative and I am created in His image." In my life, this belief goes yet a step further as I consider how deep the creative urge runs in my life: "Because He creates, I too *must* create!" When I consider this, I become aware of another profundity: "I am never truly happy unless I am creating something!"

The image of God

When I make a statement like this, I am often greeted with responses like "Well, that's OK for you, you're a creative person!" That can be a nice thing to hear—good for the ego, flattering even, as if it sets me apart somehow from lesser mortals. But it isn't true. If I read **Genesis 1** correctly, I discover that when God formed man of the dust of the ground and breathed into Adam—and later Eve—His own breath, He imbued not just a special few but all of humanity with qualities and characteristics that are His alone as part of the "image" we reflect. Male and female, we were created in His image, gifted with the ability to live, reproduce, think, choose and create. As Paul put it, we have the "mind of Christ" (see **1 Corinthians 2:16; Philippians 2:5**) and that creative spark within is part of that special gift.

It is little wonder that Satan hates humankind with such a passion. Himself a product of uncontrolled blind ambition, he arrived on planet earth filled with hate for the Son of God and determined, not surprisingly, to make as his special points of attack, the very things God created and gifted to humanity in that sinless world. Variously described as a dragon or serpent, and as a deceiver, persecutor, killer, murderer and liar, it would appear he possesses no creative ability of his own.

Where God creates, Satan can only destroy or "de-create." God creates life; Satan works to end it. God creates us in His image; Satan seeks to disfigure that image. God gives us marriage and the family unit; Satan seeks to ruin the divine pattern through lust, adultery, violence, abuse, addiction and infidelity of every type. God gives us a wonderful world to live in; Satan persuades us to destroy it through greed and ambition. God gives us the Sabbath as the memorial of His creative work; Satan sets up alternative forms of worship or persuades the followers of Christ to defile the Sabbath in any way possible. God imbues us with creativity; Satan has us use that creativity to invent ever more elaborate ways to degrade, wound and destroy ourselves and others. Jesus offers us life; Satan delivers death.

The ministry of reconciliation

So what does this have to do with ministry? Everything! Simply stated, the God who spoke the world into existence (see **John 1:1-5; Genesis 1:1**) and created us in His image is the same God who calls us to ministry. As collaborators with Satan in the fall, we are all now invited to work with Christ to share the good news of redemption to this damaged world. Just as all have sinned and fallen short of God's glory (see **Romans 3:23**), so all are offered the opportunity to be a part of a royal priesthood (see **1 Peter 2:9**), personally commissioned by Jesus to go into the world to make disciples (see **Matthew 28:18–20**). Paul calls us to join with him in the "ministry of reconciliation," a term that implies a bringing back together or a restoration of the way things once were (see **2 Corinthians 5:18–20**). To put it another way, we are invited to use our creative impulses to counter the destructive impulses of Satan, through the power of the Creator God.

I find it curious that many seem to feel they need permission to be creative in ministry. I would suggest that creativity in ministry is an expectation, even a requirement. Jesus' delivery of the parable of the talents (see **Matthew 25:14–30**) and its positioning immediately before the sheep and goats judgment scene (see **verses 31–46**) seems to declare His intention that we should use all the gifts at our disposal in the faithful delivery of our mission to the world—and more so given how close we are to the end of the story. It is a divine imperative that we keep in step with the Spirit (see **Galatians 5:56**) in every part of our lives, including the creative impulse so unique to God and consequently to us. To deny use of this faculty, especially in ministry, would be to deny God's special gift to us above all other creation.

Creative ministry

For reasons only to be marvelled at, the Creator Himself has seen fit to involve us in His work of redemption. He gifted us for the task, provided us with a "Comforter" to be our guide along the way, and provided us with a blueprint of how it all looked in the beginning. A study of God's creative process reveals four powerful overarching creative ministry principles: illumination, empowerment, excellence and diversity.

• Let there be light!

A quick read of **Genesis 1:1–3** and **John 1:1–5** reveal a clear ministry principle—that light drives out darkness, light is good, and that the true creative process thrives in an environment illuminated by the light of the Word. Every creative ministry effort must be subjected to scrutiny under the clarifying light of the Creator's Word, the only reliable "lamp to guide my feet" (**Psalms 119:105**). We ignore it to our peril. The tests of Scripture should be applied to all our efforts. We must never set aside the counsel of the Word for the sake of "creative license." We should "fix your thoughts on what is true, and honourable, and right, and pure, and lovely, and admirable. Think about things that are excellent and worthy of praise" (**Philippians 4:8**).

• Your turn now!

Once He had a well-illuminated workspace, God set about creating the perfect environment to sustain, inspire and nurture His later creations, us included. He provided everything necessary for us to thrive and grow, to learn of Him, to walk and talk and live with Him. Then He provided a weekly memorial for us to be reminded of His creative energy in providing this place for us. Interestingly, He then set us loose, inviting us to name, arrange, order, nurture, care for and husband this place. In other words, He provided the raw materials and the creative spark. Then He stepped back to see what we would do with it all.

• And it was very good!

After each major step in the creative process, God stood back, had a good look at what He had done, and declared it "good." At the end of the entire process, **Genesis 1:31** tells us that God looked over all He had made, and it was "very good." There was only one time when God noticed a flaw in His creation, something that was "not good" (**Genesis 2:18**) and He immediately set about rectifying the problem. The result was the creation of Eve. As a creative ministry principle, this evaluative process is key. God did it and the result was excellence. We would do well to follow His example, striving for excellence in every aspect of our ministry. Let's not get so caught up and single minded about our creations that we are not prepared to see flaws where flaws exist. Creative people have been known to fall into this trap.

• Same but different!

One of the things I love most about Lego is that I can use the same basic pieces to create millions of different things. I can make a car or a rocket or a house or a dinosaur from the same components and I can do it a thousand different ways. Same bits, a hundred different houses. Some would argue that we only need one kind of house—a functional one that provides warmth and shelter and a place to raise the kids. In the same way, we could argue that we only need one kind of dog to be our friend, one type of cat to ignore us, one type of bird to fill the skies, one type of fish to inhabit the oceans, and certainly only one race of people—ours, of course—to populate the earth. Yet before sin entered the world, God created multitudes of species of life on this planet. Why? Was it all just about functionality? Or was it about beauty and lavishness and texture and taste and smell and a crazy variety and whimsy that made His heart soar and His lips curl up in a smile, so much so that as He looked out at His amazingly diverse creation He could not help but blurt out "Wow—that really *is* very good!" In the same way, He gifted His servants with a diverse range of talents and creative abilities and let them loose on this planet. Same mission, but different gifts. Some would argue that all should speak in tongues, or that all should be evangelists or teachers. But the principle of Scripture is diversity—in creation, in giftedness, in ministry, in creativity.

The tools of the trade

I said earlier that I like to make things. In fact, for a number of years I made a living from making false teeth. Experience has now taught me that with the right tools and materials, I can create almost anything. Whether it's an item of furniture, taking a beautiful picture, writing a drama script, planning a worship service, drafting a sermon, or building up a young person to be a leader in the church, the principles and the motivation are the same:

1. Illuminate your work area—measure every idea, plan and dream against the Word.
2. Empower others without micromanaging the results. Gather the resources—both people and things. Bring them together, inspire them, spark the flow of ideas, nurture them along the way, but let them have a go. This is God's way.
3. Recognise that there are many different ways of approaching a problem or achieving an outcome. There can be great strength in diversity.
4. Evaluate every step of the way. Strive for excellence in all things.

God created us to experience true joy in our lives, delighting both in His presence and in the wonderful world He had created for us. Jesus declared that He had come to restore all things. "The thief's purpose is to steal and kill and destroy. My purpose is to give them a rich and satisfying life" (**John 10:10**). It is no exaggeration to say that I thank Him daily that He gives me this opportunity, and—even more than this—that He considers it the highest praise when I use His unique and precious gifts to me, joining with Him in sharing the good news.

—Tony Knight loves to nurture his God-given creative spark through writing, woodwork, and especially nature and wildlife photography. He reads a book a week to keep his mind fresh, and thrives when surrounded by creative and innovative thinkers, an experience he gets to have every day as he serves the Adventist Church as its national Youth Ministries Director in Australia. He lives in Melbourne, Australia, with wife Jacqui, and daughters Tasha and Ellesha, various four-legged pets, and a great big workshed.

CREATIVE LEADERSHIP FOR THE NON-CREATIVE LEADER

Creativity and Leadership

Glenn Townend

During the 1970s, string art became popular. I would copy and measure up designs on a board, marking exactly where each nail would go. After painting the board and nails black, I would thread cotton between the various rows of nails like an intricate spider's web and be amazed as various patterns and shapes emerged.

At the time, I lived in Papua New Guinea and spent most of my limited skill copying other people's designs. In a rare moment of inspiration, encouraged by my parents, I used a picture of a bird of paradise and designed a string art version. These sold in the local markets—I was a better entrepreneur than artist—as my only triumph in the art world.

At the same time, I had a dream of being a guitarist. My parents bought me a classical guitar and spent a small fortune to teach me how to read music and play classically. Today, I can strum along using chords but I still cannot read music. At best, it is a "joyful noise."

But, like all human beings, God did gift me with talents and abilities. One that He and the Seventh-day Adventist Church has given me the opportunity to exercise and develop is leadership. So what is the role of leaders in relationship to creativity and the arts? And does a leader have to be a creative artist to allow the creative energies of others to prosper? After all, God the Creator created every human being in His image. Each human being is potentially an inventor. If leadership is about developing a team and working with God to bring out the best in every person, how do you do that in the arts where—like me—you may have very hidden talent?

Bible leaders and creativity

According to the biblical record, the creative arts flourished in Israel during the reigns of David and his son Solomon in the 11th and 10th centuries BC (1 Chronicles 14–26). David was an artist. He was an excellent musician called upon when still a boy to soothe the then-king with his music (see 1 Samuel 16:14–25). He was a poet who authored many of the psalms, probably writing music for many of them as well. Writing in the desert or in the palace, his psalms express raw and vivid emotions, yet they all reflected on his relationship with the Author of life whom He worshipped whatever his feelings. At times, David's joy was so exuberant that He danced in worship (see 2 Samuel 6:14). Most of David's creativity was directed to God in worship but he also appreciated beauty and its source. His palace was made of the most precious minerals, exotic stones and expensive timbers (see 1 Chronicles 14:1, 15:1, 17:1).

David's son, Solomon, was also a reflective writer. Song of Songs exquisitely celebrates human love. His knowledge of nature, human nature and governance reflected God-given wisdom in proverbs that are good advice today. David made plans to build a temple in Jerusalem for the Almighty God and devoted most of his wealth to that, but it was Solomon who worked with the world's best craftsmen to build the temple. The descriptions of the cedar-lined walls carved with angels and flowers and covered with gold are still amazing (see 1 Kings 6–7).

> Jesus blends in with society and changes it from within. John stands opposed to society and changes it from without. John sees the differences—and it bothers him.

In the New Testament, the apostle Paul knew contemporary poets and quoted them when trying to connect with people who read these poets (see Acts 17:28, Titus 1:12). He encouraged the early churches to sing and he quoted psalms and the lyrics of an early Christian song that he may have authored (see Philippians 2:5–11, Ephesians 5:19, Colossians 3:16).

There is no doubt creativity and the arts flourish when such a leader has artistic skills and models creativity. But while many of the Bible's leaders wrote, few others shared such creative talent and passion. So what of leaders like me who cannot hold a tune or explain depth and symbol in a song or a painting?

Jesus and John

In his re-telling of the story of Jesus, Luke offers us some insights into how to lead in a way that encourages creativity in every way, including the arts, from the comparisons he draws between the respective ministries of Jesus and John the Baptist.

In Luke 7, the imprisoned John the Baptist sent two of his disciples to ask Jesus, "Are you the Messiah we've been expecting, or should we keep looking for someone else?" (Luke 7:19, 20). In other words, "Are you really the Messiah?—because from what I am hearing and where I am at, I am not sure." The way Jesus did ministry was very different to the way John had gone about his ministry.

The story line in the first part of the book of Luke's gospel, leading up to this question, switches from John to Jesus three times (see **Luke 1–4**), suggesting that a comparison between the two is intended. There are many similarities between their lives, ministry and message but there are also quite a few differences.

John is a wild man of the desert, dressed in camel skins and eating what he can find. He is such a powerful preacher with a relevant message that he attracts people from all walks of life—peasants, religious leaders, foreigners, tax collectors—come to hear him in the desert. He asks them to repent, change their lives and be baptised as a sign of that change (see **Luke 3:1–14, Matthew 3:1–12**). There is no record of John leaving the desert to mix with people.

On the other hand, Jesus looks like a normal person, eats normal food and accepts invitations to eat with religious leaders, as well as tax collectors and prostitutes. Like John, He does teach in the open air but He also goes to the synagogues and temple to teach and heal.

Jesus blends in with society and changes it from within. John stands opposed to society and changes it from without. John sees the differences—and it bothers him. Jesus does not meet John's expectations. How can such different styles of ministry both be from God? And that is the source of his questions.

When John's disciples relay this question to Jesus, He does not answer immediately, He just heals people. Actions always speak louder than words. His verbal reply then reminds John of Isaiah's prophecy—that this is exactly what the Messiah is expected to do (see **Isaiah 35:5 and 61:1, 2**). Jesus knows the heart of John's struggle is the difference in style of their ministry and concludes with a word of encouragement: "God blesses those who do not turn away because of me" (**Luke 7:23**).

When John's disciples leave, Jesus turns to the crowd and contrasts John the captive with Herod the captor using a series of rhetorical questions. Jesus confirms John as the prophet predicted by Malachi to come before the Messiah. Despite appearances, the captive has more power than the captor. Jesus then gives the best affirmation of John and his ministry that anyone could wish for: "I tell you, of all who have ever lived, none is greater than John" (**Luke 7:28a**). John is affirmed as the forerunner to Jesus, even though their styles of ministry were completely different.

Different songs

Jesus concludes His comparison between Himself and John by quoting a common market song sung by children: "We played wedding songs, and you didn't dance, so we played funeral songs, and you didn't weep" (**Luke 7:32**). In the ancient marketplaces, there were no childcare centres. As the parents traded their fruit, vegetables, linen, spices, leather, timber furniture and the like, the children were left to care for themselves in the alleys behind the stalls. When children play without adult supervision, they make their own rules and the natural leaders carry them through but not everyone agrees with the rules or the leader promoting them and conflict usually ensues. This marketplace ditty expressed this truth, suggesting that whatever music is offered some do not want to sing or participate. When the flute played bright music, no-one danced. When a funeral song was sung, no-one cried. Some children—some people—are just hard to please.

John's approach to ministry was more like the dirge. As a Nazarene, he did not eat bread or drink wine. He kept himself pure by not mixing with people and living in the wilderness. He was straight and strict—and people thought he was demon possessed.

On the other hand, Jesus' approach to ministry was more like the song of the flute. You would dance if you had been paralysed and could now walk; you would dance if you were blind and could now see. Jesus ate and drank with all manner of people with no thought to their social status. People thought He was too soft or lenient in lifestyle and He was called a glutton and a drunkard—hardly a description one would expect of the Messiah.

But Jesus clearly articulates His point: "But wisdom is shown to be right by the lives of those who follow it" (**Luke 7:35**).

We humans often evaluate ministry—including creative and artistic ministry—on the method and style, without thinking about the end result or the fruit.

Both Jesus and John had a clear message and a listening audience. Both are needed for effective ministry.

Fixing ministry?

From time to time, people come to me and share their thoughts on a recent visit to a church or ministry. I think they believe a conference president has a magic wand and can fix things with a wave of my hand. "You would not believe what that church was like," they begin. "They only sang hymns, the worship leaders all wore ties, there were no women involved in leadership and the program was rigid. It was terrible. You ought to remind these people that we live in God's grace and there is freedom to try new things." I listen carefully without making many comments. I then respond with the latest facts about the fruit of this ministry. This church has baptised 10 people this year and their tithe has increased by 13 per cent. The unspoken message is this: *God seems to be blessing them, so why should I interfere?*

Others come to me with other reports. "You would not have believed what it was like when I visited a particular ministry," they begin. "The music was just like you hear on the radio and it was loud—just like a nightclub. The beat of the drums is still reverberating in my ears. People wore whatever clothes they wanted, there seemed to be no decorum at all. It was not what God would want." Again, I listen carefully to what is said and respond in a similar fashion. I happen to know that 25 young people gave their hearts to Jesus and are now in a weekly Bible study as a result of this ministry. The unspoken message: *Do you really want me to close something down that God is using to bring people to Himself?*

God uses different methods to reach different types of people. Jesus and John were both sent and used by God for His purpose but their methods and style of ministry were completely different. God ordained the different ways they did ministry, because he wanted people in His kingdom. If we are to fulfil the commission God gave to us to make disciples of all people, we need freedom to be able to reach all people where they are. Methods and style of ministry are not as important as whether this ministry is effectively reaching people for Jesus and His truth.

Both Jesus and John had a clear message and a listening audience. Both are needed for effective ministry. If we have a clear message but no-one listening, we have not connected and no-one's life will be changed by Jesus. If we have lots of people listening, we have connected but if there is no clear message we will not be effective and no-one's life will be changed by Jesus.

The style or method does not matter. Jesus did not rebuff the criticism that He was a glutton, a drunkard and friends with the outcasts of society. What mattered to Him was that some of those people's lives were changed because they met Him. He simply continued His ministry. If you are called to ministry and have the balance of message and audience, just keep doing it—and let God make the ministry effective (see also 1 Corinthians 9:19–23).

To the glory of God

The arts should flourish within Christian community and ministry because God is the Creator, Jesus is the head of the church and the Holy Spirit is with us. If a leader can lead by example within the arts, they should do so. But if not, leadership must do their best to teach the principles of Scripture that allow freedom in the style of ministry, creating an open and accepting environment for creativity.

The arts in the Bible were usually used to glorify gods. Apart from Israel, most other nations modelled, carved and drew their gods (see Isaiah 41:7, 44:9–20). But the one true God is awesome and beyond human comprehension and cannot be depicted in earthly art (see Exodus 20:3-6, Isaiah 40:6-31). Yet those who worship and honoured the one true God created poetry, music and beautiful buildings that were instruments to connect people to God. This art created the environment where the Almighty God dwelt. They revealed and portrayed a God who was mysteriously distant, great, mighty and holy but also close, loving and understanding.

Within a creative and accepting environment, the church can aim for excellence in the arts. I dream of more young people who can create video clips that become viral and share God's message in a new and creative way. I dream of more artists who will paint Jesus in modern-day scenes that we connect with, and churches and schools will hang them on their walls. I dream of more Adventists who sing in community choirs and play in community orchestras. I also dream of each local church having a choir, a band, brass or string ensembles, quartets and trios—young and old with voice, guitar, cello, drums, trumpet given the opportunity to praise Jesus in song and music! I dream of Adventists winning talent shows. I dream of more Adventist artists—painters, sculptors, photographers—who are world-renowned and invited to hold exhibitions in major galleries. I dream of Adventists producing a movie on the life of Daniel that breaks box-office records. I dream . . .

However, there are still some of us in the church who have Puritanical roots. Like John the Baptist, we do not want to be worldly in any way. We see how the creativity is used today for self-indulgence and so reject the arts rather than commit this sin.

There will be churches that still hang the 50-year-old pictures of Jesus in the Sabbath school rooms and people will still sense the peace in Jesus' face. There will still be churches that have a pianist who makes a mistake in every verse of a song but those songs will be sung with sincerity and reverence.

I remember visiting a village church in the highlands of Papua New Guinea one Sabbath when I was a boy and hearing the people sing with heart, gusto and volume. I commented to my dad that the song sounded like "Jesus loves me"—and he told me it was. It was off-key in many places and had no proper timing but it reminded me that the Bible is correct in urging that whatever we do, we must do it with heart and do all to the glory of God (see **1 Corinthians 10:31**).

In ministry, in worship, in creativity, in art, whether we are doing it is always more important than how. A creative leader encourages this faithful doing—makes space for it, defends it and urges it to be better, blesses it, prays for it and celebrates what God is doing among us.

—Glenn Townend has been the president of the Western Australian Conference for 10 years and before this was a pastor in 13 different churches around Australia. He is still learning to lead, listen to God and allow freedom at the same time. Glenn is married to Pam and they have three adult children.

ROOM FOR THE SPIRIT TO BLOW THROUGH

Creativity and the Local Church

Ryan Bell

Let's play a little word association game. What are the first 10 words that come to mind when you hear the word "church"?

Did the word "creative" or any of its related forms make your list? Taking into account the fact that you're holding in your hand a book on creativity, opened to a chapter on creativity and the local church, you are probably among the few people who might have listed that word. But factoring out these circumstances for the moment, how often do the words *creative* or *creativity* come to mind when you think about your church?

A quick, unscientific experiment conducted with a random sample of my friends—some members of my church, some not; some Christians, some not—revealed that not a single one listed any form of "creativity." Lots of other important words came up consistently—like God, Jesus, Eucharist and salvation—but not *creativity*. If someone had given me this same test, I'm not sure I would have listed *creativity* either. It's just not part of what we ordinarily think of as a central component of church life.

Perhaps you are blessed, as I am, to be a part of a highly creative congregation. Maybe you are one of the creative people struggling to find a point of connection in a less-than-creative church. Or you might be a faithful Christian for whom all of this sounds disturbingly vague, such that almost anything might slip into the church under the heading "creativity."

But creativity is as important to a healthy local church as the doctrine of Creation is to a healthy Christian theology. Creativity is something we should expect to find in congregations everywhere. We should be surprised when we don't encounter a culture of creativity. Church leaders should be cultivating an environment where creativity can flourish to the glory of God for the simple reason that God is creative. It is basic to God's character.

What do we mean by creativity in the local church?

Creativity refers to the creation of something new and valuable to the community—a song, a poem, a play, a painting, a dance, a dish for potluck, a speech, a story, a film or a social space. Though some people have specific creative gifts and some have cultivated their creative impulses and observational skills, we are all naturally creative beings. Practically speaking, creativity means many things, but let's start with where we often find creativity in the local church.

Children. Every church I know celebrates the creativity of its children. Children freely express themselves in paint and crayon and clay. They sing songs and do skits, all related to their emerging faith in God. I remember making a birdhouse out of popsicle sticks. Not the most theologically profound piece of art I've ever encountered but it must have had something to do with God's loving concern, even for the most humble sparrow.

Even in the most traditional churches, children perform their music and dramatic arts to the delight of parents, grandparents and friends. We expect our children to be creative and we celebrate it, even though it's usually far from a polished performance. We intuitively know children should be creative. Sadly, as we get older, we accumulate inhibitions. Somewhere along the line, we avoid taking risks and stop expressing ourselves openly.

Though some people have specific creative gifts and some have cultivated their creative impulses and observational skills, we are all naturally creative beings.

Music. The other area where creativity is welcomed and celebrated in the church is in music. Musicians—at least of certain varieties—have been welcomed as those who contribute to our spiritual growth and our experience of God in worship.

But here the relationship between the church and creativity begins to wear thin. Only certain types of musicians have been broadly welcomed—usually, organists, pianists and musicians who play classical European orchestra instruments—and only certain types of music—that which explicitly speaks to our relationship with God. Only recently—and only in some places—have artists who specialise in the other instruments or musical genres found their gifts accepted by the church.

In many churches, this is where the experience of creativity ends. Those whose creative pursuits are in the fine arts (painting, sculpture), visual arts (film, photography), creative writing (poetry, fiction, screenwriting), graphic design, architecture and performing arts (acting, dancing, choreography) have found little acceptance. Even if these artists have not been outright rejected, there is typically no space for their expression in the traditional local church.

James, a successful actor, was surprised when he first came to the Hollywood Adventist Church. He told me that he had never in his life experienced a church community that acknowledged his artistic gift as a legitimate contribution. Naturally, he has become one of our leaders and for a while led a weekly Artists' Workshop in which emerging screenwriters wrote two-page scripts and emerging actors would perform them, under his guidance. Friends of our members who had never been to our church came consistently and the classes grew.

This lack of acceptance is not always a result of explicit hostility to the arts—although that is sometimes the case. Sometimes it is lack of awareness of the existence of other artists in the community or, more importantly, how to deploy these artists in ways that support and build up the church or express God's love in the community.

Church leaders as spiritual environmentalists

The Spirit of God is the active agent in the creation of our world. In Genesis 1:1, 2, we read:

> In the beginning God created the heavens and the earth. The earth was formless and empty, and darkness covered the deep waters. And the Spirit of God was hovering over the surface of the waters.

God's Spirit has been hovering over the creation ever since. As God's Spirit lives in us, we are partners with God in the ongoing creation of the world.

(Please pause here and read those previous two sentences again, then reflect on the implications for at least 30 seconds before moving on.)

Creativity is a Spirit thing. Another way to say this is, creativity is *spiritual*. Creativity happens when the Spirit is at work in a person's life. This doesn't mean that every work of art is endorsed by God or has the mark of the Holy Spirit clearly on it, or that every artist must acknowledge the Holy Spirit by that name, but it does mean that the creative impulse is part of our created-in-God's-image nature and—when cultivated—it can produce remarkable results.

What this means is that church leaders are environmentalists. We have a responsibility to cultivate a *spiritual space*, where people are free to express what God has placed inside them. By creating a permission-giving environment and issuing an invitation, the church can draw out from people their creative impulses. Creativity thrives in an environment of freedom and permission. Anyone who has ever tried to play an instrument knows that creativity takes practice but it also takes lots of failure. Church members need a church culture where it's acceptable to offer creative suggestions without fear of condemnation.

As environmentalists, our role is also creative. Through storytelling and teaching, we can create a biblical, narrative framework within which our members' creativity can freely and safely be turned loose. Church leaders provide the canvas on which our creative members can paint. The canvas is made up primarily of the overarching story of Scripture—how God created a good and beautiful world that was marred but not destroyed by sin, which God has been working with His human creation to restore ever since. God's creative project is nothing short of the full restoration of creation to its original beauty and, in this, we have the privilege of partnering with God.

I hope it is becoming clear that cultivating an environment where our members can explore their God-given creativity is central to the church's discipleship task. I have discovered that when we do this, we are actually helping our members grow closer to God. This makes sense, doesn't it? If we are created by God to be creative, then the act of creation should make us feel close to our Creator.

All this may sound complicated. It is difficult, but not complicated. It means giving up some control in exchange for some freedom for our creative members to express themselves. It means that church leaders—who are the rightful gatekeepers and "protectors" of the church—must stand aside and create room for what they can't always understand. In short, we must *trust* our artists and "cultural creatives" in the church.

One of the brilliant artists in my church, Paul came to me with an idea one day. I was about to do a series of sermons on the Apostle's Creed (not a typical topic for an Adventist Church but we were exploring what Christians believe and we turned to this ancient statement as a conversation starter) and he suggested that we challenge our members to create a piece of art that expressed what they believe about God. I thought it sounded fantastic. I knew nothing about putting together an art show—but Paul did. The result was remarkable. We had dozens of submissions, some from the Hollywood community and surrounding area. More than 100 people came out for the exhibition.

Mentoring the artists in your church

Many pastors and church leaders are understandably overwhelmed by all of this because they don't think of themselves as artists. But you don't have to be an artist yourself. You're probably more of an artist than you know, but leaving that aside for the moment, you don't need an Masters of Fine Arts from Columbia University to cultivate an environment of creativity in the church. In fact, acknowledging what you don't know about art is the first step toward a much stronger relationship with your artists.

Step 1: Focus on what you know: the biblical story, theology, mission. This is our role in mentoring our artists. They know their trade and we know ours. Together, God can do great things for the kingdom.

Step 2: Get close to your artists. Let them teach *you*. Be humble and learn from them. My wife, Elysabeth, is a fine artist. Spending 17 years around her has been the best education I could have ever received. Through her and the other artists in my life, I have discovered that I am also an artist. I have grown in my artistic sensibilities and general knowledge of the arts. I never imagined I would be a filmmaker, for example. Yet in the past three

A few years ago, the filmmakers in my church got together and created a short film in 48 hours, start to finish. We began the night with a text of scripture, a list of locations and a list of actors. Forty-eight hours later, we were screening the film, called *The Perfect Day*—complete with original music—in the chapel of our church. It's not perfect, but it was a tremendous learning and relationship-building experience that none of us will forget. I even played a bit part!

years, I have been the director and producer for several short spots (when I say short, I'm talking about two minutes. And, no; no Academy Awards . . . yet!)

Step 3: Support your artists as they take their gifts out into the world. The church's role is not simply to colonise its artists and use their work for the church, but to nurture the soul of its artists and release that creative vision into the world where they can bear witness to the *Creator* God. This might take you to places you don't typically frequent—but this, too, is a witness! When I first moved to Hollywood, I had no idea how much time I would spend in bars and other music venues supporting the singer-songwriters in my community. The more church leaders support the artists in their midst by honouring the work they do in the world, the more likely those same artists will be to bless the church with their talents.

Step 4: Never let the desire for a technically perfect performance get in the way of people expressing themselves, even while church leaders always need to push their members toward excellence. For most young artists, authenticity is far more important than trying to be cool. You're probably not going to beat Hollywood at its own game, so it's better not to try. No-one wants to embarrass themselves in front of a crowd. They want to do their best. By placing more accomplished artists in leadership with emerging artists, everyone can grow together.

Fear: the enemy of creativity

While the word "creativity" didn't come up in my word association survey, a few other words did. More than once I heard: *judgmental*, *conformity* and *fear*. These are creativity killers.

The Apostle John tells us, "Such love has no fear, because perfect love expels all fear" (1 John 4:18). Creativity is

I never learned to draw well. Once when I was serving in the children's program at camp meeting, the leader announced that each of us were going to draw something related to the Bible story we just read. The children squealed for joy and I broke into a cold sweat. *I can't draw!* Eventually my fear subsided—aided in part by my pride, which wasn't about to get shown up by these children!—and I drew something. It was probably pretty bad, but I did it, and it felt good.

a gift born of love. Whether it's a short story, a poem, a song or a painting, these creative gifts come from the heart. On the other hand, fear destroys creativity. Fear of failure. Fear of what others with think. Fear of judgment and ridicule. Fear paralyses us and robs us of the divine spark.

Fear is not only contagious, it's also palpable. People can feel it. Even if the words they hear say, "Go for it! We want you to share your gifts!" they will not contribute in a climate of fear. It is not worth it. Sadly, the world outside the church is often more supportive and accepting of artists than the church, which is why many of them vote with their feet and take their gifts elsewhere. The greatest challenge to cultivating an environment that draws out creative people is lowering the fear level.

If creativity thrives where there is room for the Spirit to blow through a congregation and stir up what is there, it is likely going to feel like lines are getting crossed. Creative expression often feels messy and "out-of-control" to those of us accustomed to managing God for others. But the Spirit of God can be trusted. We needn't fear. If we are surrounding our congregations with the love of God and sharing God's vision of a healed creation, God's Spirit can do miraculous things.

—Ryan Bell is senior pastor of the Hollywood Adventist Church in Los Angeles, California, USA, and a clergy leader with PICO, a national network of faith-based community organisations working for social justice. He is also adjunct professor in the Global Studies Department at Azusa Pacific University and a regular contributor to the Religion section of The Huffington Post.

IN OUR HANDS

Creativity and Faithfulness

Moe Ioane Stiles

In my early years of full-time ministry, I remember sitting with my new "worship" team to discuss the calendar for the approaching year and working out what we were going to do, which themes we were going to explore and praying for where God wanted to lead our church. Our conversation turned to creativity and what we wanted to put into our worship programs to make them God-glorifying, interesting but also sensorily-engaging.

One of the challenges we faced in that meeting was resources—mainly human resources. Many church conversations about creativity revolve around talented musicians, storytellers, scriptwriters and actors and the various types of visual artists. It is daunting to even think about creativity outside of these "art forms."

I was confronted by the dilemma that many of our communities have faced: a limited view of creativity, assuming it is only found in these few areas of giftedness. But I was also confronted with the fact that we are in a culture in which people's distrust of religion and church affect how we must communicate when we are talking about and sharing beliefs that make an eternal difference.

Some people have the knack for producing something that I would not be able to create in my wildest dreams. We should celebrate them and their giftedness. If you're reading this and you fall into this category or you have been affirmed with these gifts, praise Jesus for you. We need you! You have something to contribute in the communication of Jesus.

But we also have been stumped by the notion that because we don't have these people in our midst—or so we think—we have to settle for mediocrity, without thinking about or intentionally focusing on creativity.

Creativity questions

So what is creativity and what is it for? What difference will it make? Does it have a place in our church community? And what resources do we need to make sure this is explored and encouraged in our church family?

We only have to look into the creation story in Genesis to see that creating and recreating brings goodness. God saw what He had done and said "it was very good" (see **Genesis 1:31**). Throughout Scripture, we see creative and re-creative work wherever God is involved in the hearts and lives of people.

Creativity brings joy, beauty and life in a world where these are needed. It also allows us to communicate what words cannot fully express. In a world where godly beauty is desperately needed and we have a life-giving message to be shared, creativity plays an enormous part.

At its core, evangelism is simply sharing Jesus. But how we do this is not confined to one model or methodology. We are each created uniquely and with this comes the challenge of portraying this same message in ways that different people can understand and receive. We must imagine every angle, method and medium by which the person of Jesus is shared to breathe life into the world. So if there is a place for creativity to be explored, it should be in our church community.

> We must imagine every angle, method and medium by which the person of Jesus is shared to breathe life into the world.

This is why we might have got it wrong with our assumed understanding of creativity, that our "creatives"—musicians, visual artists, actors, poets, chefs and florists—are the only ones who have creativity in their bones. Every one of us can create and re-create to bring beauty into our community, to communicate the life found in Jesus. Someone once commented that "Creativity is life, not a hobby." We are creating everyday. And what we are creating must communicate life, love, beauty, justice, joy, peace and goodness.

We are all called to the work of creativity and re-creativity—a life, not a hobby—with the resources we are given wherever we find ourselves. This realisation is life changing and, in turn, a creative life assists in kingdom building.

A biblical example

In the book of Exodus, we find Moses called to lead the people of Israel out of Egypt. Most of us are familiar with the story and the famous question God asked Moses. We are also familiar with the excuses offered by Moses as to why he was not the right person for the job of freeing the children of Israel. "Then the Lord asked him, 'What is that in your hand?'" Moses' reply is simple: "A shepherd's staff" (**Exodus 4:2**).

The people of God were in slavery. There was a cry coming out of Egypt from the people to be saved and rescued. The solution from God is found in the man of Moses, his staff and his brother Aaron. Moses was reluctant—to say the least—and gave God all the excuses he could imagine. But God had an answer for him.

When God calls us to bring life into a situation in desperate need of Him, He comes with ways to equip us for this calling. Moses was called by God to lead His people out of Egypt—and God's response to his excuses and his fears was to ask what was in his hand. God told him to "take your shepherds staff with you, and use it to perform the miraculous signs I have shown you" (**Exodus 4:17**).

"What is that in your hand?" is an important question for our own creativity challenges. Moses only had his staff but it was something he knew how to use. God knew Moses' limitations but He also knew what Moses could do with His leading, using what he knew. For each of us, God begins with what we have in our hands. It is yet another way that He meets us where we are.

In our calling to communicate Jesus, God uses what we have in our hand. In our privilege of partnering with Him to respond to oppression and injustice, God uses what we have within our reach. In our ministry of bringing freedom, creating beauty or whatever it is God wants to engage us in, God uses what we have among our resources. God always works with what we have in our hands.

Further, God brings people to assist with what He needs to achieve through us and them. God brought Aaron because Moses was nervous about speaking in front of people due to his stutter. God also used Moses' wife to save his life when God was about to smite him (see **Exodus 4:24–26**). However amazing and bizarre and "creative" her actions seem to us, she assisted Moses in the bigger task ahead, allowing him to live so he could bring the children of Israel out of Egypt.

Creativity and faithfulness in practice

In 2012, I was able to be part of two international short-term mission trips with my husband's school and the Adventist Development and Relief Agency (ADRA). On both trips, I experienced the creative use of the resources on hand to achieve the task—because that is all we had.

In the African nation of Tanzania, for instance, we were to assist in building part of the wall for one of our schools, so students are protected from kidnapping and murder. On arrival, we had questions regarding the methods for building the wall, especially in relation to scaffolding. In one place there was a drop-off on one side of the wall, so we needed to ensure that construction could be completed safely.

But the local tradesmen had already thought through the process. They were familiar with the project and the site and had already built part of the wall. Using what we had right there and then, we used the bricks for the wall together with planks of wood as makeshift scaffolding, and we had a wall by the end of our time. God had prepared a team for us to work alongside, to ensure protection of those students. We had to get creative but it worked.

Too often we think bigger and more is best. My dad always says, "Little is much"—and this is especially true when God is with us. The trusty staff in Moses' hand—old, worn and familiar—was pointed out to Moses as a tool to be used to bring freedom to the people of Israel. God used his staff to perform signs, to bring water out of rocks, and to part the Red Sea and the Jordan River so the children of Israel could cross safely. These were things Moses would never have imagined as he carried that stick across the desert while herding sheep.

However, while there may well be moments of miracle, creativity also requires faithfulness. It is easy to say, "Use what God has placed in your hands," but it is harder to face the fact that it is going to be hard work. This is where our faithfulness needs to be put into practice.

As we read the story of Moses, he faced many challenges, particularly from the people he led and their seemingly endless complaints. These were the very people who needed freedom, which he had brought to them with the help of God, but it never seemed enough. Yet Moses persevered faithfully using that one trusty and familiar tool, as God continued to lead.

Easier said than done. We cannot afford to become discouraged and let go of what we have when that can be used to bring healing, hope, joy, beauty and freedom. There is a place for what we have to offer, and we must continue to bring together what we have imagined for our church community. Imagine what we can do with all of our creativity—and what we can share with the world!

Creatively simple

I recently visited both my birth country of Samoa and its sister island Vanuatu. I was confronted by how rich both cultures are, even amid a lack of obvious resources. They do not run "church" as we would have it in many developed nations, but their faithfulness in worship and commitment to serving Jesus is clear.

Whatever they have is used creatively, beautifully and simply—and I found it refreshing. Exotic flowers and plants are used to brighten the church. The fragrance of the flowers is delightful and fresh and fills the space. Colours come not from lights but from materials woven together and plastered on the front wall of the church. The statement is clear—this is something that we took time to create for God and this place is for God.

> We cannot afford to become discouraged and let go of what we have when that can be used to bring healing, hope, joy, beauty and freedom.

What follows is a flood of beautiful harmonies that drown the one or two guitars played during the worship service. There are no worship leaders but the whole building is filled with rich melodious sound. At the end of the worship service, the members file outside and pray with and for each other.

My heart was filled and overflowing with an encounter with Jesus that was simple yet profound! I was again confronted by people who are creatively using what they have in their hand and in their reach to bring glory to God and bring justice and healing to a world that can seem so dark and hopeless.

When we keep our creativity and worship simple, it allows the Holy Spirit to do what He needs to do among our community and the people involved. It also frees us to not be so busy working for God that we forget to include God in our doing for Him! My creative faithfulness is challenged when I am busy running around thinking up all sorts of wonderful creative ideas to put into a project, event or program. I've often caught myself, realising that

I have forgotten to stop to seek His guidance, His wisdom and His creative power for the task He's assigned to me. Building God's kingdom needs God himself. Sometimes our best creativity might be found in this kind of simplifying and re-focussing

For His glory

So what is in your hand? What has God placed within your grasp that can be utilised creatively to reflect His character? And how is this bringing life and justice into the world that so desperately needs Him? How is what's in your hand blessing you and the community you are placed in?

Faithful creativity is not handed over only to our "artists"—as important as what they do can be. Creativity is most importantly about serving as we are able with whatever we have. So "whatever your hand finds to do, do it with all your might" (**Ecclesiastes 9:10**) and "do it all for the glory of God" (**1 Corinthians 10:31**).

—Moe Ioane Stiles is a passionate lover of Jesus, and happily married to Adrian Stiles, a high school principal. She serves as the director of Youth Ministries in the Victorian Conference, based in Melbourne, Australia. Moe is passionate about seeing young people have an encounter with Jesus and live out their lives following His footsteps, making a difference in the world they're placed in as the hands and feet of the Saviour.

CURATING WORSHIP EXPERIENCES

Creativity and Worship

Nicki Carleton

I am blessed with two unique ministries: curating alternative worship gatherings and interactive prayer rooms. I use transformance art to change the culture of prayer at schools, churches, festivals and—my favourite—to redeem rarely-used hospital chapels from dusty and cold to fragrant, vibrant, healing sacred spaces. The purpose of these two ministries is to *create an experience*, allowing people to feel deeply and grow spiritually in a safe place. My calling is to disciple others and, because discipleship is about relationships, it cannot be taught through knowledge and facts alone. It must be learned by experience.

When I was younger, I gravitated toward events that were creative. I felt alive when I was in a group being creative, doing things differently. I finally discovered I was a kinaesthetic sensory learner and if I didn't do it, feel it or experience it, I found it difficult to learn. Fortunately, I had some powerful encounters with Jesus while I was growing up that left me bewildered and intrigued, and that gave me a taste of creative worship.

I remember I didn't feel quite right one day. As a young adult, I looked around my church and realised that much of our ministry was designed for auditory learners. I felt a burning in my spirit that asked, "Who will help the creative people fall in love with Jesus by allowing them to engage with Him through their natural learning styles?" Being a kinaesthetic learner, I already knew there were many more ways we could receive the gospel.

God was asking me to "build the house of prayer." While I was unsure what that actually meant, I was encouraged by **Exodus 31:2–5**, which revealed that the first person described as filled with the Holy Spirit was the artist Bezalel and he was *taught* by God to create the art for the temple. So my learning journey began. I had no idea what I was doing but God carried it to completion (see **Philippians 1:6**). I just stayed faithful, and listened and watched in amazement!

It was damp and cold, yet we were outside at Camp Somerset for the final evening worship. We each lit our candle from the youth leader's candle—representing the Holy Spirit—and placed it in the bonfire with the intention of setting it ablaze. To our disappointment, it was a failure. It seemed the bonfire was not going to be ignited. So as I placed my candle in among the branches, I gathered some other candles so the flame was brighter and slowly it started to ignite the fire. As others did the same, we marvelled at how we burned brighter with each other, even when we couldn't do much by ourselves. We needed the power of community.

What are these experiences?

A prayer room can take many forms. Commonly, I work with rooms filled with interactive stations to help engage and inspire people to pray. This might involve sectioning off parts of the room, intentional lighting, atmospheric music, setting up various media to allow participants to respond—such as paint, collage, crayons, writing walls, pinning notes on wire and sand boxes—and using different types of stimuli to help guide and focus prayer—such as Scripture, images from magazines, a cross, a table setting. Even though many people may be in the room, it is very personal. It is a sacred and holy space because God's presence is there, and He speaks because people are open to hearing.

A space like this can help people think differently about their relationship with God and how they interact with Him. It can also cause them to reflect on their relationships with themselves and others. The safe environment allows people to feel more fully—expressing grief or anger or laughter, unplugging from social media and the other "noise" in their lives to find themselves in God's arms. Significantly, teaching using the senses has a 90 per cent retention rate,[1] time slows down and worries melt away because the right side of the brain is being engaged.

While prayer rooms can be designed to suit any age, it is a particularly incredible opportunity to positively influence children's worldview, their faith and their understanding of ways they can interact with God. A room like this teaches that prayer can actually be fun and more natural—and they can begin to see the effects it has in their lives.

In response to a prayer space that had been created for this purpose, one theology graduate shared, "The prayer room was the most incredible spiritual experience of my life." I know it has been effective when a young teenage boy affirms, "That was so awesome." Some young people have gone on to build their own prayer rooms at summer camps, in their basements and at retreats. It is a ministry that anyone inspired by God can run.

In a similar vein to prayer rooms, alternative worship events are unconventional church gatherings where people get together expecting to worship in a different way. The creative options are endless. It might occur outside, using theatre, making up music together, going on a guided spiritual journey through Paris, or at an art gallery. I love doing extravagant worships on mission trips, using unique aspects of the culture or local beauty to symbolise aspects of God.

Under the "Tree of Knowledge of Good and Evil," we confessed our sins and kicked the "devil scarecrow" on the way out. We wound our way through the orphanage's landscape as the sun was setting. As I read Bible texts, our journey took us past the pit, to the "crossroads of life and death" and through the "waters of baptism." We found candles and communion waiting under the magnificent "Tree of Life" and discussed the blood of Jesus covering us in His covenant. Some prayed and cried as we lay watching the twinkling stars. As people slowly left, they took a promise that had been nailed to the tree.

The possibilities for interactive creative worship gatherings are endless. RED—our alternative worship church in Chattanooga, Tennessee[2]—revolves around teaching spiritual parables through art. After a homemade lunch together, our curator shares a topic and we use an artistic medium to create a response. Each week is different—from glassmaking, to welding, to paper cutting. Fascinating revelations are shared from each person's unique journey. The finished community art piece would be then placed in our "church" building—a fair trade shop and art gallery. Even years later, I look at a piece from a RED experience and remember the message and sometimes receive a new and fresh revelation.

Permission to worship creatively

God loves beauty and creativity and wants to share that with us. I want to revive this lost art of spiritual wonder, so my job as curator of this type of gathering and space is to inspire, guide, encourage and bless people. This works primarily by *creating a culture that gives them permission to worship* in the way they were designed, to walk in their unique identity and fulfil their destiny by bringing joy to God's heart. I believe worship is very individual, cultural and should be up-to-date. (There are forms of worship that have not been invented yet!) Your worship will be different from everyone else on the planet. Celebrate that fact.

So how do you worship God? If you are not sure, I encourage you to find yourself in a field or beach somewhere completely alone, where you can yell, dance and jump, run and sing as loud as you need to. Where you can also listen to God as He speaks to you and affirms who He created you to be and how much He adores you. As you come together in a group setting for worship, you will then be able to honour your gifts and know what's right for you so you are comfortable, not wearing an awkward hand-me-down style of worship.

Aside from giving yourself permission to worship freely in your own space, we need the permission and blessing of those in leadership when we are starting something new under a church banner. We are a body and always need to operate as one. Gradually introduce creative worship ideas to your church community, recognising that we are all learning together and are at various stages of exploring the significance of creativity in worship.

If you are leading your own gathering, you have the blessing from God to be as creative as He inspires you to be. As Francis Schaeffer said, "The Christian is the one whose imagination should fly beyond the stars."[3] As you explore creativity in the different areas of your life, you will also be giving permission to and inspiring others to respond creatively. In the worship environment, people need permission to be creative. Permission to feel, permission to have fun, permission to doubt, to love, to worship freely and to grow.

When starting out

If I have been given two hours of a bunch of people's precious time, I can either design the program to entertain them so they don't get bored, or I can think of ways to confuse, delight and transfix them, to allow them to experience God Himself. I definitely choose to deal with people's hearts—this is where healing and transformation begin. So I have to figure out how to get myself out of the picture and help them interact with Jesus.

First, I usually ask God what area they need to grow in and He inspires me to do something creative. He helps me think of ideas that are fresh and bring new ways of looking at old practices that might have lost their meaning. So let me share what my journey has taught me to this point and why I love curating worship experiences:

1. Invitation over instruction

Being invitational rather than instructional is extremely important and can make an incredible impact on whether people feel safe. A creative culture doesn't happen spontaneously. We can't tell people to worship louder, be creative, be more loving or be anything. As a facilitator, curator or guide, we can only help create a culture in which those things thrive. It takes intention to establish and grow such a culture in our community and that intention needs to be woven throughout the entire event.

If you choose to have a singing team at a gathering in the traditional sense of worship, the musicians develop a culture as well. Note the difference between worship leaders and song leaders. Song leaders may instruct people how to sing the songs and participate in the program, but worship leaders worship God and invite others to join in. The focus is God and His glory. Worship leaders tend to be less anxious and they don't have to be perfect singers. Because their focus in leading worship is to invite individuals in the group to worship God, they are not the focus or the entertainment. On several occasions, I have arranged for the worship band to be in a different room or behind a curtain or facing the same way as the audience.

2. Use what you've got

Leading a gathering can involve a lot of time, energy and other resources, but it can also be simple and easy. I use a lot of upcycled materials, turning trash into useful objects of beauty that stimulate the senses and imagination. This is an act of redemption, reminding me of the ways God wants to transform my brokenness into something of worth and value. The ordinary then becomes sacred. On many occasions, I have used beautiful and free chapels, a waterfall, mountaintop or a beach as inspiring settings for worship. A bit of imagination with the Holy Spirit's inspiration can turn anything into a learning opportunity and worship experience.

Sometimes I just come with questions. Not knowing the answers is OK and a lot less pressure! Allowing people time to explore and doubt and question and receive answers from God is so important. As people are on different journeys, what they need from God at any one time may be different from someone else, so I allow them time to absorb a revelation that is truly personal at that moment. Worship is a bit like jazz, everyone knows the key—the boundaries—but when you all start jamming, let it evolve and listen in awe as God shows up.

I remember running a retreat for tertiary students and each afternoon we would have three hours of silence. In the evenings, we had an "unplanned" worship where we would expect God to show up and just waited to see what happened. Each evening was different but one evening was particularly powerful. The women and men decided to separate and share their hearts with the mentors about their relationships and private lives. The men then decided to pray for the girls so called us all back into the worship room. They gathered around the kneeling girls and prayed the most beautiful prayers I have ever heard. I remember one man saying, "On behalf of any man who has ever hurt you, I ask your forgiveness and I promise to protect and respect you and bless you from now on." As some of the girls wept, I realised that the Holy Spirit had shown up and was healing deeply wounded spirits.

3. Be still

Quietness can be awkward when we haven't learned to listen to God. But as we embrace it and find it is part of our worship culture, we find great refreshment when we are given permission to relax and rest from our busy, noisy lives. Teaching people to plug back in to God is rewarding. It is learning to be mindful and intentional.

Working with clay, picking up rubbish or painting can give people space and quietness to be present to God. Give the Holy Spirit space to speak and reveal the answers, perhaps during the singing or before the final Amen. Allow people time to process their experience or to internalise knowledge that has been learned.

4. Safety first

Do you feel safe to fail? Expectations can be dangerous, so if you allow your worships to have unexpected endings you may be allowing space for miracles. Even if you think you have failed to get through the program, teach an art form or explain the point, surprising lessons can still be learned. You are not a failure but exploring freedom, creativity and developing patience! It's important to give God space to flow so He can reveal Himself "between the lines."

Do you feel safe to be messy? Being creative often involves some chaos. You will find through creative worship experiences that it is not the end product that counts, it is the internal process, the journey, that is the point. So take your time, don't rush, don't judge, be gentle with yourself and others. Didn't finish a project this gathering? Finish it next time. Enjoy the adventure!

Do you feel safe to feel? Acknowledging our feelings is the key to healing. Are we encouraging masks and perfection or are we giving people permission to be brave enough to be honest and to be real—to cry, to dance, to be loved and to hold each other's truth respectfully? We are designed to delight in beauty, for our spirits to erupt with joy and wonder, to be challenged out of our comfort zones so we can flourish. As God breaks into our lives, our emotions are calmed, chemicals balanced, neurons reformed. Attitudes are changed, shame and fears begin to dissolve, the world looks different . . . and we learn the meaning of redemption.

Passive no longer

For many people, church worship is a passive experience. They go and listen to other people sing, other people pray, other people share their stories. I have a natural desire to be included in the conversation. I want to share, I want to be heard, I want to be loved, I want to be prayed with, I want to cry or laugh and feel safe enough to be me. I want to create worship experiences where I can do all those things with other people, where I feel comfortable, where I can be present to God. If I have two hours to curate a worship, I want to create community by nurturing honest relationships and even do something functional like build a community garden. Sharing life with other people takes skills that need to be taught and discipleship is the result of mentoring not just preaching. The love of God cannot be only taught, it must be experienced. Allowing other people to experience the joy of what you have experienced is a priceless gift.

Like Mary breaking the expensive perfume over Jesus' feet (see **John 12:1–7**), creative worship experiences are acts of deep symbolism, because words cannot always express what is in our hearts. They may seem a bit extravagant and are highly sacrificial . . . but it's worth it to see people fall in love with Jesus.

—Nicki Carleton is a sojourner. A passion for discipleship has taken her on some extreme adventures, the most challenging was deep into the unexplored regions of her heart. Being transfixed in wonder is her favourite pastime, usually involving snow, flowers or clouds. As a transformance artist, she helps people enjoy praying and listening to God by curating interactive prayer rooms and alternative worship gatherings. Find out more about her creative ministry at <www.BlissfulMinistries.com> and <adoredandtreasured.blogspot.com>.

1. Michael J Gelb, *How to Think like Leonardo da Vinci—Seven Steps to Genius Every Day*, Dell, 2000.
2. The curator Linda Sines has lots of alternative worship ideas at <www.instantred.com>.
3. Francis Schaeffer, *Art and the Bible*, IVP Classics (2006), Intervarsity Press, page 91.

THE ART OF PREACHING

Creativity and Preaching

Alex Bryan

Human creativity is the first and foremost expectation of Scripture. Genesis informs us that Adam and Eve are told—by the same Breath that breathed them into being—to name animals, tend plants and subdue the earth. "Be fruitful and increase in number," God commands. *Re-create from God's original creation!* He challenges the first humans not only to be *creationists* (believing that God did indeed make the universe) but also to be *creators* (behaving like God did, with *creative activity*).

So a confession: I am an artist. And so are you. We all are—though research suggests much formal education tends to beat it out of us before we get to our double-digit years. And, in truth, sin's effect everywhere and always is to reverse God's creative intent—including the reality of our own creative purpose and potential. But we must not forget that we are born painters, sculptors, woodworkers, glassblowers, stonemasons, architects, engineers, chefs, wordsmiths, athletes, dancers, drummers and virtuoso violinists. Every human being is created unique. Therefore, every human being is made an artist unique.

My "paint" is preaching. I speak publicly for a living and—more importantly—as a calling. Voice is my vocation. Preaching aright, I believe, is not merely the bland recitation of monochromatic truth. Rather, I hold conviction that the colours of God are rich and varied. The melodies of God are bold and beautiful. Homiletics—the study and work of preaching—is a craft. And so, the preacher is—and should be—an *artisan*.

Sermons ought to be art. The gospel is beautiful, and ought to be preached dressed in beauty. Pulpit prose should be engaging and exquisite. Preachers should also be poets: words shaped with wonder, grammar encased in grace. I believe care should be given to both style and substance. Aren't the Scriptures both beautiful and true?

Preaching as art

So let me share some personal reflections on the art of preaching—for it is the artwork I know best. My hope is that as I share my creative process, this will help you ponder your own creative calling, whether you are preacher, paediatrician or plumber. This is a *personal testimony* given to elicit your own artistic reflection.

First of all, I try my best to pay attention. All the time, in every situation. I'm always on the lookout for raw material. I relish the art of others and particularly the raw works of God in nature. My smart phone has become valuable in my travels as a tool to capture creative images, people, ideas and more.

I listen. I read. And ask loads of questions, especially of the biblical text. Poetry must be read slowly. Museums and galleries include benches for good reason: masterworks require attentiveness and time. We need to sit, to take in, to absorb. (This is why Twitter tweets and Facebook status updates are often the antithesis of art. Too quick. Too shallow. Too cheap.) For example, I love the observation of former *Adventist Review* editor William Johnsson in his commentary on the biblical book of Hebrews:

> The book of Hebrews is a marvel and a mystery. The majesty of language, the breadth of ideas, the stately flow of argument—at once we sense that we stand in the presence of a master writer. . . . The document will not yield its message easily, however. Its close-knit reasoning calls for *a degree of concentration* that we are less used to than our forebears were. The modern age with its Madison Avenue veneer has dulled our powers.[1]

Johnsson's point is the book of Hebrews—like the Bible as a whole—is an incredible literary masterpiece. The Bible is not only theological wealth; it is a vast library of creative genius. So we must approach it with reverence. We must commit ourselves to the first discipline of all faithful creative work: we must pay attention. Anointed observation is the mother of anointed productivity.

A second commitment I seek in the work of preaching I learned from an old college professor: de-familiarise the familiar. The point here is to surprise. I want the listener to say, "I've never heard it that way before" or "I've never seen it from that perspective" or "I've never thought in that particular manner until now." The goal is to say old (true) things in new (fresh) ways.

Art does this *holy work*. I love Anne Lamott's observation, which has become a bit of a preaching litmus test for me:

> Let's think of reverence as awe, as presence in and openness to the world. . . . Think of those times when you've read prose or poetry that is presented in such a way that you have a fleeting sense of being startled by beauty or insight, by a glimpse into someone's soul. All of the sudden everything seems to fit together or at least to have some meaning for a moment. This is our goal as writers, I think; to help others have this sense of . . . wonder, of seeing things anew, things that catch us off guard, that break in on our small, bordered worlds.[2]

Good preaching, of course, must remind us of what we already know, what we have long felt, truth that is already discovered. There is importance, I believe, to regular liturgy and traditions, which signify unchanging religion. This permanence, however, must be careful not to become cold, lifeless, and forgettable. Clichés kill.

When the congregation is two steps ahead of the preacher something is amiss—and unholy boredom sets in. Artistic sermons—and worship services—call us to a more meaningful concentration. They also alert us to the possibility of seeing God and His world from a wholly new vantage point. In both ways, we find ourselves growing a Christian curiosity.

Third, I believe sermons should meet the great artistic standard of Philippians 4:8: "And now, dear brothers and sisters, one final thing. Fix your thoughts on what is true, and honourable, and right, and pure, and lovely, and admirable. Think about things that are excellent and worthy of praise."

Let's unpack those descriptors:

- *True.* This goes beyond doctrinal accuracy. Does the sermon *ring true*? Does it tell the truth about life? Does it neither understate the case nor exaggerate the point? Does it seek to be honest both to the biblical intent and the contemporary context?
- *Honourable.* Is the sermon respectable? Does it honour God? Does it honour the congregation? Does it honour the community outside the room? Does the preaching meet the standard of *nobility*?
- *Right.* Put another way, we might ask, "Does the sermon *do somebody wrong*?" Human beings have a sense of what is "right on" and what is "way off."
- *Pure.* Does presentation of God's word exclude impure thoughts, ill motives and secondary agendas? Is the pastor making sure the sanctuary has not become a home for a *bully pulpit*?
- *Lovely.* Was the sermon thrown together at the last minute? Is the presentation nothing more than some Ellen White quotes strung together or a "rant" against some problem in the world or the church? Does the congregation *feel* a sense of loveliness coming from the sermon? Was it a masterpiece?
- *Admirable.* Were the themes presented aspirational? Did the rhetoric lift the congregation to higher ideals and lofty living? Or did the sermon appeal to base desires, to fear and to lowest common denominator living?
- *Excellent and worthy of praise.* Did the preacher care enough to write an "A+" manuscript? Was the sermon well prepared in such a way as to receive a quality grade in a university-level public speaking class? Did the woman—or man—honour us with careful, prayerful work?

These objectives may seem overly rigorous. But, in my view, they are just right. Remember the artistic and creative excellence of the Old Testament sanctuary? Every detail was carefully considered by God and executed by the men and women who wished to honour Him and His work in the world. It seems to me the Word of God should be presented with a very high standard of creative excellence.

Fourth, I believe artistic sermons ought to stimulate a church full of artists. Jesus' parables were not the final word, but the first word. People left His creative storytelling saying, "What did that mean? We've got to talk about this some more!" The teaching method of Jesus did not stifle conversation; rather, it stimulated dialogue. The Bible itself is written in such a way that it produces point and counterpoint, debate and argument. This is why Sabbath schools can be such amazing hours of holy interaction. When the Bible is opened among a group of people, there's no telling where the interaction will go! This is biblical creativity at its best.

So, too, sermons aright offer Sabbath lunch the possibility of an engaged reflection on the text. Creativity begets creativity. Good thinking invites good thinking. And, ideally, a creative contagion breaks out in the church—fresh ways to serve the poor, to sing in worship, to connect with young people, to share the gospel with the world. In this way, preachers are not simply artists but also benefactors, curators and promoters of creative expression.

Please join us

I share these four reflections on my own artistic life in the hope that you'll reflect on your own creative work (and perhaps give some thought to creativity in your local church context as well). Unfortunately, this is not something we have done well as Adventists. We have had an awkward approach to art and creativity.

However, even as we wait faithfully for Jesus, Adventism is in a new era where younger generations are eager to contribute fresh expressions of our timeless truth. I see Adventist young adults sorting out how to faithfully look forward to the Creator's second coming, while living as faithful creators in the here and now. They are finding ways to blend our traditional practicality, austerity and eschatological focus with fragrance, colour and vision. They see the scriptures both commencing and concluding amid artistic beauty. They seek a biblical faith—an Adventist faith—baptised in such beauty. Between Origins and Omega, they strive to live a life of Originality.

I believe we are on the verge of an Adventism still fully committed to our historic ideals and embracing a new one: Present Truth in expression. I want to contribute to that by my art, leadership and encouragement—and I invite you to join with us in this ongoing creative project called Adventism.

—Alex Bryan is senior pastor of Walla Walla University Church in College Place, Washington, USA. He is author of The Green Cord Dream *and co-chair of The One Project <www.the1project.org>.*

1. William G Johnsson, *In Absolute Confidence: The Book of Hebrews Speak to our Day*, Southern Publishing Association, 1979, pages 9–10 (italics mine).
2. Anne Lamott, *Bird by Bird: Some Instructions on Writing and Life*, Doubleday, 1994, pages 99–100.

AN ITINERANT POLLINATOR OF GRACE

Creativity and Storytelling

Dick Duerksen

I am a pastor without a church congregation. Instead, I have spent my life pastoring from behind administrative desks, and on committees where I am slowly learning the value of listening.

On occasion—first at academies and small churches, then in large gatherings around the world—I served as "guest preacher." Rather than preach expository sermons as my homiletics professor had taught me to do, I told stories. Stories from the Hebrew scriptures. Stories from the life of Jesus. Stories of angels and demons and saints and sinners. Hopefully, stories of hope.

I preached carefully but far too long, testing the skills of technicians whose cassettes held only "60 minutes of truth."

One afternoon, a Master Preacher asked me to "tell a story to the children who come to church because it's a great place to get Cheerios." I told the story of David and Goliath, and pretended to be the audacious "Big Man." The kids' eyes bugged out and they crashed with me to the carpet like an avalanche falling off Mont Blanc. Luckily, the pianist began keying the offertory or the rug rats might have cut off my head and brought it triumphantly to the pastor.

The pastor's first words were, "The Bible has just come to life on our platform."

Since then I have preached many more stories. I've discovered that when I share the stories of God and His friends, I am able to speak to every issue Christians confront. I doubt that I could ever preach a convincing three-point sermon about sexual addiction, but listeners understand the issue when they join me for a walk through the temple with Bad King Manasseh.

The New Testament writers record very few of Jesus' "sermons"—but they share scores of His stories. Those parables and re-telling of current events, stand as His most compelling messages. Through them, Jesus was able to discuss every issue of the day, using each tale to show the relevance of God's grace.

Stories. Always stories. I've learned we all come to church for the Cheerios.

Stories come with velcro—pictures, sounds and scents to captivate eyes, ears, minds and hearts.

I discovered the power of *story-velcro* on a weekend retreat with 50 theology students and their "would-be" spouses. They gave me the challenge of my life: "Tell us a Bible story," they asked. "Make the Bible come to life."

My prayers quickly led me to the story of John Goldberg, the paralytic. Simon Peter told the story to John Mark when they were writing the gospel (see **Mark 2:1–12**), and it seemed a perfect way to help future pastors learn how to walk in Peter's sandals.

Here's the study process I use for preparing a story sermon like this one:

1. Read John Goldberg's story in seven different versions of Mark's gospel. Some folks honestly believe that "if the King James version was good enough for Paul, it ought to be good enough for me." I do not believe that, and am dedicated to helping Bible readers explore Scripture through the hearts of many different translators. Begin with the original language, if you can. Add the King James, the New International, *The Message*, *Clear Word*, the New Living Translation, and any other version you have. Lay them all out and compare them side-by-side. Each one provides different insights into the passage.

2. Check <Bibleinfo.com> for all the other times "paralytic," "roof," "forgiveness" and a dozen other words from the stories appear in other places through the Bible. I am regularly amazed at how other parts of the Bible help me understand the story I am studying.

3. Google "roof construction in Galilee," "why are paralytics unclean," "Peter's fishing boat in Galilee" and a dozen other questions that have come up as I've thought about the story. It takes time to sift through the internet "chaff," but I discovered that Capernaum's roofs were made from stone slabs—and that the "roof-raising" was often a community event much like an Amish barn-raising.
   The internet provides a score of other details that give texture and life to the story. Paralytics were "unclean" because their disease was usually the result of lifestyle choices. The sails of fishing boats were often used as doors for houses and sheets for beds.

4. Write the story as if it were happening today—and as if I was "there." Include all six senses in what I write.

   Taste: the dry-mouth hunger Goldberg and his family experienced as outcasts, unable to go into the market, unable to visit family.

Sound: the scraping of the stones being shifted to make a hole large enough for a man on a stretcher to drop down through Peter's roof.

Touch: John Goldberg feeling his friends place their strong fisherman hands under him and lift him onto the rough sail-cloth stretcher.

Smell: scores of unwashed people crowding around Peter's house, each one eager to listen, each one demanding to be in the front row.

Sight: dusty chaff sifting down in the first shaft of light glowing through the new hole in Peter's roof.

Emotions: Mrs Goldberg and the children—as friends take John away to ask Jesus for healing.

5. Read the story in the writings of Ellen White. She writes as if she had been there or as if she had seen a video of the event. If I read Ellen White first, I'm tempted to assume she's "the last word" on the story, and stop studying. When I save her writings for last, she always adds something new and often straightens out my crazy ideas.
   By the way, Ellen White really liked this story. She says Goldberg was the one who suggested that his friends take him up on the decaying roof and drop him "right in front of Jesus." She also says Goldberg's moral choices had made him a paralytic. She says he was like a leper, an outcast everyone believed was so evil and so thoroughly rejected by God for his nasty lifestyle, that it was OK for mothers to point Goldberg out to their sons and say, "Stop that, or you'll grow up to be like John Goldberg!" It was a warning that made all sons tremble.

Before I tell the story, I must discover the single point that makes it worth telling. This is not something I bring to the story, but *the truth* that comes from within the tale itself.

By now the story has become *my story*. I am there, peering through the broken roof with Goldberg's four fisherman friends. I can smell the dirty sandals and hear the hostile breathing of the scribes. I also have too much information and the story is too long.

If I tell the John Goldberg story "as is," people will yawn through my multiple-point storytelling. So I trim, trim, trim and turn the story into a tighter tale—one that gets to the point without losing the pleasure of *being there*.

Before I tell the story, I must discover the single point that makes it worth telling. This is not something I bring to the story, but *the truth* that comes from within the tale itself.

Miss Townsend, my seventh-grade English teacher, required that we write *the truth* in one sentence.

Here's my thesis sentence for John Goldberg's story:

> God draws sinners to Himself so He can forgive and empower them.

Once I have the thesis sentence, I write at least five headlines that could be used if the story were on the front page of the *National Enquirer*.

High School Lothario Forgiven!

Church Leader Repulsed

Party Organiser Loses Roof

Goldberg Is Back!

God Breathes Sawdust

"Good stories are totally unpredictable, filled with surprises," Miss Townsend taught us. "A good story captures you and makes everything else seem irrelevant. You want to gather in every word, revel in the colours and textures, then wipe away the tears that come when the surprises reach out and squeeze love into your heart."

To discover the unpredictable surprises, I have immersed myself in the story. I have prayed through it as if I were John Goldberg, as if I were Peter, as if I were the Rabbi who pronounced him unclean, as if I were John's father or his best friend. I can now tell the story by heart—without notes—because *I was there*.

At this point in the creative process, I cover the story with prayers and let it sit for a few days.

When I return to the story, it feels new and fresh. I read it through, feeling each of the senses, and checking to be sure the point comes through clearly from within the storytelling. No explaining or moralising allowed!

I told my John Goldberg story to a group of pastors one afternoon at a retreat centre in the mountains of California. They were entranced and tearful, and the story sparked a 30-minute discussion about forgiveness. Afterwards, one of my pastor-friends said, "Dick, I have finally figured out what you do. God did not call you to pastor a church congregation. He called you to bring the Bible to life, to be *an itinerant pollinator of grace*."

Creative pollinating takes time, focus and hard work. If I listen closely and tell what He shows me, the pollinating will succeed—and many others will begin to tell the stories of His grace.

—Dick Duerksen is a storyteller, professionally for Maranatha Volunteers International <www.maranatha.org> and in many other places around the world where he is invited to speak. With his wife Brenda, their responsibilities and invitations take them on many journeys around the world, providing them with unique opportunities to enjoy and photograph nature, places, and people. Find Dick's photography gallery at <www.MountainFriendsPhotography.com>.

TO STIR AS WE HAVE BEEN STIRRED

Creativity and Culture

Robert Wolfgramm

Creativity does not come cheaply or naturally. Rather, it is a gift and an assignment from God. Creativity expresses itself in service for His people, but is such that it cannot be coerced. A Christian artist—in whatever medium—is someone who has received a talent or gift and has become aware of its desire for expression, of being "stirred" in the heart, as Moses put it, to go on an assignment—a mission—with it. Jeremiah said he could not hold in his gift; it was like fire in his bones (see **Jeremiah 20:9**). He had to express himself, let it out and complete his mission.

The Christian artist is also aware of the original source of his or her talent—God Himself. As such, he or she is obliged to develop it. Not in some haphazard way, but specifically in orientation to serving the human sanctuary, God's body and bride on earth, the church.

The case of Moses is illuminating in this regard. The Bible tells us that, at one point, God Himself told him to "write down" a song and "teach it to the people of Israel" (**Deuteronomy 31:19**). We are then told that without fuss, "that very day Moses wrote down the words of the song and taught it to the Israelites" (**Deuteronomy 31:22**). It was a song written for a purpose, an assignment completed as part of a larger mission. The Christian artist being one who is "stirred" by God, in turn, stirs their church with their art, with their "workmanship" by composing it for them, displaying it to them, reading it to them, or singing and playing it to them.

Some history

This is a one-to-one divine initiative but artistic response does not take place in a vacuum. In the history of the Christian church, this dialectic has not always been easy to accommodate. The assignment and gifts of Christian artists have not always been enthusiastically received in their congregational and ecclesiological contexts.

The divisions and tensions in relation to the arts and Christianity have a long and tedious history. By the 17th and 18th centuries, we see two rival traditions emerging in response to church-based creativity: one is Apollonian, legal-bureaucratic in character, and defined by discipline and symbolic similitude; the other is Dionysian, of the charismatic spirit, and defined more by the approximation of realism and reflecting a freedom of expression.

In worship, this dichotomy was represented by the split between "high" church culture and "low" church culture in the 18th and 19th centuries. High-church creativity was seen in orchestras and choir, in the "classical" music of Bach and Handel, who put intellectual complexity into the harmonic and melodic structures of their heritage. Low-church culture was the music of congregational hymns, of tent revivalism and religious "enthusiasm" (as Luther called it). It was free-spirited by comparison—religious creativity marked by emotional ecstasy. On the other hand, high-church culture was predominantly one of emotional restraint, "Calvinised" and "iceberg style" (as one historian put it).[1]

But this dichotomy was also apparent in biblical times. Michal's criticism of her husband's naked dancing before the Lord after his military victory over the Philistines was as much about disgust at his "low" cultural expression—unrestrained, charismatic enthusiasm—as about his apparent nakedness (see **2 Samuel 6:16–23**). This behaviour was considered unbecoming of one who had penned "high" culture expressions of art, namely glorious psalms that were written for choir and orchestra.

By the 20th century, this high–low disjuncture had become an elite–folk-popular or high–mass culture distinction. High or elite cultural expression was now seen as one with a long and rich European historical heritage. It was the product of deep emotional expenditure, was rooted in divine contemplation, and led to mental and social elevation. On the other hand, folk, popular or mass culture was seen as fundamentally shallow, an artifice, manufactured by the children of the industrial revolution. Considered "light" in its intellectual content, it was easily mimicked and reproducible, and was for sheer secular entertainment and sporting pleasure. It was not "serious" music or art.

So what did I do?

This was the dichotomy and background against which I commenced high schooling in Australia in 1965, with a minimal interest in music. I thought there were only two instruments in the world that mattered: the ukulele (which I could play) and the guitar (which the Beatles played). By sight, sound and definition, the "uke" was a mass-culture/low-culture object designed for little more than party amusement. By contrast, the guitar could serve two masters—either elite or popular—depending on whether it was in the hands of Segovia or The Shadows.

That was until I came to live as a boarder with the family of Sydney Adventist teacher and musician, ("Uncle") Dave Caldwell. He was a cellist—the cello being a serious, high-culture instrument that I didn't even know existed.

Uncle Dave insisted I take an instrument and that I learn to read music. He changed my life forever. Unable to get a flattering sound out of a trumpet, I settled on a B-flat and then an E-flat bass, doing hymns and marches, but mostly learning about music and how it worked, from pen to performance. I learned about scales, keys and transposition and became a member of the Advent Brass band in Sydney for three years. From this tuition, I had the privilege of marching in Anzac Day parades, of playing in rotundas, at church functions and in competitions in the Sydney Town Hall.

It was a rich introduction to both sides of the creative and cultural cake. Brass bands sat somewhere between Uncle Dave's cello orchestral work, on one hand, and his fondness for folk hootenannies, on the other. On some occasions we were rubbing shoulders with Bach, Vivaldi, Beethoven and Dvorak, the next we were blowing chord harmonicas or strumming ukes, guitars and banjos with Woody Guthrie, Pete Seeger and Bob Dylan.

My cultural experience took a decidedly "pop culture" turn in 1967 when I began teaching myself guitar and left the brass band. Fellow school students, Lowell Tarling and Louis Rao, were my immediate inspirations and models. I was amazed at how pretty girls seemed to be attracted not only to the Rolling Stones and Bob Dylan, who were at the peak of their creativity, but to Lowell and Louis who sang their pop songs on guitars. It seemed the charisma of pop was not only manufactured, it was transferable!

> This was a remarkable concession to the times because our church, like all Protestant Christian churches, was committed to the idea that cultural deprivation was good for you.

In 1968, my adventure in popular culture advanced further when, as a student at Lilydale Adventist Academy, I formed a band with three friends. Using hired amplifiers and a bass guitar, we won the Warburton SDA Church Talent Quest that year, playing an instrumental cover of the Beatles' song "Daytripper."

Looking back at it, this was a remarkable concession to the times because our church, like all Protestant Christian churches, was committed to the idea that cultural deprivation was good for you. All transistor radios were suspect. Even vinyl records were dubious unless they conveyed classical and "acceptable" music to believers' ears.

I compensated for this cultural deprivation by trying my hand at songwriting. At age 15, the first songs I wrote were three-chord Dylan-inspired protest songs and four-chord Beatles-inspired "silly love songs"—as Paul McCartney later summed them up. They were constrained by my context of course, but I had no interest in going into elite/high cultural creativity and expression, except where this was forced on me by those who wanted me to help express what was in them. The only option for those of us who wanted to "belong" to our faith fellowship and to our generation simultaneously, was to conform to the strictures and musical tastes of church leaders and suppress the conviction of what we wanted to express from within ourselves.

Ultimately, I couldn't take this latter course of action. It was not my assignment or gift. The fire in my bones was encouraged by friends and I began writing my own "Christian-experience" songs. Then I began to write more biblically-based, "gospel" songs, at the same time as continuing to be involved with classical music.

In 1971, I started at Avondale College, where my precarious settlement between the high-church Apollonian tradition and rock's Dionysian impulse became even more marked. Forming a songwriting team with Lowell Tarling, we took up performing around the area. In deference to our context and obvious college constraints, we also wrote and produced a contemporary-style folk-cantata for mostly classical instruments. Like *Jesus Christ Superstar* and *Godspell* of the time, our libretto, theme and story were definitely high-church culture: the Passion. My melodic and harmonic hopes were for rock-style musical structures, but obviously, these had to be toned down or transposed into folk and quasi-Baroque, classical modes.

We called it *Threedom*—a loose collection of songs until Melbourne businessman Peter McDougall hired me for end-of-term holidays and paid me to score it. Peter bought the necessary pens and manuscript paper and set me up in one of his offices. He sat opposite me on the phone all day doing business, while I sat at my desk with my guitar doing classical arrangement, as it were.

Avondale's music department director, Alan Thrift, was a tremendous support, but others were not so trusting. The college formed a special music committee to ensure *Threedom* lived up to Adventist values. One song was cancelled because it was considered too "far out." A debate raged back and forth between us about whether we were being sacrilegious to voice the part of Jesus in our story in the first person. One staff member sat through rehearsals and made notes that would turn up in my mail as the committee's suggestions for "improving the cantata."

Lowell and I were also regular "street preachers" in Sydney, Melbourne, Newcastle, Wyong and other centres. As street preachers, we not only witnessed through personal testimonies and group singing on city streets, we took on the job of writing and performing original Christian songs. Lowell and I also gigged in coffee-shop poetry readings, as well as at various church-organised functions. By 1977, our songs were being sung and shared among street preachers and youth groups in Sydney and Melbourne. Street preaching was seen as a low-church cultural enterprise—noise and entertainment as "bait" for passers-by. Through this mass-culture exhibitionism, a "fish" may be "hooked" for Jesus.

Our creative work together continued after Avondale. In the late '70s, Lowell—who had been writing and producing Sydney-based oratorio-plays of his own—introduced me to a high-school student named Sally Hilder. We recorded a first album—on vinyl and cassette—of Tarling–Wolfgramm songs, with Sally as our feature vocalist. With friend and financial adviser, Genna Levitch, we launched *Galilee Recordings*. It was released through Spotlight Records, a trailblazing non-denominational Sydney-based Christian music distributor. It was our debut in the "contemporary Christian music" scene—and the first for an Adventist outfit in Australia.

Encouraged by the positive reception we received for the album, we recorded more and, in 1978–79, my solo album *Bob* was recorded and released, which gave me opportunities to perform with some of the biggest names in contemporary Christian music at that time. In the summer of 1979–80, again funded by Melbourne street preachers, we went back into the studio with Sally Hilder and other friends and recorded a final album. *Persecution Games* was a concept-protest-album, developed with Lowell Tarling as a tribute to Lindy and Michael Chamberlain. Pop-artist Martin Sharp who had worked with Eric Clapton and his '60s psychedelic group Cream donated the cover art. This was the best work we had produced but—as rightly predicted by our financial adviser—the album sold least well. Early 1980s Christians did not know what to make of its bitter-sweet lyric and metal-aggro attitude. In one of Melbourne's top record stores, it was filed under "Punk & Disorderly"!

Throughout this recording career, the point of my recorded work and performance was to document my Christian convictions and beliefs as they had developed during my years from late school songwriter to street preacher, hopefully for the benefit of others. The point was never about becoming a star but to be a ministry.

What did I learn?

As I look back on my active music years, I can see that my church—indeed the Christian church as a whole—has changed for the better. We easily forget how conservative churches were in the '60s and '70s. Today, many churches are more open to different styles of worship music and Christian creativity. But there is always more work to be done. Our sanctuary, our ark, our temple is never completed.

Churches are now able and willing to discriminate between the multiplicity of contemporary popular music forms, which were simply lumped under the rubric of "rock—the devil's music" when I was younger. Popular music now includes styles from folk, country, blues, jazz and gospel—all of which have mixed and metamorphosed into hybrids, fusions and sub-styles. In turn, each of these music genres is differentiated by performers affecting more subtle styles and ideologies associated with ethnic, age, gender and geographical factors. And all of which enriches the creativity potential of the church.

And this is all to the good. For many church people whom I encountered when I was writing, performing and producing, the word "rock" was just a cipher—a shibboleth—that allowed them to ignore hard thinking and substantive analysis of the matter. Labelling "rock" music allowed them to dismiss without knowing. Generally, little attempt was made to distinguish a better popular song from a boring one, a constructive from a destructive one. There was little if any acknowledgment of the fact that culture—whether high or low, elite or popular, folk or mass—is an arena of creative contest, of cultural ambiguity and of discursive contradiction. And there was almost no recognition of the fact that music itself mirrors both the good and the bad in society, in people and in nature. This blind absolutism meant that Christians having a more intelligent critique and a more contemporary praxis and orientation to their art and their creativity had to look elsewhere.

Generally, little attempt was made to distinguish a better popular song from a boring one, a constructive from a destructive one.

But there were exceptions. While some of our church members were literally pulling the plug on my guitar amplifier (while street-preaching thirty years ago), Uncle Dave Caldwell was pointing out to me the Baroque aspects of Beatles music. While many churchgoers were condemning heavy rock for being "too loud," "too showy" and "too heavy," some commentators and friends were pointing out Purcell-like descending chromatics and Vivaldi-like arpeggios on the latest Deep Purple album.

Culture—popular or otherwise—is a field with many players driven by many different motives. Creative expression is neither *a priori* good nor bad, moral nor immoral. The point is to *test to see that which is good*, to find that expression that uplifts, and to do it for God's glory. Whether it be classical, ethnic, world, techno or hip-hop, style is irrelevant. The essential danger in creativity is not the medium, but the response it elicits. The Christian artist works under the sovereignty of God. His or her art is to be directed to His glory. The worst outcome for any creative person is not if their art is ignored, but if their art has "traded the truth about God for a lie" (**Romans 1:25**)—if the end result of their art encourages audiences to worship and serve "the things God created instead of the Creator himself" (**Romans 1:25**).

In articulating a philosophy of creativity, the Christian church would do well to recognise the complexity and slippery ambiguities inherent in cultural analysis. The church needs constantly to re-think its approach, reacquire its artistic consciousness and extend the spectrum of music—as with other art and creativity—we officially sponsor and promote, so it reflects the range of music actually out there in our pews and schools. Any policy that narrows expression of the broadness and variegation of the creative gifts of the Holy Spirit risks self-defeat. We must not pursue a narrow and "safe" aesthetic to conform to the reactionary values of an ageing elite. A healthy church policy cannot ignore the needs and talents of a plural and multicultural membership.

The critical condition of our world is such that newer sophisticated analysis and praxis are called for. A tele-technological consciousness—emailing, downloading, skyping, twittering and so forth—now defines the global village. It has sprung from 20th-century scientific advances, from the expectation of democratic principles, and is coupled with multicultural political and social hybridities. It will continue to destablise hitherto authentic expressions of so-called high church Christian culture.

Call it "postmodern" if you like, but whatever it is, repeatedly pontificating an agonistic moral panic about it and its alleged apocalyptic effects on the church won't work. That just dampens and insults the creative spirit. Instead, the task is to put some realism into our cultural perspective: to respond to the perversity of this fading world by re-articulating and re-signifying what it means to be "creative" and "Christian." As Dylan put it, "The times are a-changing" indeed—and the church knows this as much as anyone else. The mission is for us to continually inspire creativity that responds with Christocentric joy and enthusiasm—to stir as we have been stirred.

—Robert Wolfgramm was born in Fiji and is presently retired there after 42 years of schooling and working in Australia. He was the recipient of the Gabe Reynaud Award at the Manifest Creative Arts Festival in 2012, recognising excellence in using the creative arts for ministry. His musical tastes are multicultural, but his particular interest is in gospel, blues, jazz and folk idioms of the 20th century. Occasionally, he writes a song and pens an essay.

1. William H Sweet, *The Religion of America*, Baker, 1979, page 230.

SHARING

COLOUR ME IMPRESSED[1]

Creativity and Communication

James Standish

Have you ever heard of a nation called Cymru? Granted, it isn't the largest nation on earth, nor the most influential. In fact, its entire population would fit into Sydney (Australia) with plenty of room to spare. And it is less than one-seventh the geographic size of the South Island of New Zealand.

At this stage you may be excusing yourself for never hearing of this obscure land. But here is the kicker: you do know this country. In fact, many Australians and New Zealanders have a little Cymry blood running through their veins. You may know its Prince well—he even lived in Australia for a while as a boy and has since made high-profile visits around the world—and I'm sure you know of a few other Cymry. Take, for example, Shirley Bassey or Duffy. But maybe most startling, Australia plays Cymru regularly in our most celebrated sporting rivalry, but most of us don't realise it.

Where is this mysterious land?

It sits right next to England, and in the English language, it is called "Wales." Of course, Wales is a bit of a misnomer as it merely means "foreigner" in Anglo-Saxon. Imagine having your national identity perpetually carved in stone as a "foreigner" in your own land! If that were not indignity enough, when the England and Wales Cricket Board fields a team, it's simply called "England." No wonder the Welsh identity is so wrapped up in rugby union, where at least they play under their own name, albeit the English version of it.

You might think that this little land of curious names like Llanfairpwllgwyngyllgogerychwyrndrobwllllantysiliogogogoch, beautiful scenery, heroic history and powerful

> voices is a bit of backwater when it comes to our faith. After all, what have the Welsh ever given Christianity?

Stop reading now

Take a pause.

Look at the preceeding five-paragraph excerpt and try to imagine what kind of document it came from. The truth might be a little surprising. I'll give you the answer later in this piece, and along with it, where to discover the most profound Welsh contribution to Christianity (here's a hint, it involves half a billion, every single year).

But for the time being, all you need to note is this: the excerpt comes from a piece whose purpose is nothing to do with advancing the cause of cultural literacy, proclaiming the contributions of the Welsh to the world, or even providing insight into Christian history. Nothing whatsoever.

So why begin the piece with this little mystery about the Cymru? Because most of us love a tease. We are curious creatures. If someone throws out a few clues, we like to follow them. I suppose it's our inquisitive nature.

So starting with something likely to be unfamiliar, presented in a breezy style and weaving in a little mystery is enough to capture the interest of most people. And if we ever want anyone to read anything we write, listen to anything we have to say or watch anything we produce, making it a little interesting up front is a good place to start.

But drawing in interest isn't always as easy as it sounds. Some of us are dead boring, if truth be told. When we're given a microphone at church, our instinct to drone on in monotone kicks in. When given a chance to write, our stories lie lifeless on the page, our efforts to inspire come across as worn-out platitudes, our hopes to move others in prose turn out to be prosaic. So how do we take dull sermons, stories, articles and all the rest, and breathe a little sparkle into them? We are called to use all these vehicles to inspire and engage, so surely a truly faithful response should be a sparkly one.

A creative writer

Jonah Lehrer thought he had the answer. He wrote the *New York Times* bestseller entitled *Imagine: How Creativity Works*. In it, he explores all manner of influences on the creative process. Apparently amphetamines can help—but there is a brutal law of diminishing returns. Maybe more critical in the creative process is the colour of your room.

Mr Lehrer reports on a study that found we're best at solving insight puzzles in light blue rooms. Who knew? Shower time is also great for creativity, as is simply taking a break and thinking about other things. In fact, Mr Lehrer reports that many of the most profoundly creative insights in the history of humanity have come at a time when no-one was particularly working on them. So, while a change may be as good as a holiday, it turns out a holiday is also an excellent agent for change.

In summary, if you want to be creative without pharmacological assistance, paint your workplace a light blue, take lots of long showers and, whatever you do, don't think about what you want to be creative about. At least, not when you want to be most innovative.

What I love most about Mr Lehrer is that its turned out that he is particularly creative himself. For the first time in history, his book contains Bob Dylan's detailed description on the creative process that lead to the writing of his masterpiece "Like a Rolling Stone." It is almost too good to be true.

Alas, it is too good to be true. It turns out there is a reason the quotes have never been published before: Bob Dylan never made them. As punishment for fabricating Dylan quotes, this brilliant young writer who flew so high, so fast, has recently had his Icarus moment—a very sudden and punishing fall from grace. His book has been pulled from distribution and the e-version discontinued.

> If you want to be creative without pharmacological assistance, paint your workplace a light blue, take lots of long showers and, whatever you do, don't think about what you want to be creative about.

Personally, I think the literary world is being a bit rough on Mr Lehrer. After all, his book was all about being creative, wasn't it? And how much more creative can you be, than making up quotes from absolute thin air?

And it would seem a practice that Dylan himself would approve of—he being not at all averse to making up fictitious stories about himself. My favourite Dylan autofictography[2] is his early claim to have travelled America as a young carnival performer.[3] That is, I think, far more interesting than the truth of Dylan's rather mundane Minnesotan middle-class upbringing.

Creativity rules

If you want some pointers on creativity and you don't want to find them in a book called *Imagine* containing imagined quotes, let me offer you just three simple rules of creativity. These I will modestly call the Immutable Mutually Reinforcing Laws of Creative Communications—or IMRLCC for short.

The IMRLCC are a good starting point for any project involving communication of any kind, anywhere, at any time. Now, if that isn't broad enough for you, let me add, it is a magnificent starting point. Hence, without delay, here are the IMRLCC:

1. Tell people something they don't already know; or
2. If you can't do that, tell them something they know, but in a way they've never heard/thought of before; and

3. No matter what you do, put a bit of bounce, vim, velocity, panache, pathos and/or passion into it!

There. Simple. No need to drop acid or repaint your home. No need to study the fabricated quotes of Bob Dylan or to spend the rest of your day in the shower. Just start whatever project you're involved in with a question: *Do people already know what I'm trying to communicate?*

If the answer is no, you are in good shape, just go to rule 3, and throw yourself into it. Remember, what you are communicating doesn't have to be new, it just has to be new to your audience. Cymru has been around a very long time, for example, just most of us don't realise it.

If the answer is yes—that is, your audience already knows what you are about to tell them—you are on dangerous ground. Indeed, you are at a very high risk of delivering a bland, mundane, tedious, pedestrian product. But go to rule 2 and see if you can give it a unique, captivating new twist of your own, with the help of the Holy Spirit. Ask for the Spirit to provide profound new insight.

Can you relate it in a dynamic or engaging new way? Are there new facts or information that provide something brilliant or challenging? Is there something in your delivery that breathes new life into your old material? But be very honest with yourself before assuming you do have something grand to add. Think of the vast weight of all the banal sermons you've heard in your life. The truly terrifyingly trivial TV shows you've wasted precious time watching. Remember the pieces you've begun to read, only to have your eyes glaze over (assuming not this piece, as you have made it this far . . .).

If you don't have anything better than the same kind of stuff that lulled you into a stupor, have the courage to abandon the project at this point. No matter what that project is—a call to offering, a sermon, a story, a book, a TV show—please be merciful and let it die a natural death before it inflicts harm on anyone. It is far more noble to communicate nothing than to risk the outrageous slings and arrows from an audience at the receiving end of tired clichés that are so familiar they can repeat them back by rote.

Of course, when stuck for good ideas, there is a source you can always turn to—a source so overwhelming endowed with creativity that He created creativity in the first place. You can't get much more creative than that, now, can you? And, He's promised, He's always ready to lend a hand.

In the somewhat unlikely event you really do have a brilliant insight or delivery, some twist, something remarkable that breathes new life into well-worn material, then go to rule 3. Give your new insight bounce, vigour, vim and panache—and see it fly.

Back to the beginning

Now, what were those first five paragraphs taken from? I'll give you one final hint: they come from the cellar of communication. What are you are least likely to read, most likely to drop in the bin? What do you hate to get and what simultaneously makes you cynical, miffed, riled and repulsed? Yes, they are the first five paragraphs of that tedious irritant—the loathsome, lowly fundraising letter.[4]

In truth, the letter the excerpt was taken from was designed to communicate one thing, and one thing only: *Please give us your money.* But sometimes a little creativity improves an ugly duckling into a slightly unsightly swan. And if a little creativity can do that for fundraising letters, it can be done for absolutely anything—even sermons. So release your creative juices, follow the IMRLCC like your life depends on it and, if you're so inclined, please do send money. Lots of it.

—James Standish currently serves as director of communications for the Adventist Church in the South Pacific, editor of Record *and host of* InFocus. *He has a Juris Doctor, cum laude, from Georgetown University, Washington, DC, an MBA from the University of Virginia, and a bachelor's degree from the one and only Newbold College, England. He is married to Leisa G Morton-Standish and they have two daughters, Shea and Skye.*

1. Rather unoriginally taken from the Replacement's song of the same name.
2. Fictography: a fictitious biography. Autofictography: a fictitious autobiography, also known as a resume.
3. I write this from memories of hearing Bob Dylan wax eloquent about "his" colourful youth in an archival interview, but I haven't located the text of the interview. Could it be I've unconsciously created a fictitious account of his autofictography? If so, give me credit for creativity, and if not, please don't judge my limited appetite for Dylan research too harshly.
4. Just in case you're wondering about the precise source, it comes from a fundraising letter I ghostwrote for It is Written Oceania. If you want to know about the profound contribution the Welsh made to Christianity, you'll have to contact It is Written Oceania for a copy <www.itiswrittenoceania.tv>. But be forewarned, once on the mailing list, I have an unending string of fundraising letters coming your way!

REACH OUT AND COLLABORATE WITH SOMEBODY

Creativity and Collaboration

Kyle Portbury

A wise old BBC film director once said to me, "Creativity is measured by your ability to harness the talent of those around you toward accomplishing a common goal." Be that making a film, writing a book, painting, drawing, sculpting, singing, dancing, 3D modelling, using your iPad to learn to play guitar—you name it, all these creative endeavours are enhanced by the input of someone else.

Steve Jobs didn't sit in a factory in China making your iPhone, Mick Jagger gets no satisfaction without Richards, Watts and Wood, and Eddie Murphy can't play every role in his movies—OK, bad example but you see where I'm heading.

Collaboration is vital to the success of any creative project and your collaborators are limited only by your willingness to reach out and connect with them. You usually don't need to look far. But it's the reaching out that sets a creative practitioner apart from a creative procrastinator.

OK, take five to go tweet that pearl of wisdom . . . Tweeted? Good, now that it's trending globally, let's refocus.

Just ask

We've all met them—and maybe you're one of them—the person who's always talking about what they're "going" to do, if only they knew the right people or had the right family name. My first challenge to you is simple: Don't be afraid to ask.

In 2008, I was living and working in London and I had the misfortune of producing a pilot drama series. I say misfortune with a smile now, but at the time it was anything but funny. The director—also the financial backer—turned out to be slightly crazy. And when I say "slightly," I mean straitjacket nuts. Just how crazy I discovered daily during the course of the production.

One morning during the pre-production phase, he walked into the production office and shouted, "We must have Joan Collins in this show! We simply must!' Turning to me, with the crazed look of a seagull that's just sensed a hot chip is about to come its way, he exclaimed excitedly, "Kyle, get her on the phone."

Well, I certainly didn't have Joan Collins' number on speed dial. Where do you even start looking for it? It's not like she's listed under "C" for Collins in the phone book. I looked. The numerous Joan Collinses listed ranged from a carpet cleaner to a lawyer. Suffice to say, none were romance novelists. Rather adamantly, I reported back to my wonderfully unhinged director, "There is no way we're getting Joan Collins to do this show—you know that, don't you?"

> Naivety will get you a long way in this regard: the less you know, sometimes the less you realise what you're asking for.

His reply was possibly the only sensible thing the man said the whole shoot: "All I know is that if you don't call her, she definitely won't be doing it, will she?"

Even for a crazy guy, I couldn't really fault the logic. It's great advice: don't be afraid to ask. What's the worst that can happen? Nothing? That's what you've got now and at least if you've asked, there's a chance they'll say yes and something will happen. At worst, they'll say no politely. And maybe the next time you ask—which, of course, you should—they will be available. They may even recommend someone else who can potentially help. Asking creates possibilities.

Naivety will get you a long way in this regard: the less you know, sometimes the less you realise what you're asking for. When I first graduated from The Drama Centre London, I was lucky enough to get funding for my first short film and I set out assembling the cast, crew and key heads of department. I had met a well known and accomplished composer through my directing mentor and had struck up a few conversations with him on different occasions. So when it came time to think about music for my first film, in my naivety I thought, "Well, everyone else is on location so I guess the composer writes the score on set too, right?"

I sent him a text to see if he could meet with me and, that same day, I found myself his guest at the British Academy of Film and Television Arts (BAFTA) on a particularly bright sunny day in London. I asked him if he would be interested in coming down to Cornwall and writing the score for the film while we shot it. Four films later and we are still working together. Incidentally, he still comes out on location to write music, which—as it turns out—is not common practice. Who knew?! But my naivety has lead to a collaboration that has been incredibly rewarding for both of us.

On our second film, he climbed Mt Kilimanjaro with us. How many composers can say that? And let me tell you, a few of his contemporaries questioned the necessity of the climb until he reached the summit and then they were all jealous. When we began working on the score back in London and we asked, "How do we communicate this emotion or theme?" We were able to say, "I know, remember when we were struggling to breathe at 19,000 feet above sea level and hallucinating about cats in bowler hats? Yeah, that's how this moment should feel—like that."

(The cats didn't have bowler hats but it does make for a better story, doesn't it?)

Asking. It's a simple concept but often hard to do. Don't be afraid to ask—or do be afraid and ask anyway. You never know what might come out of it.

I eventually found the contact details for Joan Collins and called her agent, a lovely man who told me Joan would be delighted to do the project—for a price. Taking the bait, I inquired as to what that price might be.

He replied, "Son, Joan doesn't get out of bed for less that $25,000."

"Well," I replied, "don't bother waking her up."

Honesty increases influence

There are few creative endeavours that are truly solo sports. Even a published novel takes a team—after all, it doesn't edit and market itself. The creative process is a team game and brings all sorts of people, from different backgrounds, together to make something that will hopefully captivate an audience. So it is important to be honest and open with your collaborators. Seems pretty logical, right? You want to know who you're working with, just like they want to know who they're working with?

But you'd be surprised how many Christians will not mention their faith to their colleagues. I'm not suggesting you must blurt out a list of your beliefs at your first meeting, but don't get to the end of a project having never mentioned Jesus. Now you might be thinking, "What if I am not making a Christian program or writing a Christian book? The project is still shaped by your core values, beliefs and influences. And do you really think you're never going to chat about something other than what you're both working on?

What are you afraid of? That they'll think you're weird? Guess what, *everyone is weird*. Believe me, you don't have that market cornered. As I write this, I'm sitting in an airport lounge in New York looking at a room full of weird people. Like the guy sitting directly across from me. He's cleaning an apple with a napkin and a bottle of mineral water, really! And even worse, I'm writing about him like a stalker . . .

I was watching *Oprah* a little while ago (don't hold it against me) and the vice-president of production at Columbia Pictures was on the couch being interviewed. Turns out he's an Adventist and at one point in the chat, he starts telling Oprah about how he got his first internship with Will Smith. He didn't intend to begin a conversation with her about the Sabbath but when you are spiritually honest, conversations happen. Suddenly he finds himself telling Oprah—and 50 million viewers—that his conviction to honour Sabbath did not prevent him from receiving an internship with Will Smith's production company, and that 10 years later, he is now producing Hollywood films and still turns his phone off between sunset Friday and sunset Sabbath.

Did DeVon Franklin feel weird? Of course he did—have you seen *Oprah*? I rest my case. While this may be an extreme example (likely you won't be in conversation with Oprah on national television . . . this week), the principle holds. Don't be ashamed of who you are.

Now the guy isn't making "Christian" films, but he is making films in harmony with his core values. He hasn't compromised his faith for the sake of working in the film industry. He is certainly not putting his career in front of his relationship with God. He is also clearly choosing collaborative partners who respect that. It's vital that you don't sell your integrity just to get on the ladder. **Mark 8:36** seems to concisely sum up what's at stake: "What do you benefit if you gain the whole world but lose your own soul?"

Don't compromise who you are to impress your collaborators. If they are uncomfortable with who you are, it's unlikely to be a successful collaboration anyway. You're going to spend a lot of time with these people and they'll find out your "dirty little Sabbath-keeping secret" eventually. At times, I've made some amazing connections through openness about my faith. Be comfortable in your faith and be unashamed to acknowledge it.

> Don't compromise who you are to impress your collaborators. If they are uncomfortable with who you are, it's unlikely to be a successful collaboration anyway.

Prioritise people

Possibly the most overlooked aspect of collaboration is the importance of reward. It is easy when you have limited financial resources to assume that all artists must accept the position of "starving" artist at some point in their pursuit of an artistic life. And while there may be some value in authentic struggle and sacrifice for your art, in the real world, everyone's got to eat.

I was in the audience watching an interview with a well-known young Australian filmmaker. He was speaking romantically about the artist's struggle and how anything is possible, even if you have no money. It became apparent that on his journey to success, he had used a lot of people and taken advantage of them in order to create his art. So while a bunch of film aficionados sat around telling him he was an amazing artist, I couldn't help thinking there was likely another group of people thinking he was something else.

The Sistine Chapel wasn't painted out of Michelangelo's love of art. It was only possible because of patronage. Someone had to fund the thing. So ask once—and only once—for someone to work for nothing. Do not, under any circumstance, go back a second time and expect someone to work for free. Now I don't mean that if they do you a "freebie" the first time, you must pay them an outrageous amount next time. But do pay them, even if it is a nominal amount.

I can't stress this enough. For you to grow as an artist, you need to learn that art has a cost. You might have to give them $100 out of your own pocket but this is more respectful than expecting favours. And if you ask them again, you better be prepared to pay them a bit more.

This is possibly why many low-budget productions fail to reach completion or creative goodness. Often we do not recognise other people's time as a valuable resource with a dollar figure in our budget. I know people who've had a $10,000 budget and think nothing of spending some of that hiring a RED camera but will then ask a cinematographer to work for free for a couple of days. What is more valuable—a piece of technology that will be outdated three months before it's released or the skilled professional whose experience and understanding of the craft could make your film look good with a candle and an iPhone?

People are the most important resource in your project. If you're working in a professional context and you don't have enough money to pay your people, then you possibly don't have enough money to make something. There are many factors that make a good piece of art but understanding the correlation between time and money is crucial in growing and developing as a professional. Don't exploit people but rather treat them fairly and with respect (see **Malachi 3:5**). This is probably the least-held principle of collaboration in the creative arts, but it's so important to growing creatively.

Be discerning

Go back in time—even as little as 20 years—and there was a certain mystery to being an artist. Equipment was expensive and not readily accessible and training in a recognised pathway or an apprenticeship under an old master were hard but vital roads to become an artist. This mystique certainly had it's issues but it did ensure that only the most skilled practitioners made their way into the respective industries.

Go back 500 years and who was the church collaborating with? Names like Michelangelo, Raphael and Leonardo Da Vinci. They were the best of the best. In today's terms, it's like hiring Martin Scorsese to direct your film, J K Rowling to write your young adult literature or Banksy to inspire Generation Next.

Today the democratisation of art, coupled with a societal mentality that "everyone has a story to tell" has seen an explosion in "artistic" expression. It's never been easier to pick up a camera, a brush, a pen or a keyboard and call yourself a director, painter or writer. You can self-publish, gain an audience and become known seemingly overnight, all without having to go through the fire, so to speak.

There are many opportunities that come with this accessibility and some talented individuals who are able to make valuable contributions this way. But it is imperative that before you approach collaborators, you ask, "Does this person have the ability, the experience, the solid foundation to grow both of us?"

Just because they call themselves a cinematographer doesn't mean they actually understand the fundamental principles of how light interacts with the surface of a camera's sensor to create the information we call an image. There are a lot of people out there who talk a good talk but they haven't put in the work. Picking up a $1500 camera with some nice lenses makes you no more a cinematographer than picking up a scalpel makes me a surgeon.

So be discerning.

Creating together

If we cast our minds back 11,080ish characters, to the wise old BBC film director's comment—"Creativity is measured by your ability to harness the talent of those around you toward accomplishing a common goal"—you will find much wisdom. Read between the lines: *creativity is not about you, it's about others*. If you apply that principle to your collaborations and how you approach any creative project, you will have more chance at creating something that resonates with others. After all, isn't the point of creativity to create something that someone else can relate to?

Your ability to relate to people is vital to the whole process. Get this right and the process is the reward. The final product is—as it should be—the cherry on what was hopefully a very tasty cake you were privileged to enjoy with some great people who made it with you.

—Kyle Portbury is the creative director of film and television at the Adventist Media Network in Sydney, Australia. He is a multi-award winning feature and documentary director. Kyle most recently directed the Complete Health Improvement Program (CHIP) series for Sanitarium Health and Wellbeing and won the prestigious CINE Golden Eagle for AMN's documentary series, Beyond the Search. *He is soon to begin filming* Tell the World, *a period drama focusing on the lives and struggles of the founding pioneers of the Seventh-day Adventist Church.*

CREATIVELY CHANGING LIGHT BULBS

Creativity and Problem Solving

Scott Wegener

How many creatives does it take to change a light bulb? (The answer a little later.)

Everyone is creative. God made us that way. Believing you have little creative ability probably comes either from a misunderstanding of what creativity is, or not realising there are methodical steps that can lead to creative results.

Some are so effortlessly creative that it's hard to comprehend how they arrive at such an outside-the-square result. However, these "creative geniuses" are usually following—albeit, often subconsciously—the steps we'll soon look at. This means anyone can potentially reach such radical creativity if they just know how.

What creativity is

One aspect of creativity is to invent something to conquer a challenge. It is imagining a solution—or a better solution. It may be something new or it might just be an alternative, something other than what already is. It could be called inventive problem solving.

Perhaps this is a different way of looking at it but the purpose of many creative endeavours is essentially to solve a problem or achieve a certain outcome. Consider some examples:

- You're in an airport, luggage is checked in, your flight is delayed for five hours and you have little money at your disposal. You have children in your care who are becoming bored—quickly. Creativity to the rescue.
- You'd planned to cook a meal for a family arriving soon and discover some ingredients missing you thought you had. You have no time to go and buy them. Creativity to the rescue.

- You need to make an ad to convince more than 50 per cent of your church's members to attend a business meeting. Creativity to the rescue.
- You want to create an artwork, song or article that communicates God's love to people who have never grasped the concept before. Creativity to the rescue.

Even being creative "just because" might still be solving a problem—especially when it comes to overcoming procrastination.

Making people buy or think positively of a product is generally a marketer's creative challenge.

The creative challenge for a comedian is to make people laugh, while a game creator's creative challenge is to make something fun and engaging for a specific demographic to play.

A teacher's creative challenge might be to help students learn some specific "boring" information, while a parent's creative challenge is often to encourage their child to eat their vegetables, among many other challenges.

This kind of creativity creates a useful solution that currently does not exist in response to some form of challenge. But enough definitions and theory, on to the first step in the creative process.

Step 1: Define

The best place to begin in solving a challenge with creativity is to be clear about these two things:

1. What the current situation or challenge is.
2. What the desired outcome or solution is.

As well as speeding up your journey to a solution, knowing where you are and where you need to end up will also give you a more focused solution. Unfocused creativity can take us off track. While you could end up with a solution far better than planned, you could also end up deciding on a "solution" that doesn't actually solve the problem.

So before you get too creative, be clear on where you are and where you want to be.

Step 2: Create

There are four main methods that help deliver a creative solution.

a. Detective method

For some, this will be the first port of call, especially when there is a tight deadline to meet. Others will use this as their last resort when attempts to come up with their own creative solutions start to fail. The mantra for the detective method of creativity is: "Go online or get living examples" (or GOOGLE).

Whether to save time or to help when you're stumped, seeing what already exists will often create a solution for you. Using the internet or asking friends or experts for their creative solutions for the challenge ahead of you can really give you a kick start, if not provide a complete solution. Sometimes the foundation of an existing solution can be adapted to be better suit your specific needs.

Of course, if you're going to borrow other creativity, you should make sure you give credit where it's due, asking permission beforehand if necessary.

b. Stocktake method

The stocktake method consists of three basic steps:

1. List how many different attributes exist in the current situation.
2. Explore how each listed attribute could be replaced with a variation.
3. Experiment with different combinations of attributes and see what you end up with.

Let's look at some examples from the challenges listed earlier:

We need an ad to convince more than 50 per cent of church members to attend a business meeting.

Step 1: List the attributes we have to work with. There's the ad format and the tone of it, the church members that need incentive to come, the meeting's advertised agenda, and its time and location.

Step 2: Explore the variations of each of the listed attributes.

> The ad format: A bulletin paragraph, a printed bulletin insert, posters, a promotional video clip, an email out, up-the-front announcements, an acted drama, a song, a sermon, personal phone calls, text messaging, Facebook posts, PowerPoint slides or something else.
>
> The tone: stern, friendly, mischievous?
>
> The church members who need an incentive: food, giveaways, concert, games, trivia, craft, child minding, linked to some other activity or event .
>
> The meeting agenda: boring, critical, entertaining?
>
> Time: weeknight, Sabbath afternoon/evening, Sunday morning/afternoon/night?
>
> Location: Church hall, carpark, parkland, restaurant, forest, beach?

Step 3. Experiment with the variations we came up with for the attributes of our challenge.

It could be: a drama that promotes a fun afternoon in the forest, with trivia games intermingled with the business meeting.

It could be: personal phone calls regarding the critical nature of the upcoming meeting and free pizza to all those who attend.

It could be . . .

There are so many other variations! (Although, clearly not all will be practical solutions.)

Another example: Stuck at the airport with some children you need to entertain.

Step 1: List what's available to work with. Let's start with our personal inventory: a pen, box of mints and wallet/purse (and contents).

Step 2: Explore what can be done with the pen (or the other items). Write, draw, colour, score, spin, roll, click, throw, drop, catch, balance, pull apart.

Step 3: Experiment with what you can do with different possibilities to make up many activities.

That was just one item in our personal inventory explored. We could also look at the attributes of the building around us, the signs, the people . . . it's a wonder we don't have to pay to enter the terminal with the amount of fun and games that can be played there.

All we need to do is a simple stocktake of what we have and what is around us, explore what could be done with each and then combine different variations to create a solution.

Create an artwork, song or article that communicates God's love to people who have never grasped the concept before. To me, this is the ultimate challenge.

One more example: Create an artwork, song or article that communicates God's love to people who have never grasped the concept before. To me, this is the ultimate challenge. Not just for the difficulty level but more so the wonderful eternal result, if it is achieved successfully.

One work of art, song or article will not communicate God's love to everyone, so first you need to define who you wish to communicate with and what you want to communicate to them. Can the stocktake method help find a creative idea for such a work of art? Let's try.

Step 1: List the attributes in the challenge. The medium, the style, the colours used, the actual subjects/objects/shapes painted, the current thoughts of the audience and the message to be communicated. While all the attributes of this artistic challenge are important, perhaps the thoughts of the audience you're trying to reach is something to research carefully. This will give you the best chance to connect with your audience.

For example, what moves them, motivates them, makes them laugh, frightens them, entertains them, angers them? And what are their preconceived ideas about your message?

Once you have all the variations, the final challenge is to piece together the best combination of the attributes to most successfully reach the audience with your message.

For each of these examples you can hopefully see there is a somewhat methodical way to go about being creative. Methodical creativity might sound like an oxymoron, but this is what's happening in the minds of many of the most creative people—usually at amazingly fast speeds.

c. Brainstorm method

If the above seems all too regimented or you just can't put your finger on a solution, it might be time to set your brain's rational governor to "off" and let your thoughts roam unrestricted for a moment.

Brainstorming is the process of listing idea after idea, as they come to mind, no matter how random they might be. It can be done individually but a group brainstorm will usually get more ideas flowing and take you to concepts you'd struggle to ever invent yourself.

Writing random ideas down in a brainstorm may get you a creative solution but despite the whole point of the process being "free thinking," here's some structure to guide the freedom into something useful:

1. Define the issue and desired outcome first.
2. List the known or obvious solutions, even if they don't completely solve the challenge or problem.
3. Start listing "crazy" variations to these solutions.
4. Continue on with any ideas or concepts that come to mind, without stopping to discuss or discount good or bad ideas.
5. When all the ideas come to an end, spend a minute or two exploring each idea:
    - Is it worth exploring further or ignoring?
    - Are there any elements to the idea that can be used elsewhere?
    - Are there any elements to the idea that mean it won't work? If so, explore what would be needed to make it work with that inhibitive element or how it could be replaced.

Sometimes a great idea or two will become obvious during a brainstorming session, sometimes it will still be hard work, with a solution possibly coming to someone in the group days later.

Here's an example of a quick brainstorm's results when trying to find an interesting way to begin a chapter for a book about creativity (perhaps you're in the middle of reading it now?):

> Famous quote twisted, story, example, joke, song, puzzle, different language, web address, GPS directions, ten commandments, analogy, metaphor, wrong topic, creativity for dummies, creativity 101, light bulb, apple fall on head, flashback, quiz, cartoon, school, blackboard, detention, driving test, personal trainer, gym membership, poem, point form, fanfare, infomercial . . .

There are several good ideas and the rest probably wouldn't work so well. But essentially it helped me choose an angle to open this chapter.

Oh yeah, and how many creatives does it take to change a light bulb?

A: Who says it has to be a light bulb?

(And there's a nod to the stocktake method.)

d. Inspiration method

Finding the creative solution you've been searching for is not always easy. As well as trying the other methods, sometimes creativity just happens in random places.

For some, creativity comes most often in a quiet or uninterrupted place, like in the shower, in bed at night, watching the ocean or clouds, or driving the car. Other times, you might find inspiration as you see or hear different things or interact with different people. And sometimes inspiration comes from experiencing a movie, song, artwork or simply seeing someone else's solution to a similar problem.

Given its fickleness, this is a difficult method to use if you need quick results. But being still and letting inspiration strike is another important method for finding creative solutions.

Step 3: Evaluate

Once you have your creative solution, evaluate it with your initial brief to see if it is an acceptable, workable or worthwhile solution. After the solution has been implemented, it's also a good exercise to evaluate how well it works or has worked. Maybe it's not too late to implement some of the variations you thought up along the way, if it is not working as you envisioned.

Finally, the first thing

All said and done, the ultimate source of inspiration for creativity comes from God. Assuming you're looking for a creative solution to a noble challenge, pray. God has more creativity than we can handle. The ultimate thing you can do before you even begin an attempt to be creative is pray for inspiration, then delve into and experiment with one or more of the methods suggested above.

And when inspiration does strike, even if you didn't pray, give Him the glory. Without God and the abilities He's given us, we wouldn't have any creativity!

—Scott Wegener is an award-winning writer (for originality and creativity), game creator and drama director at his church in suburban Melbourne, Australia. He has worked as a website developer, editorial assistant and other creative things. Scott loves the attention to detail and storytelling of Disneyland and has published a book called Things to Do in Theme Park Queues. *Visit <ScottPublished.com>.*

FROM DEEP WITHIN THE SOUL

Creativity and Writing Stories

Kay D Rizzo

After a late night of table games with friends and too many bowls of popcorn, I awoke at 3 am with an intensely vivid, full-blown book idea swirling in my brain. I hopped out of bed, rushed to my computer and typed as fast as I could so as not to forget the details of my exciting and inventive plot line. Two hours later, as the last vestiges of darkness lingered in the pre-dawn sky, I put my computer and my brain back to sleep.

Later in the brilliance of the mid-morning sunlight, my 16-page, single-spaced plot about a dysfunctional humanoid whose purpose for existence was to plant thoughts, both good and bad, into people's brains appeared much less dazzling than it had been at 3 am. Was the idea creative? Undoubtedly. Have I written and published this bizarre storyline? Only in this article. Will I ever use it again? Maybe yes, maybe no.

Whether writing sci-fi thrillers, magazine articles, novels or biographies, creative storytelling plays a major role in a writer's success. It's what one does with the idea that matters. I've had students in my writing classes who spin the best scenarios for proposed books, but never put their fingers to the keyboard to make it happen.

Like an artesian well, human creativity springs from deep within the soul. An endless supply; the more that is released, the more bubbles to the surface. The inherent need to be creative is a God-thing implanted in all people's DNA by the Creator, as His children made in our Father's image. Creativity is as natural as breathing. Watch a toddler coax his grandma into reading a second bedtime story—that's creativity in its purest form.

From that first glimmer of an idea to the final published work, an author's creative juices must be tapped to produce satisfying results. And that wellspring of creativity isn't limited to the written word. Whether writing a sonnet, raising a child, composing a cantata or designing a garden, the spark comes from the same source.

Minus creativity, a writer's end product would be little more than a well-organised shopping list of facts and figures. And, as any political viewer knows, even so-called facts and figures can be "creatively" manipulated by political spin-doctors.

I've observed that creativity works much like popping corn in an open pan. When heat is applied, it will burst in multiple directions simultaneously. The same is true of the germ of an idea. The brain will explode with plausible and not-so-plausible ways to develop it. Encountering unexpected situations, hearing people's remarks, scanning newspaper headlines, viewing TV shows, reading well-written books—it doesn't take much to inspire my thought process. Even *Uncle John's Bathroom Reader* can provide the heat to explode a day's supply of idea kernels. All of life is material for a writer. Every experience is fodder, meaning everything an author writes contains autobiographical insights into the writer's personal life.

A starting point

With so much information bombarding the brain, it takes skill to cull the potential winning book ideas from the dross. So where does a writer begin?

As a Christian writer, my first consideration is summed up with, "Do all to the glory of God" (see **1 Corinthians 10:31**). No matter how imaginative and original an idea may be, if my labour doesn't ultimately glorify God, I consider it a waste of my time and creative energy. I could crank out two to three romance novels for the popular market in the amount of time it takes me to write one romance that reflects my personal values and will be an example of character building for young women who read it. This is important to me since I have far more possible book ideas than I have days to live, even if I were to live as long as Papa Methuselah.

> No matter how imaginative and original an idea may be, if my labour doesn't ultimately glorify God, I consider it a waste of my time and creative energy.

Once I am certain a book idea sufficiently brings glory to God's name, I consider the following questions: Do I wish to "live" the story for at least a number of months? When co-authoring a biography, will I enjoy working with the other individual? A co-authors' relationship must function like a good marriage. If personality quirks prevent unity of thought or egos take precedence over the project, I would rather switch than fight.

An additional, important question: Is the book's theme saleable? Is it significantly unique to similar books on the market? As traumatic as surviving breast cancer is for the patient, the story will need an unusual twist to attract the interest of a publisher. If not, months of time and energy will be wasted and the manuscript will languish in my computer archives.

I will decline writing any biography that is little more than a public relations piece glorifying a person or a story that doesn't have some redemptive value. In the case of a biography, if the person's story doesn't uplift the reader in some way, I consider it unfinished. God needs more time to write the final chapter in the subject's life before it's made public.

Is this a Pollyanna-ish view of life, that happy endings are the only stories worth writing? The biography *I Will Die Free* is hardly a tale of lollipops and lilac blossoms. God is glorified in Noble's journey from the faith of a young pastor to a man who found joy in spite of his circumstances.

To effectively retell the horrid events of Noble Alexander's incarceration in a Cuban prison for 22 years, I had to "live" the experience, so readers could feel the extent of his suffering. For example, before writing Chapter Three of the book, I stretched out on the floor of my darkened office in the middle of the night and imagined snakes, rats and unidentified creepy crawlies of every ilk skittering and slithering across my body—a night vividly etched in my memory yet today.

Some may call this creative storytelling but, for a Christian writer, a better term may be "sanctified imagination." This additive comes when the element of prayer blends with one's natural creativity. I had never visited Cuba, never been stripped of my freedom, never been thrown in a dark and filthy six-by-six-foot prison cell. I had to depend on Holy Spirit input. Later when Pastor Noble read Chapter Three, he said the picture I'd painted with words was so accurate he again felt the trails of slug slime across his bare calves.

Whether writing a biography or fiction, or weaving anecdotes throughout a book on an inspirational theme, it takes "sanctified imagination." A writer uses this gift to reconstruct necessary conversations to which he or she was not privy. He calls on sanctified imagination to rightly portray a subject's behaviour as he or she interacts within their era and situation.

My mother-in-law was a spunky lady. When I wrote the 68-year-old woman's biography, *Someone to Love Me*, I had to visualise her as a pre-schooler, a teenager and as a young bride. After a heavy dose of research on New York City life in the early 1900s and putting in requests for an extra large dose of divine guidance, I could set free my imagination, with satisfying results.

Fiction and truth

Some would suggest that Christian writers should stick to true stories. So should Christian writers dabble in fiction? How does the Christian writer delineate between writing factual stories and fictional tales?

The book *Helter Skelter*—about the Charles Manson murders—was clearly factual, but I wouldn't want to read it, let alone have written it. By contrast, a fictional book like *Pilgrim's Progress* excels in glorifying God by highlighting the principles of truth about life and about God.

Jesus, the Master Teacher, couched divine concepts regarding salvation in stories. As our Creator, He understood the thinking processes of the right brain and left brain. He knew a visual illustration would stick with His listeners long after He returned to His Father. His people would forget a plethora of words and abstract ideas, but they would remember important lessons whenever they saw a pearl dangling from a woman's necklace, a field filled with thistles and thorny bushes or a bridal procession on a darkened road. The listeners would recall and be blessed again and again.

And, of course, not all of His stories were illustrations taken from His surroundings. Not all were factual. He used a familiar fable of His day—the Rich Man and Lazarus—to explain the truth of living a righteous life while on this earth. While a preacher of our era might use Santa Claus as a metaphor of how God knows everything we do, no-one in today's audience would believe the illustration to be anything but fictional. So Christ's audience understood the point of the rich man's conversation with his former servant.

So Christian writers can use a fictional story to more clearly illustrate heavenly truths. When writing a biography, a biographer must stick closely to the events of the person's life because it is someone's life. An example of fictionalising events in a man's life would be Mason Locke Weems view of George Washington refusing to lie after he cut down his father's cherry tree—a moral tale for children everywhere, but fictional nonetheless.

The events in a person's life don't always fit into a neat little package that will illustrate an overall theme. By using fiction, as Jesus did, an author can build a story that will drive home divine truth like forgiveness, redemption, grace and love.

An example is George Elliot's *Silas Marnier*. The miserable and miserly recluse finds love in the person of an infant. As the child grows, a heart-change occurs in the man until he is willing to give up the very object of his affection for the good of the child. Another fictional story that illustrates the real truth of divine grace is that of the bishop's candlesticks in Victor Hugo's *Les Miserable.*

Often the dénouement of the story determines the value of the end product. Christian romance writers in the early half of the last century used a pat formula: wealthy heathen falls for beautiful but destitute Christian girl; she converts and marries him and is no longer poor. Hardly a realistic lesson a parent would recommend for a daughter. The genre joined the run of "dime novels" of the era, which created an unrealistic world with no redeeming virtues, let alone no illustration of God's truths.

"What is truth?" Pilate asked in exasperation (see **John 18:38**). An author who uses his or her creative juices to touch the lives of his readers, regardless of his chosen genre, must repeatedly ask himself the same question, "What is truth?" Do the words I pen reveal God's eternal truths? Will my reader catch a kernel of truth from my story? Once he or she is certain the project answers Pilate's question in some small way, for him or her, the universe is the limit. The Christian author can revel in his or her wildest and craziest ideas. They can go wherever their creative, Holy Spirit-led sanctified imagination may lead.

—Born and raised in Troy, New York, Kay Rizzo wrote short holiday skits for her grade school classmates to perform. Writing for profit began years later with a short story submitted to Guide *magazine. God has blessed her efforts with 50 books and more than 1000 magazine articles published, while maintaining an active speaking schedule throughout North America, the Caribbean and Australia.*

A STORY LIKE JESUS

Creativity and Imagination

David Edgren

> One day some parents brought their children to Jesus so he could touch and bless them. But the disciples scolded the parents for bothering him. When Jesus saw what was happening, he was angry with his disciples. He said to them, "Let the children come to me. Don't stop them! For the kingdom of God belongs to those who are like these children. I tell you the truth, anyone who doesn't receive the Kingdom of God like a child will never enter it." Then he took the children in his arms and placed his hands on their heads and blessed them (**Mark 10:13–16**).

What would it have been like to be a child in this story? Imagine the emotional roller coaster you would have ridden. When you woke up that morning, Mum tells you, "We're going to see Jesus today"—imagine your excitement! You get dressed in your best clothes. Mum brushes your hair. And finally, after a long morning, Mum says, "OK, let's go!"

She tries to carry you but you're too wriggly with expectation. She lets you walk, even though it's a long way. You're so excited and can't stop talking about seeing Jesus. Then, when you finally get there, some men say Jesus is too busy to see you.

Imagine the crushing feeling. Can you feel the tears welling up in your eyes? As your mother leads you back out of the crowd, you hear another Man's voice. He says, "Let them come. Do not stop the children! I want to see them!" What a feeling! *He wants to see me!* Mum lets go of your hand and you weave through the legs and hands and robes, until you break through the crowd—and there He is!

Jesus wanted to be with children and they wanted to be with Him. Because He told great stories. Because

He cuddled them. Because He laughed when they did. Because His smile was as sincere and kind as His eyes. Children wanted to be with Jesus because He loved them—and they could feel it.

In one of His many stories, Jesus said people have four responses to His teaching. Some, like a rocky footpath, barely take notice—nothing sinks in. Others, like shallow soil, burst into action with new life but fizzle when things heat up. A third kind of hearer, surrounded by thorns, is choked to death before they can mature. And finally, there is a fourth listener who, like good soil, is healthy and ready for the Word and becomes both blessed and a blessing as the harvest multiplies in them and through them. This is who we, as parents, teachers and leaders want to be—good soil growing the Word in our lives and in our children.

While He held a child on His lap, Jesus said, "For the kingdom of God belongs to those who are like these children. I tell you the truth, anyone who doesn't receive the Kingdom of God like a child will never enter it." Why? What intuitive receptivity or ability do children have that adults lack? Somehow, kids "get" the kingdom of God. The story gets through. Children are good soil.

It would seem, those who believe most authentically, make-believe most authentically.

Like a child

In 2007, Oxford University initiated a focused anthropological study entitled, the "Cognition, Religion and Theology Project." Their goal was to understand why humans, across the globe and through time, have faith. Every culture has religion. Why? What is it about humanity that results in us having belief in a higher power? Where does the reality of God or gods come from and why do humans, across the cultures, believe?

In July 2010, Oxford University held a "Cognitive Science of Religion" convention to reveal their findings. A total of 41 papers were presented on various aspects of human faith and religion. Intriguingly, much of the research focused on children and their faith. It seems—the scientists discovered—to understand human faith we must first understand a child's faith.

Various findings suggested that in imaginative play all children include a "God" figure—a higher power or omniscient being—even children from non-faith backgrounds. Their invisible friends are more likely to be immortal than natural. One paper memorably quipped that invented playmates tend to be more "godlike than doglike." Children's imaginations do not create pets to play with, but instead wonder and wander toward God.

Another interesting finding about the faith of children was that children understand God's immortality before they understand human mortality. Eternal life makes more sense than human death. Scientists were amazed by this finding. To Christians, it is perfectly reasonable because we know God's original plan for life did not include death. Childlike faith understands this intuitively.

It would seem, those who believe most authentically, make-believe most authentically. Jesus calls us toward an experience of faith in which the imagination is fully engaged—like a child. Notice what Jesus did not say: He did not say the kingdom of God belongs to children. He did say, "The Kingdom of God belongs to those who are *like these children*. I tell you the truth, anyone who doesn't receive the Kingdom of God like a child will never enter it."

What is the similarity Jesus is calling us toward? In storytelling, a story becomes effective when the listener exercises the "suspension of disbelief." This is the ability to enter the story-world—to let go of "reality" while enjoying the story. You have undoubtedly experienced this during a movie or while reading a book when your mind stops saying "This is just a story" and starts allowing the story to come to life—allowing it, in effect, to be true.

Most children are able to suspend disbelief as quickly as you can say, "Once upon a time . . ." Adults take a bit longer. This ability to fully enter a story and forget the cares of the world, for a time, is part of what it is to be human.

One Christmas season I was acting in a walk-through Christmas pageant. Each group of people came to our scene for a few minutes, then continued the story by walking to the next scene. As Herod, it was my job to exude a selfish arrogance that betrayed my words that I too wished to "go and worship the child."

Once the audience had moved away, I would leave the stage. But, in one group, a little boy did not stand and leave with his group. Instead he remained seated on the grass and stared at me as I sat on my throne. As his group entered the next scene, his sister rushed back and grabbed his shoulder, "Come on! We've gotta go!"

The boy jolted back to reality. Confused, he looked at his sister and, in a startled voice, said, "He's not the real—" then his head snapped back to me and he proclaimed, "You're not the real Herod!"

This is the suspension of disbelief, as only a child can do it. He was so lost in the story that it took a shake and a shout from his sister to get him back to reality. Those who believe most authentically, make-believe most authentically. Good soil brings the story to life. And this is the childlike reality we are called to imitate. We are to be engaged with the story like a child. Childlike faith—the faith required to get into the kingdom of God—is a faith that gets lost in the story.

Disciple-making storytellers

If God truly wants us to get lost in the story of His presence, power and provision, there should be somewhere we can turn to engage in the story. And there is. The Bible is full of stories. About 75 per cent of the Bible is story! Why so many stories? Because God knows we need stories to hang our faith on. He made us as creatures of story. I know I am on the right track when I find myself lost in the epic story of God and His kingdom.

So how can we engage with the Bible in a way that disciples our children and us? Perhaps the easiest way is to ask your children to tell the stories with you. They will need paper, pens, paths, paint, seeds, songs, waves, sunshine, noise, trees, rain, pictures, fruit, fields and time—lots of time. Because kids really get God's kingdom and to tell kingdom stories takes time. As adults we get too easily caught in the trap of explaining and proving. Children, on the other hand, get lost in exploring and playing.

If you are a parent or involved with leading children, please take the time to make-believe your way through the Bible with them. In every family, church, classroom and at every stage of childhood, this retelling and re-enacting of the story will look, feel and truly be different. This is OK. In fact, this is important. The story of God's kingdom is one that builds layer by layer with each telling.

Let your imagination come back to life—become good soil, once again. Enjoy the Bible as the storybook of the ages. Let it speak to you and through you in a way that is beyond belief. Tell the Story. Tell it with your life and with your lips. Tell the Story well. And it will make belief.

What about adults?

While children engage with the kingdom of God almost intuitively, many adults seem to have lost the skill. Kids just get God. They take little time to go from hearing the story to believing it to be true. An ancient Jewish teaching story about truth goes something like this:

> Truth, naked and cold, had been turned away from every door in the village. Her nakedness frightened the people. When Parable found her she was huddled in a corner, shivering and hungry. Taking pity on her, Parable gathered her up and took her home. There, she dressed Truth in story, warmed her and sent her out again. Clothed in story, Truth knocked again at the doors and was readily welcomed into the villagers' houses. They invited her to eat at their tables and warm herself by their fires.

Adults engage with truth and belief in much the same way as children do, it just takes longer for the truth to have its way with us. We need to be softened through the power of parable. Our imagination needs permission to become involved in shaping what we accept as reality.

The scientific method has so overpowered our thought world that, even as Christians, we have become convinced that empirical proof is required to prove truth. Can it be tested? Has it been tested? Can I redo the test and get the same results? Then it is true. This is the scientific method.

The scientific method has so overpowered our thought world that, even as Christians, we have become convinced that empirical proof is required to prove truth.

Stories of faith operate on a different level of thinking. Religious truth does not typically do well on the empirical tests of scientific reasoning. Faith and science often seem at loggerheads and, with scientific method as our reasoning strategy, the stories of our family, history and faith often get set aside by those who are "facing facts" or "growing up." Story, it would seem, is no longer an acceptable garment for truth.

So do stories still live in the hearts of people today? Or is story-based truth dead? Is there anywhere in our world we can go to find myths to build our character, stories to shape our identity and our passion for living? Is there a place we can go today to hear stories of things beyond belief and yet grasp them as believable?

We do not scientifically believe a boy bitten by a spider can shoot webs out of his wrists and scale buildings with his bare hands. Yet, globally, we sit for 90 minutes, enthralled as Peter Parker dons his Spiderman suit and fights evil—and we leave thinking, "I too believe that great power must be accompanied by great responsibility."

Yes, humanity is still very involved with the myth-making of superheroes, gods and goddesses. For well-told stories, our modern-day world goes to the movies. If we compare or equate theatres with churches, scriptwriters with theologians and actors with pastors, we become very antagonistic and uncomfortable. And we run the risk of missing what is really happening.

People are not going to the movies to find their gods. They are going to the movies to find themselves, their values, their identity and their purpose. They are looking for a good story to hang their life on. The church has, unfortunately, stopped telling the story in all its compelling glory and fallen into the scientific method mind-trap.

Using such parables

We do not scientifically believe that a child was quietly sent here from a distant part of the universe, raised by human parents, that he walked among us as a man, looked like us, acted like us and yet when the moment of need arose he was revealed to be very unlike us as he emerged from a nearby telephone booth wearing his red cape and blue suit with an S emblazoned on his chest.

Perhaps you were thinking of someone else. Someone who was sent from above as a baby, lived with unassuming human parents, grew up incognito in a nondescript village and revealed his true identity and purpose as an adult—miraculously healing people, saving people, raising the dead and ultimately emerging from death Himself. What would happen if this superhero—this Jesus of ours—was allowed the "suspension of disbelief" by the world today? What if His story was allowed into the hearts and minds of today's seekers of identity and purpose? What would today's myth-loving moviegoer do with Jesus if they really let Him in?

A few years ago, I took a youth group in Tasmania to see *The Passion of the Christ* on opening night. We were in the first group to see the movie. When the movie finished, we all sat quietly through the entire scrolling of the credits. Nobody left until the credits stopped and the lights came on. Afterwards, the theatre owner said to me, "In my 20 years of running this theatre, I've never seen anything like it. People just sat there."

A few minutes into the credits, a teenage girl stumbled to the front, fell to her knees facing the screen and wept. Another girl came and comforted her. Everyone else watched from their seats, stared into the screen or just closed their eyes in silence. No-one wanted the lights to come on. No-one wanted to go back to reality. No-one wanted the suspension of disbelief to end. They wanted the story to be true.

As Christians, we work so hard to get people to this point. We hope, pray and struggle to convince people, hoping they will realise their dire need for the story to be true.

Because we know the Story is true.

And when a friend or family member reaches the point of desiring the story of Jesus—accepting that this story is true and is worth building their life upon—we have a wonderful opportunity.

We must tell them the Truth in all its glory. And it is here that we blunder. Far too often, in our desire to tell them the truth of Jesus, we—as products of our scientific era—try to prove it to them. We pull out our charts, our historical data and our proof texts. And in so doing we suck the air out of the room and the door slams closed. Their suspension of disbelief—their openness—crashes back to reality. The good soil grows thorns and becomes rocky once again. Their search for values, identity and purpose is hijacked by a science lesson. They were looking for a hero, not a proof text. They were seeking a Saviour, not a formula. They were hoping for a new reality, not a refresher course on this one.

We must share Jesus in a way that engages people with a story they can hang their faith on: "Jesus always used stories and illustrations like these when speaking to the crowds. In fact, he never spoke to them without using such parables" (**Matthew 13:34**). Help people transition from the suspension of disbelief into accepting a new reality by sharing truth, not naked and cold but wrapped in story. Draw them to the presence of the God who is Love the way Jesus did—through story.

Providing facts without story leaves too much to chance. Like the Master Storyteller, be patient enough to tell a story—the right one—that brings life to truth. Be wise enough to save the story until the moment when it can be savoured. People don't need new facts, they need a new story. It's easy to tell the truth. But to have the truth welcomed, embraced and embodied—that takes a story.

—David Edgren is a storyteller and pastor. He tells stories at schools, camps and churches and writes stories in books, articles and chapters for compilations like this one! His books include 28 Stories, The Perfect Lamb *and the "Adventures in the Bible" series. Pastor Dave lives with his wife and three kids in Melbourne, where he serves as church departmental director of Sabbath school and Children's Ministry.*

LIKE LITTLE CHILDREN

Creativity and Children

Karen Collum

> It is late on Saturday night. My four-year-old twins are perched on the edge of my bed, eyes wide with excitement at having spent a night out with Daddy at a church social. They talk of table tennis and pizza and running games, giggles punctuating their sentences. The laughter fades away and is replaced by a seriousness and sincerity that draws me in.
>
> "Mummy," says Matthew in a hushed voice, "I wished upon a star tonight that I could be a dinosaur."
>
> "And I wished upon a star that I could be a rocket ship," says Jacob.
>
> I am captivated by their imagination, their reckless abandon of wishing and wondering and believing. Without the chains of adult realism or the straitjacket of possibility binding their thinking, my two beautiful boys truly believe that anything is possible. In that moment, they are the embodiment of a precious God-given gift: creativity.

Given the biblical account of Creation begins with two adults, it would be easy to assume that the adult human is God's masterpiece, but after partnering with God in growing four children within my womb and parenting for seven years, I am convinced His life's work is best displayed in a child. Children question without embarrassment, wonder with a complete lack of self-restraint, and postulate what and why and how without a thought as to what is "possible." Creativity is not just something they possess or tap into or exercise; it is the very essence, the embodiment, of who they are.

Have you ever watched children play make-believe? They embrace the pretend completely, method acting in a way that would make an Oscar winner proud, convinced that they are a superhero or doctor or Mummy or the family dog. The conversations flow easily without the self-awareness that tends to inhibit adults trying to do the same. (Anyone who has sat in a professional development course involving role-play can attest to that.) They give of themselves completely to their creative pursuit and quite literally end up in another world, a world of wonder and delight, of heroes and villains, of the known and unknown.

Sadly, life tends to quell this creativity and, as the years go by, we as a society and sometimes as individuals value rationality over creativity and logic over imagination. Yet aren't we all still at least partly the same person we were when we were young? Yes, there are bills to be paid, rational decisions to make, logical paths to follow for our wellbeing, but too many adults have sacrificed their creative selves, a part of themselves that only exists in faded family photos of when they were a child dressed up as Superman. It doesn't have to be this way and I don't believe God wants it to be this way.

When He was on earth, Jesus valued children. He blessed them, laid hands on them, prayed for them and welcomed them into His arms. Jesus even said we should be like them (see **Matthew 18:3**). I think this applies to creativity, but it also applies to the other half of the equation as a Christian creator: faith.

> Faith is my counterbalance, the margin around my creative pursuits that keeps me on God's page in how I exercise my creativity.

There are many people one could define as creative but who use their skills to hurt or harm or attack or drag people down. Faith is my counterbalance, the margin around my creative pursuits that keeps me on God's page in how I exercise my creativity. My children once again inspire me with their faith and challenge me to have a child-like faith of my own.

Just today, Jacob looked up at the sky and asked, "Mummy, where does Jesus live?"

"I think Jesus lives on that cloud," said Matthew, pointing to a particularly bright and fluffy cloud floating in the sky over our house.

As we talked about heaven and how wonderful it's going to be to meet Jesus in person and what animals we'll get to see, I longed for the simplicity of their faith. Their belief is absolute and unflinching and yet I see myself in Jesus' words—"Oh ye of little faith"—time and time again.

This was demonstrated powerfully for me when my eldest son, Samuel, was a toddler. As I hung the washing out one beautiful summer's day, he pottered around the clothesline playing with sticks and rocks and leaves. He came across a dead beetle on the path and crouched down, a sad expression clouding his face.

"Oh, poor beetle," he said.

Then his face changed and the sadness was replaced with vigour. He stood up, pointed a finger at the beetle and declared, "In the name of Jesus, stand up and walk!"

I half expected the beetle to do just that because Samuel's faith was so strong. As an adult, I would never have uttered those words, content to rationalise the death of an insect and let it be. I was humbled again by the strength of my child's faith and my heart repented at my lack of belief.

What if all of us grown-ups possessed the vital combination of creativity and faith that comes so naturally to our children? What if we let go of our inhibitions and our hang-ups and our preconceived ideas and let God be God? What if we harnessed that God-given creativity that is at the core of ourselves and used that to colour the world with hope? What if we saw the world through the eyes of a child?

As a children's author, I'm in the business of creativity and I have discovered that this is possible. Seeing the world through the unclouded, unjaded, uncynical eyes of a child is one of life's greatest joys. But it doesn't just happen. I have to intentionally watch and listen and look for wonder-filled moments in the faces of the children around me. And when I glimpse those little miraculous moments, I am inspired to reconnect with that essential part of my being. In doing so, I believe with all my heart that I honour my Creator God.

My stories most often have their genesis in something my children have said or done. When Samuel was two years old, he used to sit in the shopping trolley and blow kisses to random people at the supermarket. Grumpy men would smile, tired workers would stand straighter, others would blow kisses in return or play peek-a-boo. This was the inspiration for my picture book *Samuel's Kisses*, my tribute to the power of a little person's love in changing big people's lives.

A conversation in the backyard with Samuel when he was three resulted in *Fish Don't Need Snorkels*. He looked skyward at one of the big eucalyptus trees that stood guard over our house and said in an awe-filled voice, "Mummy, a giraffe doesn't need a ladder to reach the top of the trees. God gave giraffes long necks."

Then came the day I was doing the typical mum thing of hurrying my children along after swimming lessons. My mind was on what to cook for dinner and getting the kids home in time for baths and bed at a reasonable hour. As I shepherded everyone out the door of the swimming centre, I was completely exasperated when I discovered Jacob was nowhere to be seen.

Telling the other children to wait, I reefed open the door, words of anger ready to spew out of my mouth . . . only to discover him transfixed by a perfectly symmetrical bright red leaf that had somehow lodged in the gap between two sheets of grey corrugated iron. "Look, Mummy," he said, gazing at me, his big blue eyes filled with joy, "isn't it beautiful?"

And it was. This breath-taking moment I shared with my boy became the inspiration for a picture book called *Small and Big* that celebrates the little things in life.

My children have filled me up with their boundless creativity and unflinching faith and inspire me to become like a child once more. And in those special moments when I have been touched on a soul level, writing becomes an act of worship. My stories are not necessarily overtly Christian and they don't always have happy endings, but it is my prayer that they are honest, captivating and filled with hope. I hope my readers—young and old—find themselves in my stories, as well as who they want to be. I hope I challenge them, inspire them and give them strength. I hope they get a sense of the unfailing love that God has for them and that in the end, it's going to turn out all right.

My creativity is at the core of my being and my faith is the framework through which I have chosen to exercise my God-given gift. When I honour this part of myself—the creative, vulnerable, wonder-filled me—and it intersects with my faith, an amazing thing happens: I grow. My sense of purpose, my fulfilment, my joy in the journey is increased exponentially. I am a better mum, a better wife, a better daughter and sister and auntie and friend because of what I do. And each time I rediscover what it means to be a child of creativity and faith, heaven doesn't seem so far away.

—Karen Collum is a wife to one pastor, mum to four kids and author of three picture books, numerous articles and a couple of poems. She is now learning the art of illustrating—slowly. You can find her and her books at <www.karencollum.com.au>.

CREATIVITY BEGINS AT HOME

Creativity and Family

Kylie Stacey

God made male and female in His own image and they are considered the most significant of all creation. God so highly valued humanity that He gave the directive to be fruitful and multiply—this convinces me that the family is the pinnacle of Creation and of creativity itself. So it is our priority as Christian parents to help our children understand that God loves them, and it would make most sense for them to experience this love in creative, tangible and sensory ways.

I love the text in the book of Deuteronomy that speaks of loving God with all your heart, soul and strength. It emphasises the importance of passing this type of faith onto children and encourages us to talk about God's laws of love "when you are at home and when you are on the road, when you are going to bed and when you are getting up" (**Deuteronomy 6:7**). It goes on further to describe ways of making God's love central to our lives, our homes and our families—as natural as our breathing.

Let me introduce my children: Jaxon (8), Ryan (6), Corbin (4) and Nash (2)—active, delightful, excitable, moody, noisy, teary and whiney. Living amid such energy, it's easy to neglect impressing the commands to love God upon our boys.

My husband and I do have a plan. It goes something like this: we want our children to love Jesus, to care for people in need, to develop a spirit of thankfulness, to be responsible with money, to show courtesy, persistence and respect, to obey, and to share. We ask God, most days, for the grace, love, patience and wisdom to implement this plan. Sometimes we fail—badly. Sometimes we succeed and smile as we remember the funny and quirky things that took place during the day. Sometimes we're too tired to remember much at all. But we want our children to have a faith that sticks with them for life, so, we're doing our best to nurture that faith at home, in as many creative ways as possible.

Creating daily spaces

There are so many ways to share God's love and purposes with our children, even just in the everyday moments and spaces. By creating daily spaces for creatively sharing God's love, it can be woven into the fabric of your home! Our aim is to make it part of our daily rhythms.

We love learning Scripture together. Each week as we begin learning a new memory verse, one of our boys writes it down on a piece of paper, which we then stick to the window in the dining room. Often as we are eating, the boys will begin reciting the memory verses they have learnt. Writing the verse on paper is a great visual prompt. Singing memory verses also helps your child remember them more easily.

Meals are usually hectic, but they're also a great time to talk to each other. "What's the best thing that happened today?" is a regular conversation starter. We were recently given a gift called *Table Talk*, which is a box of cards, each with a question around a theme. This has encouraged some spiritual conversations and even our younger boys have enjoyed joining the conversation.

Children love to ask questions. This is part of their inbuilt creativity and naturally curious approach to the world around them. If we take the time to listen and to talk with them, we will discover the depth of their thoughts.

- Jaxon and I are looking at an illustration of Noah and the rainbow. "Where are all the dead bodies?" he asks.
- While discussing the resurrection, Ryan asks, "Mummy, are the angels and Jesus and God all going to bring their shovels down with them?"
- My son doesn't like his hair being shampooed. He's nervous and says to me, "Mum, don't let it run into my ears because I won't be able to hear God talking."
- As we discus the Sabbath school lesson, Ryan declares, "I know what it's about. It's about the *disciplesaurs*!"

As an early childhood music educator, I'm passionate about the role music plays in the development of my children. I love to sing with them, and I love to move with them. Daily family worship is a great opportunity to nurture your child's musicality and to strengthen their relationship with you and with God.

I love to use massage rhymes and songs, particularly with infants as touch is a baby's primary mode of learning. When we touch our child in a loving way, we experience emotional togetherness. Through touch, we are also able to experience the rhythmic beat of the song, which is essential to musical development. Bouncing rhymes and songs are also effective. Place your child on your knee and enjoy the fun. Children love these types of activities because they are playful. The joy of the bouncing ride is filled with messages about how much you and God both love your child.

• "Mashed Potato"—it's the new name for Poppy, a deviation from "Sausage." We're all sitting around the fire praying and thanking God for all He's given us. Ryan prays, "Thank you for Mashed Potato and Nan." Nan's shoulder starts shaking. "And thank you for the heater, the roof, the table." Ryan pauses. Nan's whole body is shaking. Ryan is oblivious to all this, adding thanks for the "carpet and the lights and the doors." Nan's rip-roaring snort "Amens" the prayer.

It's important that family worship time is fun and not too rigid, especially with little ones.

Daily spiritual routines that remind us of who we are and who God is help keep our lives in perspective. They also connect us to each other. Each evening before bed, our family sits together, holds hands (this may change as the boys get older) and sings "The Blessing." The words are adapted from a traditional blessing:

> May the Lord bless you and keep you/ Cause His face to shine upon you/ And be gracious unto you/ Amen/ May the Lord bless you and keep you/ Look upon you with His favour/ May He fill your life with peace/ Amen.

Another way to sing a blessing and use music at bedtime is through personalised music. As I write, my six-year-old son, Ryan, is listening to his *Ryan* CD as he drifts off to sleep. The music on the CD is filled with lyrics written specifically for him. The lyrics tell him how special he is to us and to God, and how much he is loved.

This is a beautiful way to end each day.

Creating time

In our hurried world and hurried lives, we need to get creative about making time for chats, for cuddles, for those magnificently intimate moments with our children that we would otherwise pass by but are significant steps to building stronger families and stronger faith.

My husband, Brenton, and I love to take one of ours boys out for a date each month. One month, I will take one of the boys; next month it's Dad's turn. At this young age, a date usually consists of a cookie and a milkshake. The joy on the boys' faces is delightful. And they seem to walk with a skip in their step. The conversation is great, too. We have found dates with our children so worthwhile.

In addition to dates, Brenton and the boys do "boy stuff" together, such as a recent visit to a fighter jet museum at our local airport. Brenton also takes the boys to the local skate park so they can ride their scooters and to his weekly indoor cricket game so they can play in a vacant net. I love that my husband is willing, and even eager, to spend time alone with the boys. It's good for their relationship—and it gives me a break!

A cuddle in bed with your child is one of the most special and intimate times of the day. My two-year-old son, Nash, says, "Cuddle, cuddle," before I turn the light off. It's never satisfactory for me to lie on top of the doona and hug—Nash says, "Legs, legs," which means, "Please hop under with me!" Usually just as I'm beginning to relax,

- Mummy takes her tiredness out on Corbin. I use a loud voice and feel bad about it, so later I hop into his bed to apologise. "Do you forgive me Corby?" I ask as we cuddle.
  He nods his head and says, "But Mummy, you shouldn't get angry at me because Jesus won't take you up to heaven, and we need to go to heaven."

he'll say, "Go." This is all part of the fun! The older boys enjoy a cuddle, too. I use cuddle times to connect with my children, to remind them how much I love them and to wish them happy dreams.

Creating Sabbath fun

I know many people who have traditional Friday evening meals to make the beginning of the Sabbath special. Our family tried this for a few weeks but a lack of routine made it difficult. So we looked for another tradition.

We found it the next morning—Sabbath morning breakfast is now our special meal. Being "inconvenient vegans," we indulge in scrambled eggs with our baked beans, hash browns and toast. I am especially growing to love Sabbath morning breakfast as the boys become more capable of preparing the food, even though it sometimes means picking out pieces of eggshell as we eat.

Find a meal on your Sabbath that brings the family together. There is no end to the possibilities for creating your own Sabbath routines and traditions to build memories and meaningful family time together.

As a parent who sat through many Beginner Sabbath schools, I often felt frustrated being relegated to the back row. I wanted to worship with my children! When parents are involved, they bond with their children and they learn the songs so they can sing them at home. And their enthusiasm is contagious.

There is great value in including your children in all parts of church life, even when they are quite young. Forget the mentality that only the children's story is for them! Even if your church doesn't appear to target children in its programming, you can still make some creative efforts to engage them, from where you are sitting with them.

We encourage our boys to take part in the communion service at our local church. Encouraging them to consider the bread and wine as a "prayer" rather than as a "snack" helps them grow in their understanding of the meaning of the service. This is a wonderful tactile experience that all ages can participate in with just a little guidance.

- The boys sit well through the worship service this week. After the final hymn, Corbin asks, "Is church finished now? Can we turn it off?"

Creating real gifts

When I think back to my own childhood I remember a few stand-out gifts—a Strawberry Shortcake doll, a red bike and a sewing machine—but most I've forgotten. The camping and hiking trips, though, the caravan holiday around Australia, the Friday evening chocolate treats, the family concerts, the backyard cricket games—these I still vividly remember. While recently pondering the parents' struggle not to overindulge their children, my aunty Fay said to me "The great thing about giving experiential gifts is this: they can never get broken"

Thank you, Aunty Fay, for reminding me what's important. And Dad for terrifying us as teenagers playing "Murder in the dark"—that's one experience none of us will ever forget.

- The boys and I caught a bus into town. We visited the library and bought some chips before catching the bus home again. The boys were so excited. They described everything as either "beautiful," "lovely" or "amazing." A great investment for $8.
- Brenton also enjoys giving homemade vouchers for presents—he's editing this article with a "One-hour-of-help-with-your-article" voucher now. My favourites? "A back massage," "breakfast in bed" and "a hot cuppa."

Creating warm hearts

There are so many wonderful ways to foster compassion in children. Our boys find delight in walking down the road with a batch of homemade cookies they have helped make to give to one of our neighbours. This is a good opportunity to talk with the boys about the importance of sharing and about how sharing makes them feel.

Each time your child receives a new toy, encourage them to give one of their other toys away. And why not apply the same rule to yourself. As you add an item to your wardrobe, find an item you can donate to charity or give to someone else.

As my children grow into teenagers and young adults, my desire is to enjoy some family mission trips together. As a teenager, I had the privilege of volunteering in South America for a number of months. The experience showed me the realities of life for many on our planet. I believe every young adult would benefit

- Ryan receives three boxes of Lego for his birthday. The next morning he says, "Corby, this one's yours." I say, "Ry, they're yours. You got them for your birthday." "But Mummy," he says, "I got three. I'm sharing them with Jax and Corby."

from having the opportunity to experience life from a different perspective, particularly as they are making decisions about career and study pathways. I also believe it will be a wonderful time to bond and create memories as a family.

Homemade creativity

For our family, being "creative" is not just about crafts or paint or making things. It is a way of interacting with and responding to the world, to each other, to our environment and to God. It's about seeing and learning and understanding. It's about questions and thoughts and imagining and talking and listening. It's about spending our time together in exciting and meaningful ways with the intention of developing deeper relationships with each other and with God.

—Kylie Stacey lives in Sunshine, Lake Macquarie (Australia) with her husband Brenton and four children. She loves music and the joy it brings to people's lives. Her favourite times of the day are watching the sun rise over the lake and snuggles with her little boys in bed at night. Her forthcoming book of children's worship resources is called Playful Worship. *Visit <www.themusicroom.net.au> for more information about how to create your own CD filled with messages of affirmation for your child.*

LIVING

BEING HEARD AMID THE DIN

Creativity and Mission

Gary Krause

A world-famous classical violinist stood outside L'Enfant Plaza metro station in Washington, DC, holding his $3.5 million Stradivarius. It was morning rush hour on a cold winter's day in 2007. Three days earlier, Joshua Bell had sold out Boston's Symphony Hall, where merely "pretty good seats" cost $100 each.

Bell began with the technically demanding "Chaconne" from J S Bach's *Partita No 2 in D Minor*. During the next 43 minutes, he performed six majestic classical pieces. During the entire time, a grand total of seven people stopped to listen at least for a minute—another 1090 walked by.

Twenty-seven people gave money for a total of $32.17—to a musical genius who can earn $1000 a minute. Bell later joked that $40 an hour wasn't so bad, considering. "I could make an OK living doing this," he said with a laugh, "and I wouldn't have to pay an agent." But he did admit, again with a laugh: "It was a strange feeling, that people were actually, ah . . . *ignoring* me."[1]

Being a Christian witness in a post-Christian society can feel like busking to deaf ears in a metro station. We know that the melody of the old, old story is the most magnificent life-changing music in the universe—but few seem to listen. We play louder, softer, with greater virtuosity—but people still rush past, tuned to their own agendas.

Walter Brueggemann says the biblical theme of exile best describes our situation in a post-Christian society. "The Old Testament stories of exile might be a resource," he writes, "perhaps the only resource, to move us from denial and despair to possibility."[2] He adds that the prophets, "the great hopers of the exile," didn't talk policy or make recommendations. Instead, "what they offered was poetry." They sang songs.

In fact, you could sing your way through much of the Bible. It's not just a collection of propositions, doctrines and "truths." It's full of poetry, prophecy, song, story and parable. So how do we play the tunes and sing the songs that will awaken the hearts and minds of the passers by?

Shouting and whispering

American writer Flannery O'Connor reportedly once said her stories described "the action of grace in territory held by the devil." Some criticised her for shocking readers with outrageous images and characters. Among these, I found her descriptions startling—and they stuck with me—as she described "respectable people" entering heaven last, after several groups, including "white-trash, clean for the first time in their lives" and "battalions of freaks and lunatics shouting and clapping and leaping like frogs."[3] The confrontational image is certainly memorable. She said it was her way to get a hearing for the gospel among readers who didn't share her beliefs. "To the hard of hearing you shout," she commented, "and for the almost-blind you draw large and startling figures."

Parts of the Bible do the same thing. For some, the beasts of Daniel and Revelation have become tame through familiarity. But look again with fresh eyes and you might rediscover things to haunt your dreams. And revisit the prophets who shouted at the spiritually deaf and drew "large and startling figures" for the spiritually sight-impaired.

These days it may take the spiritual megaphone of an O'Connor to be heard above the static. Perhaps we need to employ the power of the arts to awaken a generation in exile and push people beyond their comfort zones—out of numbness and into seeing and hearing.

Being heard amid the din may at times require creativity that confronts and jolts the soul awake, but at other times it calls for creativity that gently stirs. There is room for nuance. For subtlety. There is a time not to shake the shoulders of our neighbour, but to whisper gently with artfully crafted words and songs and images that simply engage a person and allow them to imagine an alternative. Another American southern writer, Doris Betts, thought so:

> I—like many mothers and kindergarten teachers—have found that the whisper can also be effective. . . . [T]here's a range between times when Jesus inveighed strongly against a "generation of vipers" and other times when He might stoop and silently scratch words in the ground. At times Jesus pronounced His woes against the religious leaders. But at other times He told parables that sneaked the truth in through the back door, and gently knocked on the hearts of His audience.[4]

The creative work needn't be overt. It needn't be loud—or even obviously religious. Some of the most effective Christian voices take an approach that writer-producer T-Bone Burnett describes this way: "You can sing about the Light, or you can sing about what you see because of the Light. I prefer the latter."

When you create from the stance of faith, truth naturally sneaks in. People who may never enter a church can catch glimpses of grace through the lives of believers, and through artists, writers and musicians who craft their work as authentic Jesus followers. As Betts once said: "Most writers set out to tell a story knowing that who they are and what they believe will whisper its way in just as they do in one's daily life."[5] In this way, faithful creative practice can be just as valuable as an evangelist standing on a public stage.

Creativity and mission

At times Jesus talked "straight"—usually when sorting out the religious leaders. But He never spoke without telling a parable—sneaking the truth in the back door (see **Mark 4:34**). Although the Apostle Paul was famously outspoken, he always carefully framed his approach—speaking to pagans in significantly different ways to how he spoke to Jews. Christians engaged in mission quickly discover that truth must be re-framed for new situations. Think of Paul quoting pagan poets on Mars Hill (see **Acts 17:22–31**) or George Whitefield preaching to thousands in the "open air" and helping kick start the 18th-century revival known as the Great Awakening.

Adventists have kept the "re-framing" tradition going. When Fernando and Ana Stahl went as missionaries to the Peruvian Andes in 1909, they began using the time-honoured Adventist technique of selling magazines. The problem was that 95 per cent of the impoverished population was illiterate. So they adapted and refocused their ministry into a creative wholistic approach—starting schools, clinics, markets and, by the way, a social revolution.

> Although the Apostle Paul was famously outspoken, he always carefully framed his approach—speaking to pagans in significantly different ways to how he spoke to Jews.

Educator and congressman Jose Antonio Encinas visited the town of Plateria and saw some of their work. He wrote: "The basic thing is that [the Adventists] are transforming the spirit of the Indian, bringing him into civic life, making him aware of his rights and obligations, separating him from the vices of coca and alcohol, removing superstition, curing illnesses, showing the best way toward human dignity."

Nearly 100 years ago, American evangelist H M S Richards began experimenting on secular radio, no doubt scandalising some Adventist church members. Some 30 years later, William and Virginia Fagal began broadcasting on secular TV, copying the format of popular variety shows of the day—complete with dramatic skits, music, discussions, and special guests. They then launched a full-blown weekly TV drama—*Westbrook Hospital*. Different? Yes. Innovative? Yes. Compromising the truth? No.

In the 1940s, Australian pastor John Coltheart tried a new approach to public evangelism. In 1958, he explained to church leaders in America:

> I did a little experimenting myself about 13 years ago. I was searching around for some new approach for evangelism. Subjects such as Bible lands, archaeology and the Bible, suggested a new approach. We advertised a meeting, and three conference evangelists said to me, "You won't get anybody out because Pastor So-and-So tried that approach here five years ago, and it just doesn't work." Well, I am happy to say that approach did work, and it has since been used by many of our men. I use the title "Dead Men Do Tell Tales" . . . We have gathered huge crowds with that title.

A few years later, Coltheart used the method in London. The result was unprecedented. Phone lines rang busy for three days with people booking seats for the program, and more than 8000 people attended on the first two days: "Preceding the slide lecture proper the audiences are taken on conducted tours through many places of the Middle East and Australasia by way of scenic slides and movie films to a background of descriptive organ and piano music."

I grew up attending this type of "mission." In seven decades, it has led to tens of thousands of baptisms. And Coltheart's method is still used widely—although in many places it now struggles to get a crowd.

Thousands of Global Mission pioneers—indigenous church planters—daily explore innovative mission in different cultures and contexts all over the world. One pioneer faced a community that forbade Christian witness so he became a door-to-door salesman—selling clothing on an instalment plan. This allowed him opportunity to visit regularly to collect payments and thereby provided ongoing contact with families. These pioneers are using dozens of different methods to connect with people: music, sport, fitness, health remedies, agricultural techniques, literacy training, the list goes on.

Authentic creativity

Of course, fake or contrived witness can be smelled a mile away. American songwriter and musician Mark Heard recalls producing a record for a Christian artist. Contemporary Christian music is big business in the United States—outselling both jazz and classical music. A Christian record company executive was keen to give his client a big break on Christian radio so came to Heard with samples of what he wanted—songs with safe, warm lyrics and a predictable "synthesizer oriented" sound. Heard was so annoyed by the request that he decided to throw musical integrity to the wind and make a really big hit for Christian radio—according to the brief given him.

So he found a "really stupid and inane" chorus, quickly wrote some verses and a bridge, and turned it into a song. Heard felt the musicians were playing too creatively, and told them to dumb it down. Strictly adhering to his brief, he encouraged the backup singers to do something silly like "a bad lounge act in the Seventies."

Listening to the finished tape, he felt the dictum of "no—play something even stupider" had paid off. The next day he got a call from the executive who was excited. "Mark, we had no idea you were capable of such brilliant production work," the executive enthused. It was released and went to number two on nationwide Christian radio. It was an interesting exercise but, as he said later, "The whole process had nothing to do with Christianity or excellence." Surely a faithful response to our calling to be creative—and our best chance at being heard above the din—is manifested when we create with the utmost care, thought and ambition for excellence in our offerings of creativity.

Creative mission knows no bounds

Ironically, the Jesus People Movement of the 1960s pioneered updated Christian songs because they wanted to witness more creatively and effectively to non-believers. Today it's almost entirely an in-house industry—selling downloads to disciples, playing concerts to congregations. And the pattern has spread more widely. Walk into a

Christian bookstore and note how the vast majority of books are aimed at Christians. Saints talking to saints. In fact, I find many of these shops in the United States profoundly troubling. Looking for something that seriously engages mission? Get ready to navigate past Christian T-shirts, jewellery, test-a-mints, weight-loss books, celebrity biographies, praise music DVDs, self-help and a veritable claustrophobe of health-and-wealth tomes. And make sure you don't trip over the "Patriot's Bible" on your way out.

It's natural that a Christian bookstore will sell products aimed at Christians. But shouldn't they also help equip Christians to more effectively engage with unbelievers and with their communities? It's almost as if we've given up on impacting our wider culture—so we live and move and have our being entirely within the Christian subculture. Unfortunately, when someone bravely moves out to try new and creative ways to engage non-believers, they're often shot down in pious flames of criticism: "We've never done it that way before." "You're watering down the truth." "Just preach the Word!" However, Jesus clearly calls us to use innovation and to apply our creativity beyond just serving ourselves.

In July 1849, a young Adventist pioneer, James White, produced the first issue of *Present Truth*—the result of hard labour, experimentation and sacrifice. By December, he had stopped printing. Funds were running low and he was discouraged. Making matters worse, the oldest Adventist preacher and pioneer alive, Joseph Bates, gave no support and refused to write for the publication. He felt White shouldn't be messing around with new-fangled methods of witness when the funding could go to direct evangelism. Fortunately, come Spring, White found the courage and means to continue—and Adventist publishing went from strength to strength.

Many years later, when White's wife Ellen was about 70 years old, she wrote: "God would have new and untried methods followed. Break in upon the people—surprise them."[6] It won't guarantee people will stop to listen to the old, old melody. But we're called to keep on improvising anyway.

— Gary Krause is director of the General Conference Office of Adventist Mission (www.AdventistMission.org), which cares for the Seventh-day Adventist Church's Global Mission initiative and Mission Awareness. He is married to his best friend, Bettina, and they're the proud parents of a beautiful seven-year-old daughter, Bethany. Gary is the author of hundreds of published articles and the book, God's Great Missionaries. *Before moving to the United States, Gary worked in Australia as creative director for the South Pacific Adventist Media Centre and as an editor at Signs Publishing Company.*

1. Gene Weingarten, "Pearls Before Breakfast", *Washington Post*, April 8, 2007, <www.washingtonpost.com/wp-dyn/content/article/2007/04/04/AR2007040401721.html>.
2. Walter Brueggemann, "Conversations Among Exiles," *The Christian Century*, July 2–9, 1997, pages 630–2.
3. Flannery O'Connor, "Revelation," *Everything That Rises Must Converge*, Farrar, Straus and Giroux, 1965.
4. Doris Betts, "Whispering Hope," *Image: A Journal of the Arts and Religion*, Issue 7, Fall 1994.
5. ibid.
6. Ellen White, *Evangelism*, page 125.

ART THAT TELLS TRUTH

Creativity and Evangelism

Neale Schofield

In Amsterdam's Rijksmuseum hangs the intriguing painting "Fishing for Souls." The artist, Adriaen Van de Venne, depicts fishing boats catching naked humans and hauling them in from the icy waters of Holland.

On one side of the river are the Protestants, lined up in an orderly fashion, beneath a flourishing tree on the riverbank. Their boats are filled with successful evangelists and the painting depicts a large number of people rescued in their fishing nets—and, no doubt, happy to be.

The Catholics are on the other side of the river. The Pope is being carried through the crowd in his 1614 version of the "Popemobile," past a withered tree while dark clouds fill the sky. In front of him are several fishing boats, at least one of which is close to capsizing. These boats are in trouble, not due to the success of their evangelistic efforts, but rather their inability to be good fisherman.

The "lures" on each side seem to be the difference. The Protestants have the Bible in their lead boat, while the Ten Commandments and the Latin words *Fides*, *Spes* and *Charitas*—faith, hope and love—are sown into the nets. On the other hand, the most prominent Catholic boat is full of musicians and incense. It is virtually a floating orchestra as they attempt to lure people into their boat through the beautiful sound of their Christian songs.

The point of Van de Venne's painting? Soul winning is much more successful using the solid foundation of the Bible, Christian virtue and the Commandments than using flimsy devices such as music and the arts—ironically, represented in the medium of this painting.

To a large degree this painting resonates with many Adventists. In fact, one could be forgiven for thinking "an

Adventist might have painted this." However, when we stop and review our history as well as our current condition could it be that in the rush away from the arts the church has lost something?

The atheist provocateur, Stephen Fry makes this comment,

> God once had Bach and Michelangelo on his side, he had Mozart, and now who does he have? People with ginger whiskers and tinted spectacles who reduce the glories of theology to a kind of sharing.[1]

The question we need to ask in our church today is this: instead of using the Bible or creativity in evangelism, why not have both? Perhaps it is not an either–or discussion. The Bible is always the foundation of our beliefs. That is a given and should never be compromised. But why not communicate the Bible's message in a way that adds further colour, depth and understanding? Perhaps there are things of the Bible and of God that could be communicated more fully with the help of creativity. In fact, if we carefully examine the character of God, it seems that we should not even try to separate His Creativity from His Truth.

The arts have an incredible capacity to take a story from being grey to gripping. From reaching the head to reaching the heart. From being downright boring to fixing your attention and compelling you to laugh or cry. Engaging the arts may find you sensing yourself in the very situation and becoming part of the action.

> The arts have an incredible capacity to take a story from being grey to gripping. From reaching the head to reaching the heart.

Insights from experience

My early days were in a family where my sister was a musician while my stepfather was an artist. The house was littered with trumpets, flutes, paints and easels. In my youthful arrogance, I would look at them and think to myself, *Why don't you get a real job? When I grow up, I will be a businessman!*

After completing university study, my specialty became marketing and strategic planning. This eventually took me into the heady world of advertising. There I found my business partners were all writers, artists and film producers.

There is one business meeting that I will never forget. We presented a television commercial to a multinational food company—that makes the world's most delicious chocolates, so I'm told. It was my role to present the details of our strategy, including the target market, the key objectives and the USP—the unique selling proposition, the "killer fact" that would be highlighted in the commercial. The client listened to our presentation and some discussion took place to ensure we were all on the right track.

After all this, our creative director presented the creative concept. What happened next was a pivotal moment for me. The client rose out of his chair, his eyes lit up and his whole facial expression changed. He was captivated by the creativity. The strategy and message I had proposed moments earlier had suddenly come to life when framed within the creative concept.

At that moment, the Lord impressed me to work for Him in the area of providing evangelistic resources that are both true to the Bible and are creatively expressed.

We sometimes criticise—even chastise—our fellow church members for not being involved in witnessing to their friends. But if we were developing professional, creative Adventist resources, I believe our church members would be proud to share them with their friends. And perhaps we could also empower individuals to think of other creative ways to share Jesus, using their own unique giftedness and expression.

Think about it.

We have a special God-given message to share with the world.

As Seventh-day Adventists, we need to communicate this message in a way that captivates their attention, that pins people back in their seats. We need to share our faith in ways in which people are so interested in what we are saying that they tell their friends, "You *must* read this book! You *must* see this film! You *must* listen to this music!"

Here's the point: creativity is a vital component of fruitful evangelism.

Add to this: the creative story is much more important than the format or the media platform.

For example, I have heard many church leaders express the "need" to have "something"—a "presence"—on the internet or social media. There is an assumption that use of these vehicles will result in automatic evangelistic "success." But it is what we have to say that is most important, not the platform, forum, format or media.

If you stubbed your toe, you could put that story on social media and all over the internet, but few will read it and even fewer will be moved by it—except perhaps for your mother. Similarly, a document listing the church's 28 Fundamental Beliefs or a sermon on the Sabbath might not be as interesting to society as we think it is. But if we have a great story, told in a compelling and creative way, then we can take advantage of and best use all the new and old media technologies we have available.

Not another tele-evangelist

While in the United States recently, my wife and I turned on the television. Coming from a nation where we usually only access a small number of channels, we were fascinated to be able to flick through hundreds of channels, including dozens of Christian channels. Sadly, we had difficulty determining which were more dull—the Christian channels or the shopping channels. While I am sure many of these broadcasters are well intentioned and may well be used by God to touch some people, a bunch of preachers yelling and screaming at their audience or round-table "discussions" that were really just sermons by four or five people were not really our idea of engaging viewing.

Media commentator Mark Dreisdadt puts forward a number of reasons why Christian television lacks creativity and interest:[2]

1. Most Christian television is created to please the donors, not to reach non-believers.

2. Most Christian television is more about ministry exposure and product sales than evangelism and discipleship.
3. Many people give to Christian television ministry because they believe they have a right to exist, not because they actually watch it.

For me, his next point is the most significant:

4. Hollywood takes what is fake and makes it look real, while Christian TV tends to take what is real and makes it look fake.

There is one thing without a doubt: the devil knows the importance of creativity in advancing his cause. He uses creativity to "evangelise" the world to his own end. Think of so much of the music industry, the film industry, the top-selling books of the world.

If the Adventist church spent even a fraction of the budget of a Hollywood blockbuster on media evangelism, it would probably cause major discussion and even concern. But the devil spares no cost and employs literally trillions of dollars and some of the best creative minds in the world in the promotion and dissemination of his cause. The result? Confusion. Depression. Atheism. A growing rejection of religion, faith and God. If God does exist, He is depicted as miserable and mean. The Christian life is mocked and audiences are encouraged to throw caution to the wind and "enjoy life."

We have the beautiful privilege of sharing the good news of a God who is good and loving, Who offers something far greater than what the world offers. Why not share this in a way that can speak deeply and resonate with souls and hearts?

Of course, Jesus was the ultimate creative evangelist. He had none of the media we have today but that also freed Him up from many of the broadcast temptations of the tele-evangelists. Whoever He was with, and wherever He was situated, determined the methods He used. He would creatively communicate the message, then drive it home. Whether He used fish, dirt, spit or just brilliant stories, people flocked to hear Him and we are still captivated by His teachings.

When many Adventists think of "evangelism" the first thought of course is public evangelism. Public evangelists have long been known for their creativity, in various ways. Stories are told of early evangelists setting up large images of Nebuchadnezzar's statue from the prophecies of Daniel and having a rock come down a rope to knock down the image into a pile of rubble. Almost certainly, their attendees still have a mental picture of such a creative stunt and the imagery it created.

In my own experience in evangelism, creativity has always been a vital part of developing an engaging program. Each of the program elements such as artwork, scripts, visuals and music all play a key role. Well-told stories and creative illustrations are also pivotal to the understanding and retention of the message. More importantly, they enable the message to convict people through the power of the Holy Spirit. This is paramount in leading people to a decision for Christ.

Beyond evangelism

One of the recent projects I have been involved with demonstrates the potential for creativity in evangelism—and has been recognised as such outside the church. Adventist Media Network (based in Sydney, Australia) is an "arthouse for evangelism" so everything AMN does is designed to creatively communicate the gospel. In my view, our recent project *Beyond the Search*[3] is one of the most exciting and effective creative evangelism resources in the church today. This is a multi-platform evangelistic tool for church members to use personally, publicly or digitally, something they can be proud to share with their family, friends and community.

The *Beyond* series has already won 14 global film awards, 10 of these being secular awards. Along with receiving a coveted CINE Gold Eagle award, *Beyond* won an award from the United Nations for being a voice that is "turning dissension to peace; chaos to harmony and dreamers into change-makers."[4] The Accolade awards won by *Beyond* recognised "those filmmakers, television producers, videographers and new media creators who produce fresh, stand-out productions. It is a showcase for cinematic gems and unique voices."[5]

Beyond is just one example of the integration of creativity with evangelism. The series has been developed to share the full Adventist message in a unique and creative way. I believe it demonstrates how creativity should be used for the mission we have been given. In the context of evangelism, a message without creativity is difficult for people to hear or connect with and creativity without substance or that does not touch people's hearts is pointless.

However, we must also remember that, important as they are, being strategic and creative is not a replacement for the Holy Spirit. In fact, the only way we can faithfully use the creativity we have been endowed with is in connection with the Holy Spirit. Nonetheless, when working for the Lord, when sharing the message that is so dear to us and so important for the world, we must use the best and sharpest tools available to us.

In contrast to the opposing approaches to "fishing" portrayed in Van de Venne's painting, we are not forced to choose between sharing the truths of the Bible and the best in artistic creativity. Rather, it is the importance of the Bible's truths that calls for the best of our creativity.

—Neale Schofield is chief executive officer of Adventist Media Network, based in Sydney, Australia. He has degrees in marketing and has worked in senior marketing manager and strategic director roles in the corporate world. He has also been a church planter at "Fountain in the City" in central Sydney. Neale has been married to Coralie for 20 years and they have a chocolate Labrador named Cyrus.

1. Quoted in Mark Sayers, *The Road Trip That Changed the World*, Moody Publishers, 2012, page 268.
2. "Making religious TV work," <philcooke.com>.
3. See <beyond.info>.
4. <unaglobalwakeup.org>.
5. <accoladecompetition.org>.

THE SPIRITUAL INFLUENCE

Creativity and Design

Anthony Rigg

An overriding atheism surrounds much of the creative industry. In the architectural sector, a bastion of such beliefs, the notion of God in design is rarely—if ever—considered. And when one does broach the subject, the response is either aggressive opposition or a glazing over of the eyes, a shutting down of the brain and a crab-like scuttle to another topic. Yet I have heard it said in these same circles that their experience of a beautifully crafted space, like art and nature itself, can evoke something akin to a transformational spiritual experience.

In a moving scene shown on podcast, well-known interviewer, Charlie Rose was touring Bilbao's famous Guggenheim Museum with the building's architect, Frank Gehry. With them was renowned designer Philip Johnson. As the three gentlemen stood in the foyer looking up at the breathtakingly beautiful interior, Charlie asked the 95-year-old Johnson what he thought of the structure. With obvious emotion, the great designer replied, "Architecture is about tears, it is about love, it overwhelms." The moment captured this man—who had devoted his entire life to creative expression—being completely overwhelmed by the thing that still moved his soul: exceptional design.

If creativity can affect us so deeply that it moves and changes, why is it that we as humans find it so hard to acknowledge or, better still, actually *desire* divine inspiration? Could it be that we just don't know what inspiration feels like, so we're not sure if we've had it or not? Is it because of the subjective nature of design, that to imply that one is receiving inspiration from God suggests the design is perfect when to an onlooker it could seem strange or even faulty?

Other issues might also arise in our minds: Could the costs involved in building such creations be prudent spending for the time we live in? Why would God conceive of such things if the money should be spent on the poor and needy? What are the values or spending agendas of the heart of God? Does He have a prioritised list of projects we should be investing our dollars into?

One place to go for answers to these and other ethical concerns must be the Bible. If we look directly into God's word, we immediately come across evidence of heavenly-directed projects:

1. Solomon's temple

> Then David gave Solomon the plans for the Temple and its surroundings, including the entry room, the storerooms, the upstairs rooms, the inner rooms and the inner sanctuary—which was the place of atonement. . . . "Every part of this plan," David told Solomon, "was given to me in writing from the hand of the Lord" (**1 Chronicles 28:11, 19**).

David's drive to honour God literally built a platform for a meeting of minds surrounding architecture. How exciting that must have been for David to conceive with the Maker of the Universe the plans and details for a building that is described as the most astounding and costly structure to have ever been built! Did God know that in a matter of decades, it would become a war bounty, completely and utterly destroyed? Did that deter Him from making it a top priority for earthly expenditure? It seems not! Perhaps His desire for relationship and connection between Himself and His people was worth it. Perhaps in His mind, He wanted to give humanity a glimpse into His extravagant heart for intimacy with us, no matter the cost.

Upon completion of the temple, nation-wide celebrations marked the opening and God Himself showed up in such intensity of Presence that the priests could not enter the temple because the glory of the Lord filled it. A whole nation of people fell on their faces and worshipped God saying, "He is good! His faithful love endures forever!" (**2 Chronicles 7:3**).

Could God want to be involved in design and construction to this extent again where a whole nation might be changed, a whole culture transformed by His Presence?

2. Noah's ark

> So God said to Noah . . . "Build a large boat from cypress wood and waterproof it with tar, inside and out. Then construct decks and stalls throughout its interior. Make the boat 450 feet long, 75 feet wide, and 45 feet high. Leave an 18-inch opening below the roof all the way around the boat. . . . But I will confirm my covenant with you. So enter the boat—you and your wife and your sons and their wives (**Genesis 6:13–18**).

Design can be critical to survival—and God knows it. He downloaded such specifics that the ark Noah built withstood a storm that destroyed every other man-made thing on the face of the earth. Could it be that the same God has designs for structures that will withstand the onslaught of the natural disasters on our planet today? Could it be that He is yearning for someone to access these through intimacy with Him in order to stem the loss of life and devastation fires, earthquakes, tsunamis, floods, hurricanes and cyclones bring? Could it be that He has the solutions to housing crises for the earth's poor, for renewing slum areas, for providing shelter for those who have none, for low-cost accommodation for single mums, the elderly or the disenfranchised? It seems consistent with covenantal Love. Imagine faithful designers who work to protect, shelter and rescue people in trouble by creative constructions built in sustainable and affordable ways.

3. Moses' snake

> Then the Lord told him, "Make a replica of a poisonous snake and attach it to a pole. All who are bitten will live if they simply look at it!" (**Numbers 21:8**).

God literally used a piece of art to focus the attention of the people on Him. In a place of utter chaos, panic and death, God ordered Moses to erect a tangible symbol of His future sacrifice. This was to raise such a level of faith in those who believed and looked, that it actually attracted the healing power of God into the person, defeating death and causing life to come rushing back into their bodies! If it happened then, it could happen again. God's desire or ability to heal has not changed. His desire to use the arts is no less impacting.

4. Tabernacle of Moses

> Then the Lord said to Moses, "Look, I have specifically chosen Bezalel son of Uri, grandson of Hur, of the tribe of Judah. I have filled him with the Spirit of God, giving him great wisdom, ability, and expertise in all kinds of crafts. He is a master craftsman, expert in working with gold, silver and bronze. He is skilled in engraving and mounting gemstones and in carving wood. He is a master at every craft!" (**Exodus 31:1-5**).

One of the most exciting references in the Bible in relation to design is found in the account of a Jewish artisan named Bezelel, whom God called and anointed to complete exquisite works of design and craftsmanship. Remembered thousands of years after they were created, these pieces have become another revelation of God's delight in beauty and art. And to add an exclamation mark to the Spirit's celebration of creativity, Bezalel was the first person mentioned in the scriptures of whom it was said that he was "filled with the Spirit"!

Remembered thousands of years after they were created, these pieces have become another revelation of God's delight in beauty and art.

All these examples involved divine strategy to accomplish earthly projects. These people's lives and experiences, their accomplishments and works were not just to serve the people in their generation, but were to declare God's ability and desire to "do it again"—to continue creating. This is the core goal of testimony—to glorify God again and again in every successive generation. He cares about design and how things work, so He chooses a man or woman He can use as a vessel, not only to bring glory to His name but also to bring His Presence, salvation and healing to the earth just as David did, Noah did, Moses did and Bezalel did.

During the outpouring of Pentecost, Peter recognised the fulfilment of the prophecy spoken by the prophet Joel, "'In the last days,' God says, 'I will pour out my Spirit upon all people. Your sons and daughters will prophesy. Your young men will see visions, and your old men will dream dreams. In those days I will pour out my Spirit even on my servants—men and women alike—and they will prophesy'" (**Acts 2:17, 18**). In the power of the Holy Spirit, every person has the capacity for glorifying God and bringing about His will through connecting with heaven, dreaming with God and creating on the earth.

Transformatve design

Around the world, we see evidence of architecture that has literally changed the dynamics of whole cities. In the city of Bilbao, Spain, the city's struggling industrial port precinct was closing its shipyards and factories one after the other in the mid-1990s. The future of the local population was looking bleak and uninspiring.[1]

It was an unlikely site to be chosen by Thomas Krens, then-director of the Solomon R Guggenheim Foundation. Visiting the city, Thomas spotted the industrial wasteland on his daily run. Despite the depressive scene, the director's eyes saw things extraordinarily different to the reality confronting the locals. Following this vision, Thomas commissioned the highly awarded and somewhat unconventional architect Frank Gehry to design a masterpiece.

Disgruntled local citizens and council caused a ruckus in the planning stages, declaring the building an "eye-sore." But, almost 13 years on, the structure has been labelled a "miracle building," single-handedly reversing the city's financial woes. The museum became an instant tourist attraction, now pouring an estimated 300 million Euros per year into the coffers of the city of Bilbao.

Hailed as a "signal moment in the architectural culture" because it represents "one of those rare moments when critics, academics and the general public were all (ultimately) completely united about something,"[2] the building has redefined the city not only as home to an iconic, world-famous structure, but also by bringing about a cultural unity that has given the city a voice around the globe.

I don't know if Frank Gehry believes in a deity but, if God wants to pour out His Spirit on all flesh, we all have the opportunity to be a conduit for renewal, regeneration or even revolution. Jesus wants the effects of His kingdom to be felt on the earth *before* He comes again so that all people might come to know Him. And the primary way He has chosen to do this is to fill His sons and daughters with His creative Spirit!

God is interested in problem-solving at both the macro and micro level. The Guggenheim in Bilbao is one effective example of architecture on a large scale but what of the micro? What about the hand of God in design, say at the level of the family home?

Australian architect, Peter Stutchbury, is a multi-award-winning designer whose renown has attracted international residential design commissions. But what is remarkable about his creations is that few of his houses have ever been sold.[3] The owners are so delighted with their homes that they are not willing to move, because to move would be to compromise.

Stutchbury's appreciation of place in design, coupled with his understanding of sustainability, has refined an uncanny ability to design homes for his clients in a way that brings joy in living. He acknowledges that this "gift" is largely to do with the spirituality of his mother. How able is one, whose mind is connected with God, to design for the delight and comfort of their clients?

As a designer, I find myself incredibly moved by works that enhance the surrounding environment, intimately working with it, not against it. There is a sense of humility in architecture that is continually pointing toward things other than itself. A humble yet carefully considered home entices one into an experience rather than trying to bring glory to itself. And that experience is all the more glorious when it interacts with the fabric of nature. An outstanding example of this is the Fallingwater house designed by Frank Lloyd Wright, an accomplished and widely-recognised American architect. Out of the many potential house sites available on the owner's land, he chose to build the house directly over a waterfall creating a "close, yet noisy dialogue with the rushing water and the steep site."[5]

Learning from the Creator's creation

For the creationist, nature provides us with the most refined example of God's creative expression. All over the globe, due to advancements in biology and engineering, we are witnessing the emergence of what is an entirely new movement in design thinking. "Biomimicry" involves the examination of nature, its models, systems, processes and elements to emulate or take inspiration from in order to solve human problems.[6]

> There is a sense of humility in architecture that is continually pointing toward things other than itself.

A spearhead in this movement, Janine Benyus states, "We have approached fabrication in the past with a heat, beat and treat method, while nature on the other hand always creates conditions conducive to life itself." It is an exciting model for the future of creative expression as it plumbs the depths of the mind and heart of the Great Designer. Already we are being impacted by its effects with companies employing discoveries found in nature to solve major issues. In architecture, structures like Rem Koolhaas' CCTV building in China have adopted similar engineering principles to the way a tree is arranged in terms of molecular density. The structure of the building increases in solidity around areas where it needs strength and minimises its bulk were it doesn't.

Another more industrial example is the Shinkansen Bullet Train of the West Japan Railway Company. This is the fastest train in the world, traveling up to 275 kilometres per hour (170 miles per hour). A problem occurred when the train would emerge from a tunnel causing air pressure changes to produce large thunderclaps—a sonic boom of sorts—causing nearby residents to complain. Eiji Nakatsu, the train's chief engineer and an avid birdwatcher, asked himself the question, "Is there something in nature that travels quickly and smoothly between two very different mediums?"

His reflections led him to the kingfisher—a bird that can dive from the air into water with hardly a ripple.

Modelling the front of the train after the beak of the kingfisher resulted not only in solving the noise problem, but unexpectedly saved 15 per cent on electricity and caused the train to travel 10 per cent faster.[7]

It has been suggested that biomimicry can offer more than 30 million well-adapted solutions to human design issues. To me, it would make perfect sense that God would point human beings toward the very thing that depicts His own creativity—nature.

The call to faithful design

However, as optimistic a picture as this paints, Christians have barely made a mark in problem solving on the world stage. The overriding mindset that everything will end soon and be transformed at a later date has produced a laissez-faire attitude. This disabling mentality has so pervaded some parts of Christianity that this has created a massive gap in critical leadership around the globe and has seen the keys of culture creating and decision making being handed to unbelievers to lead many advances in technology, science, the media, politics, education and the arts.

As those who embrace spirituality, should we not be at the forefront of our industries? Not with a pompous, holier-then-thou mindset but through humility portraying to a hungry world the beauty of what can be achieved when in relationship with the Creator of all, enticing them into the same. I believe God is looking for a people who want to tap into the creative heart of God for humanity.

For the Spirit-filled architect, this might manifest in the form of designs that have been prayed about and received through dreams or inspired thought, homes that have been anointed and environments that have been dedicated as "God spaces." If we devote time to hearing from Him on behalf of those we are working for, our work should have the capability of being more relevant and life-giving than we could hope to produce in our own strength.

The motivation to reveal God to the world has to be one of love born out of personal relationship. God made each one of us so unique that if we aren't pursuing individual expressions of creativity, a perspective of God is never revealed to the world. It is not just the famous artist, songwriter or poet who gets to make an impact. It is the everyday you and me living in intimacy with the Spirit that reveals God Himself to the world.

We should be working with the Spirit to bring Jesus His full reward. If, as the scriptures say, He paid for not only humanity's salvation, but also our healing and deliverance,[8] then we—in our earthly redeemed actions—must unite with His purpose to become conduits of the re-creative power of heaven so that, at His return, Jesus receives all He paid for (see Revelation 21:24–26).

We have the incredible honour of participating in the redemption of souls through the artistic expression of His will on the earth, that people would be so moved and deeply impacted by our art as to seek out its Source. How amazing then to be able to give Jesus this gift that we will only ever get to deliver while in this unique earthly condition!

Ephesians 5:27 talks about Jesus coming back for a bride without spot or wrinkle. I like to think this could go beyond just the transformed mind and into the physical surroundings of our earth. After all, Christ did teach us to pray while as residents on this planet, "on earth, as it is in heaven" (**Matthew 6:10**). As strange as it may seem, I view well-considered architecture to be jewels on this earth, crowning it just as a bride's wedding dress is adorned with beauty.

What an honour to be invited to participate with heaven in dressing the bride for the return of the Bridegroom! This is the ultimate call to "rise and shine" (see **Isaiah 60:1**).

—Anthony Rigg is managing director and founder of Bleuscape Design, a multi-disciplinary design firm operating out of Brisbane, Australia. With a strong creative bent toward architecture at all levels, the firm's body of work spans the east coast of Australia from Melbourne to northern Queensland. His passion for creativity has also seen him contribute through writing and speaking engagements in both Christian and non-Christian circles. He currently lives in Brisbane with his wife Jaki and two kids, Jed and Eden.

1. <www.architects-talk.com/2011/01/frank-gehry-talks-about-guggenheim.html>.
2. <en.wikipedia.org/wiki/Guggenheim_Museum_Bilbao>.
3. <www.leadershiponline.co.za/articles/other/1413>.
4. <www.ozetecture.org/oze_NEW_portfolio_peter.html>
5. <en.wikipedia.org/wiki/Organic_architecture>.
6. <en.wikipedia.org/wiki/Biomimicry>.
7. <www.biomimicryinstitute.org/case-studies/case-studies/transportation.html>.
8. Significantly, the Hebrew word *sabal* means to carry, bear the weight of, and is used in Isaiah 53:4 in reference to both *makov* (pain) and in Isaiah 53:11 with reference to *avon* (iniquities/sin). He bore both on the cross!

EUREKA!

Creativity and Science

Lachlan Rogers

When Archimedes lowered himself into the bath, a number of things happened almost simultaneously. The warm water washed over his body, stimulating millions of sensory receptors in the skin. His mind, weary from focusing on a perplexing puzzle, drifted into mental repose and out of nowhere he suddenly knew, in an instant, the answer he was looking for.

Archimedes uttered the legendary cry of "Eureka!" and euphorically ran from the baths and down the street. Famously, he was still naked.

The concept that struck Archimedes in the bath is remarkably simple. He realised that an object lowered under water will displace—push aside—a volume of water exactly equal to the volume of the object. This principle is still taught in introductory physics courses today and it can seem almost obvious. It is easy to gloss over the fact that Archimedes had thought of a brand-new idea. Nobody had ever formulated this physical relationship as a tangible idea in a human mind, capable of being transferred from one person's imagination to another. This was a moment of intense creativity, as Archimedes converted a string of thoughts, observations and motivations into this new concept of buoyancy. He didn't create buoyancy—but he did create the concept of buoyancy.

Science as creativity

It is not surprising that Archimedes made his tremendous breakthrough while bathing. Quite a lot is known about how creative thought processes work in the brain, and defocusing the mind with something like a warm bath can produce the perfect opportunity for an "Aha" moment. The connections to science and creativity are vast. In fact, we can use science to better understand creativity. But this is not a chapter about the science of creativity. Instead, I am going to focus particularly on the creativity of science.

Science is a creative way of living and thinking. It is innovative and inventive and many of the other words we usually associate with creativity. It is often understood that science is about answering questions that have never been answered before. This is true—but it is also about asking questions that have never previously been asked, and that is a remarkably creative process.

It is quite possible you've never thought of science being a creative activity, partly a result of the "creative medium" being rather technical. Imagine yourself back in kindergarten grappling with the strange shapes that could be crafted with a pencil. "This is the letter A," your teacher would say, "and this is B." There was not much creativity apparent at this stage of learning to write—in fact the rules could be stifling. The shapes had to be copied so precisely, and inventing a new letter was not encouraged. A little bit later, these letters were put in groups and called "words." Here again, there was little room for creativity. Mixing up the arrangement of letters was called "incorrect spelling," not "creativity."

Only after these basic skills of the "written medium" were mastered did it became possible to write creatively. Even then, an author is constrained predominantly to use words that already exist.

The creativity of science is more like inventing new words. But science is not like writing gibberish. In order to invent new words effectively, it is first necessary to have a knowledge of existing words. Since modern science has been expanding its vocabulary for four centuries, there is a lot of learning required before creativity can be expressed. Unfortunately but necessarily, what is studied as "science" at high school is rarely anything more than learning the alphabet. Not many people stick with it long enough to see the "creative writing" of science.

This does not make science superior to other creative endeavours. Even the traditional arts vary greatly in the amount of "prior knowledge" required before creativity can flourish. Painting is perhaps one of the easiest activities to "access creativity," whereas music tends to require skill development over many years because it involves a foundational learning of a language of sorts.

There are a number of ways in which science operates creatively. The experience of Archimedes is an example of *conceptual discovery*, which differs somewhat from the more traditional notions of discovery. The moment Christopher Columbus saw land on the horizon, he had discovered the American continent. This was not a moment of creativity but of observation. By contrast, Archimedes was not the first person to ever see something lowered into a tub of water. However, he was the first to take this observation and imagine the general concept of buoyancy. This was a moment of brilliant creativity.

Science also exhibits creativity in experimental techniques. New tools are continually invented, then adapted for all sorts of tasks beyond the original design brief. This "role re-allocation" is a highly creative activity. The moment Galileo decided to point his telescope at the night sky is an example of this. Using micro pores in rocks to filter and temporarily untwist DNA strands for genome sequencing is another. A tool from geology, when used creatively beyond its context, was able to revolutionise an experimental process in microbiology. Scientists are constantly innovating new ways of using what is in their hands, much like an artist.

Mathematics as poetry

Mathematics is an endeavour closely associated with science, as many scientific concepts are described mathematically. Typically, but incorrectly, maths is thought of as being roughly the opposite of creativity. Here's another way of thinking about it: if science is like a form of creative writing, then mathematics is like poetry. It is a special form of communicating ideas and feelings that transcend ordinary discourse. It has structural and symmetrical and rhythmic beauty accompanying the beauty of what it is talking about. It is particularly creative, because it is less constrained by experimental results and observation. Unfortunately, like some forms of poetry, mathematics can be extremely difficult to access. This makes it difficult to pick helpful examples from the vast plethora of mathematically creative ideas. Returning to Archimedes yields one such helpful illustration.

Almost all of us met numbers as children in the context of counting. There were two apples or five oranges or 10 fingers or 100 cents and so on. We need to count things and numbers are useful for that. But the *idea* of a number is something far more interesting, abstract, powerful and potentially creative than just being useful.

It was Archimedes who wrote to the king saying, "There are some, King Gelon, who think that the number of the sand is infinite in multitude; . . . Again there are some who, without regarding it as infinite, yet think that no number has been named which is great enough to exceed its multitude." Perhaps he was even thinking of the figures of speech we find in the Old Testament. When Abraham was promised descendants that outnumber the grains of sand on a beach (see **Genesis 22:17**), he almost certainly understood this to mean "too many to count." Archimedes goes on to name some numbers that he proves are larger than the number of sand grains that would fill the earth, and even the universe as he understood it to be. In order to construct such a number, he starts with a meaningful "known" number and then builds it up on itself. This is like describing one million as "one thousand thousands."[1]

The point here is that Archimedes constructed a number that was too big to be useful. Even if the universe was filled with grains of sand, this number would not be reached when counting all those grains. We can do the same thing even more exotically today and give a number larger than the count of atoms in the known universe. In fact, today some mathematicians even describe some infinities that are bigger than other infinities. Such numbers are absurd, in that they are literally impossible to visualise or comprehend in a "counting" way. Despite this, mathematicians can talk about such numbers quite sensibly. They still "work" but must be created—or imagined—in the mind.

Within the history of mathematics, there are perhaps as many examples of this kind of conceptual creativity as there are grains of sand on the earth. We can take a physically meaningful concept of a vector—something with size and direction, like wind speed on the weather report—and abstract it into n dimensions. The maths still works even if n goes to infinity! We can arbitrarily redefine what "size" and "distance" mean mathematically, and construct entirely new numbers. We can build algebraic systems that don't need numbers at all, but allow us to do real mathematics with squares and boxes or dogs and cats. Mathematics, in a sense, is a creative game of imagining and describing impossible things.

So why is it closely related to science? The short answer is "because it works." If you want to describe alternating-current electricity, the best way is to use "imaginary" numbers that include the square root of minus one. If you want to explain the shapes of intricate protein molecules, the best insights come from abstract symmetrical patterns in six and seven dimensions. Over and over again, the results of wild and unconstrained mathematical creativity have proved to be the perfect tool for examining nature in "real life."

Another way to the Creator

But why should the abstract mathematical creations of our human imagination turn out to describe nature and the universe so effectively? This question is poignant because mathematicians constantly strive for higher levels of abstraction. This might suggest that history show a gradual decline in the "usefulness" of mathematics—but precisely the opposite is observed. This is a question of such profundity that it has motivated philosophers across the ages. Einstein called it the "unreasonable effectiveness of mathematics." Perhaps it is a clue that our minds are an image in some way of The Mind behind the structures and patterns of nature.

The most prominent people in science have typically been those who have created a human concept that helpfully describes the behaviour of nature. These concepts are often referred to as "Natural Laws" because the universe is so remarkably consistent that it appears to be obeying laws. This reliability and repeatability has piqued the curiosity of many scientists, because there is no inherent reason why our universe should display such consistency.

Coming face-to-face with this kind of natural reality can easily provoke a form of spiritual experience. Einstein wrote, "Everyone who is seriously engaged in the pursuit of science becomes convinced that the laws of nature manifest the existence of a spirit vastly superior to that of men."[2] Even without an Einstein-like understanding of "Natural Laws," the simplest encounter with the complexities and profound ordering of nature can turn our hearts and eyes to God.

Kepler famously described science as "thinking God's thoughts after him". Artists have often used this same quote to describe their own acts of creativity. As King Solomon said, "Nothing under the sun is truly new." (**Ecclesiastes 1:9**)—but both the artist and the scientist are in the business of recording and describing the world around them in new ways. Science not only gives us the opportunity to explore the deepest and most mysterious things of this world—like the artist, the poet and the musician—but also to exercise our creativity in a way that draws us closer to the Creator and fulfils His plan for us.

—Lachlan Rogers is a research physicist currently working at Universität Ulm in Germany. At school, he once claimed to be a "scientist not an artist," but while studying science at Avondale College he realised the foolishness of that distinction. His PhD led into research that involves playing with individual atoms in glowing diamonds. His spare time is spent cycling, taking photos and creating LEGO® towers with his son.

1. You can read Archimedes' manuscript in Stephen Hawking's book *God Created the Integers*.
2. There is a somewhat intricate context behind this quote: <quoteinvestigator.com/2011/12/16/spirit-manifest>.

MY HISTORICAL–PROPHETIC IMAGINATION

Creativity and History

Lisa Clark Diller

I am a historian. Since I study English history, many people think I should also be able to think creatively about poetry and literature and art. I can't. I don't. Not only that, but I'm not artistic in any of the other obvious ways. I'm terrible at things requiring an eye for beauty. My language is plain, even prosaic. I don't listen to or even have an appreciation for music. I grow restive at any activities requiring or celebrating "creative outlets."

While many other historians likely *do* have such imaginative skills, I am good at my job because it doesn't seem to require much innovation or any ability to "make something up" (which is at least one simple definition of creativity). Here is what historians do: we read widely and deeply into the sources, synthesise the evidence and articulate the answers to our research questions in both oral and written form. This is often just as boring as it sounds. I think of creativity—or anything requiring it—as being much more exciting than what I do.

However, because I am a Christian, and because, beginning in graduate school, I continue to be shaped profoundly by Christian scholars who have urged me to think creatively about how my faith shapes my study, I find myself constantly pushed to see how imagination and inventive thinking might make me better at my work. Historians such as N T Wright have also reminded me that working for beauty alongside justice is how we create space for the kingdom of God among us. So I have become committed to promoting the efforts of those who have skills at beauty and imagination. And gradually I have learned how I can also be part of that in my own research.

First, I have learned how the study of the past is part of the creative work of God. Because of the incarnation, because Jesus took on human flesh, the study of people—and of this world—has value. Even though no society has ever reflected God's ideals fully, by studying humans and their organisations and ideas, historians give significance to God's children. We are doing what Jesus did in coming into the world and identifying with the messed up and dysfunctional community He was born into.

But Jesus not only announced the fallenness of the world, He announced its redemption. So as a historian with an imaginative eye, I will expect to see both sinfulness and transcendence in the world. I will see both people who cooperate with exploitation and power-grabbing, and people who work against it and who, despite their fallen state, act in ways that promote beauty and justice. As followers of Jesus, Wright reminds us, we are not only to be "kingdom announcers," but also "crossbearers."[1] Historians often bear the cross of telling uncomfortable stories. This kind of storytelling can make people angry, but it can also effect a holy work of repentance within them.

A broader understanding

Historians help us widen our understanding of who the people of God are—who we see as connected to ourselves. They bridge the gap between the past and the present.

One of my Christian undergraduate professors, Ben McArthur, was the first to tell me this. "Historians are society's prophets," he urged. Historians keep us from idolatry. As prophets, we can point out the idols of our time and widen our imagination to help us worship God with bigger hearts and minds. When we study history, we are learning about the children of God in different times and places. This expands our view of who God is and how people have responded to Him.

> The best way to respect God's children in another time and place is to help them speak honestly to the living.

It widens my heart and mind to see the huge variety of what it means to be made in the image of God and to see people from very different times and places as reflecting His image. They are no more or less created in His image than am I. This causes me to see God as bigger and more varied than I would if I only stayed familiar with my own time and place. Too often, I tend to think of God as being made in *my* image.

We no longer see our own day as the primary place where God resides and acts. We develop affection and links to people who have sought God in faraway places and times. This helps keep us from the idolatry of the present, from reading the Bible as only speaking to our current time and place. For instance, historians remind us that Scripture has spoken to others, and that some people have even worshipped the triune God as illiterate Christians—without the benefit of the Bible, but no less fully submitted to God and trying to live out His salvation in their communities.

This respect for people in the past, seeing them as fully created in the image of God, and therefore worthy of esteem, may actually help me be *more* creative in my profession. In the words of Christian scholar William Katerberg, it restores some of the "wonder" of history. "History belongs to the living," Katerberg reminds me, "insofar as they are active and striving, preserving and admiring, or suffering and in need of liberation." Because, in one sense, the past is finished and there is no way of changing what has gone before. The best way to respect God's children in another time and place is to help them speak honestly to the living.[2]

When my students and I try to read and understand the texts of the past, and to allow them to speak prophetically to us, we are participating in the ministry of redemption. We do this not by believing that whatever those in the past said and did was the right thing, but by seeing it as one alternative for how to be in the world, as one way to try to make sense of being human. We can see the outcomes of choices people made and as we look at their justifications of themselves and the consequences of their actions, this can allow us to have more imagination regarding the possible penalties of our own rationales and actions today.

Historical alternatives and choices

The study of history is not monolithic. There is not only one way of viewing the past and the lessons are not singular. The job of the Christian historian is to help us be more creative in seeing how many choices there have been in the past and, by implication, how many there still are today. So when we try to understand the past, we are expanding our imagination.

Things did *not* have to be as they are. Recognising this can cause us to change how we act now and create new possibilities for the future. This is what the biblical prophets did. While they predicted outcomes based on current actions, they were always begging people to behave differently so that they could have a different result.

The prophets frequently recounted the history of God's people to them for the purposes of steering them on better paths for the future. When they did this, they helped exercise what Peter Goodwin Hetzel calls "prophetic imagination."[3] This act of imagination creates sympathy in us. Such sympathy allows us to love better, as well as to notice that there are always other ways of acting and being.

As a Christian historian, I want to focus on what the biblical prophets so often called attention to—the plight and experience of the poor and powerless. I raise my imagination above the experience of the powerful states, the elites of a society, and think about those who Jesus was most attentive to, who the prophets wrote about: the victims, the people who worked for justice.[4] I will call attention to how societies have constructed systems that exploit, have imprisoned people unjustly, have economically oppressed for their own wealth, have colonised and enslaved the children of God. Like Mary, Micah and Isaiah, I will help sing a song—a historical song—that makes way for the Messiah. While they prepared people for His first Advent, I hope to help live out the kingdom of God as we wait for the Second Advent.

Sometimes prophets—such as Sojourner Truth, the 19th-century escaped slave who worked for racial and gender justice in the United States—turn the old stories upside down in order to show how God works on the side of the oppressed. White Christian elites in the United States had often told the history of their nation as a history of the New Israel. But Sojourner Truth retold this story with the slaves featuring as the biblical Israelites, upending white Christians' image of themselves for prophetic purposes.[5]

This is also the work of the historian. We not only point out the ways in which systems in the past worked both for better and for worse, but we help reveal the ways in which systems can be constructed that better benefit the weak and downtrodden. This is the way we help widen imaginations to envision a different sort of political economy, one with more justice.

Creatively questioning today

The next creative act for the historian–prophet is to allow the past that I study to shape my vision for the present. Even more challenging, Katerberg argues that my study of my subject must shape *me*.[6] But, for example, how does studying the Atlantic economy of the 17th century make me a better person, someone better able to love?

These questions are difficult because they are not obvious. We have to be careful of the "self-evident." It is not enough to say, "The Atlantic economy was oppressive because it was based on slavery." That's the obvious work. But that doesn't help shape me or my students. We are already against slavery. But seeing the ways in which Christians were implicated in the economy, the ways in which the wealth of Western European states was fully funded by the system of exploitation, the ways in which the development of capitalism and modern nation-states *required* empire and un-free labour—this is complicated.

And it takes creativity to see how the people at the time might have chosen differently. How could a merchant in the 1690s have participated in the Atlantic economy without basing her or his wealth on slavery? Is it possible for my students and me in today's world to invest or save for retirement *without* also being implicated in systems of exploitation and pollution of the environment? Such questions are acts of prophetic imagination that the study of the past can provoke. The more I teach about the modern world, the more I see the truth of this.

Such questions are acts of prophetic imagination that the study of the past can provoke.

Each year in my World Civilisations class, around the time we study World War I, we read an essay by the Christian scholar Paul Griffiths. He addresses the question of what makes it seem possible, even obvious, for Christians to kill other Christians in the service of the state. There is a particular history that explains why we do this.

"For us, and for a long time now, citizenship rather than religion has provided the principal bond of solidarity in the service of which we shed our own blood and that of others," Griffiths writes. "In the great slaughters of the past century or two in Europe and America, Christians have killed Christians and Jews have killed Jews because they were separated by citizenship in time of war. It would have seemed odd—treasonably, seditiously odd—for an English Christian in 1914 or an American one in 1941 to have refused to kill or die for his country because he might have to kill his co-religionists on the other side. . . . We American Christians all know, deep in our bones, that when it comes to the shedding of blood, citizenship trumps baptism."

Griffiths calls for us to exercise creativity in the face of what he sees as a tragedy. "It's never clear where acts of imagination will lead," he says. "But some results are likely. Beginning to imagine the world as if religious solidarities were more important than national ones would inevitably divert imaginative effort from depicting and ornamenting the glories of the nation and of citizenship."[7] Here we have an American scholar acting prophetically—calling for creativity in viewing the past and present, all in the spirit of having a wider view of God's children.

Of course, as a Seventh-day Adventist historian, I have an even stronger prophetic view of the ugly role that might be played by my own nation-state in the world. Because I am part of the Body of Christ worldwide, I have access to an imagination that sees my fellow believers as belonging to many different political communities.

Prophetic imagining, however, not only points out the "places of death," it seeks to show how they could be "transformed into spaces of hope."[8] We can choose to look beyond the histories of the powerful to see when alternative visions of hope have been put forward and to inspire our contemporaries with the possibilities they could also, with the help of the Holy Spirit, construct in their own societies.

My creative tasks

This process has helped me change my self-image. I get to be creative and exercise prophetic imagination every day. These creative acts—considering historical alternatives, embracing a broader understanding, and creatively questioning today—also chastise me regarding my own idolatry, my desire to create God in my own image and to value myself and "my people" as more worthy than other humans. Such scholarship pushes me to work more energetically for the kingdom of God in my local community, to see beauty and alternatives for serving God all around me.

—Lisa Clark Diller is a historian who teaches at Southern Adventist University in Chattanooga, Tennessee. In addition to 17th-century religion and politics, she enjoys service/activism in her urban neighbourhood and ministry in the local church community she and her husband Tommy helped start in 2008. Her academic credentials enable her to talk about history and politics—but her passion is learning how to be part of the kingdom of God, and she loves the friendships and adventures that come with discipleship.

1. N T Wright. *The Challenge of Jesus*, Intervarsity Press, 1999, page 188.
2. William Katerberg, "History, Hope, and the Redemption of Time" in *The Future of Hope*, Miroslav Volf and William Katerberg (eds), Eerdmans, 2004, pages 58–64.
3. Peter Goodwin Hetzel, *Resurrection City*, Eerdmans, 2012, pages 40, 47.
4. ibid, page 52.
5. ibid, page 88.
6. Katerberg, ibid, page 57.
7. Paul Griffiths, "Allah is My Lord and Yours," *The Christian Century*, October 17, 2006, pages 8f.
8. Hetzel, ibid, page 138.

EIGHT PORTRAITS OF FAITHFUL INNOVATION

Creativity and Justice

Chris Blake

1—Metropolitan Kyril

During World War II, the Nazis were forcing Jews into boxcars in Sophia, Bulgaria. Distraught Jews, many sobbing hysterically, awaited their fate at the train station. Suddenly a tall man appeared wearing a black robe and a flowing white beard. He was Metropolitan Kyril, the Orthodox Church prelate.

In *Which Jesus? Choosing Between Love and Power*, Tony Campolo recounts what happened next:

> As he approached the entrance of the barbed-wire enclosure, the SS guards raised their machine guns and told him, "Father, you cannot go in there!" Metropolitan Kyril defiantly laughed at them, brushed aside the guns, and went into the midst of the Jewish prisoners. The apparently doomed Jews gathered around him, wondering what a leader of the Christian community would have to say to them at this desperate time. With arms upraised, Metropolitan Kyril recited one verse of Scripture from the book of Ruth. He helped to change the destiny of a nation as he shouted, "'Wherever you go, I will go—your people will be my people! Your God will be my God!'"
>
> With these words, the frightened Jews were suddenly turned into an emboldened mob. They cheered their Christian friend. The Christians on the outside of the barbed wire enclosures cheered with them, and they became one in the Spirit. Responding to the noise at the train station, the townspeople came out of their houses and joined the crowd.
>
> The SS troops, surveying the scene, decided that discretion was the better part of valour. They boarded the train without their captives and left the town.

2—Show us the mayhem of war. All of it.

On my office door hangs a photo of the Franklin Delano Roosevelt Memorial in Washington, DC, along with his quote: "I hate war."

I hate war, too. Much like cursing, war is the result of a dearth in diligent innovation, a capitulation to carnal impulse. Yet the myth of redemptive violence remains a sturdy icon, belying all evidence. As an elderly Iraqi man lamented, "We killed Saddam and created a million Saddams."

War has been romanticised, merchandised, mechanised, and deodorised. Innocent civilians killed are now called "collateral damage." The US Army doesn't kill the enemy anymore; it "services the target." Occupations are identified as wars. Instead of an invasion, it's a "predawn vertical insertion." Spraying an area with machine guns is dubbed "reconnaissance by fire."

We are informed of "precision bombs"—an obscene oxymoron. Guided missiles carry their deadly cargo along with the label "peacekeepers." Bullet points are for documents. Sudden death is in sports. Doublespeak erodes our corporate conscience; our language serves principally to desensitise us to what is truly happening. After all, "All's fair in love and war." (*Really?*)

Photographs, however, do not lie so easily. The Vietnam War was brought to an end largely by photographic images transmitted to horrified viewers in the United States.

So wherever warfare descends, send us back images of headless children, limb-strewn yards, mothers shrieking with unavailing grief. Show us weddings blasted to shreds, the bridal veils replaced by burial shrouds. Depict cratered houses, their walls stained red. Stay long enough to focus on teens with missing hands and legs owing to land mines. Compile a visual journal of the toxic uranium wasteland that follows a bombing run.

To be fair, portray also all the humanitarian good done by military personnel—the schools rebuilt, the remaining bridges guarded, the marginalised protected.

I'm a journalist and I say, "Show it all. Every bloody bit." I want to know where my tax dollars are going.

3—The nonviolent Philippine revolution

After the tainted Philippine presidential election in February, 1984, dictator Ferdinand Marcos announced he was victorious over the wildly popular people's choice, Cory Aquino, widow of martyred Benigno Aquino. As darkness settled over Manila on Saturday, February 22, at 6.30 pm, Minister of Defense Juan Ponce Enrile and Fidel Ramos, a much-respected general, held a press conference in Camp Aguinaldo. They announced, "We can no longer support Marcos as our commander-in-chief—because of our honest belief that he did not receive the people's mandate in the election."

It was essentially a death notice. They were marooned at the camp, surrounded by a thin circle of military men. But at 9.00 that night, Cardinal Jaime Sin made another announcement. In *Kingdoms in Conflict*, Charles Colson describes what happened next:[1]

Sin's familiar warm voice suddenly came on Radio Veritas. He ordered all nuns into their chapels where they were to pray continuously until God delivered the Philippines. Then he spoke to *all* Christians. "Go to Camp Crame and Camp Aguinaldo. Lend your support to Enrile and Ramos. Protect them and bring them food; they have nothing to eat."

Within 30 minutes, two million people were on the streets. Unarmed, often gathered as church groups, they simply waited, listening to their radios, praying and singing through the long night. . . .

With barbed-wire fences for their backdrop, they organised into shifts for the vigil. They read Scripture, sang hymns, made signs. Everyone felt the tension. This was a protest that could end in blood.

The next day Marcos' troops began to come. One long column of tanks and trucks carried a regiment of marines. . . . Groups of marines armed with automatic rifles leaped out of the trucks and jogged to the front. They took up menacing positions, guns ready. The general came forward with his bullhorn and ordered the people to disperse. The huge milling crowd, composed largely of women and children, instead moved closer. Some held out crosses; others offered flowers. Still others were praying. An old woman in a wheelchair cried out for the soldiers; kill her if they must, but not their own people. . . .

Many threw themselves to their knees and began praying out loud. The general ordered his men to start the tanks. The people prayed louder above the roaring engines. The tanks jerked forward, their treads creaking and clattering. There were high screams of horror; men held their heads, anticipating the moment when the first bodies would be crushed. But just as the lead tank reached the first kneeling bodies—many of them priests and nuns—it stopped.

For just a moment there was virtual silence. Then the crowd let out a prolonged cheer. The top of the tank opened and a helmeted, bemused soldier poked his head out, looked around at the masses of happy people, and shrugged his shoulders, as though to say, "What can we do about this?"

By Monday morning, there were dozens of such tanks on the streets all around the military camps, stopped not by antitank missiles but by the bodies of praying Filipinos. Young soldiers sprawled on top of their beached vehicles eating food offered by the people who had stopped them.

On Tuesday, Marcos fled the country, defeated.

4—Interview with Yolanda Blake, my exquisite wife and a superb teacher

CB: Not long ago, you instituted a creative policy for justice in your classroom. Please explain what happened.

YB: Too much of my time was being taken up by listening to my second-grade students [about age 7] tattling on other students, generally to get them into trouble.

CB: What did you do? How did you work out a solution?

YB: I bought an inexpensive spiral notebook and wrote "Tattle Book" on the cover. If they wished to tattle, students had to take the book to their desk, note the date and write out the problem as a formal letter to me with their signature. (Also, they couldn't read other people's entries.) They then returned the book to its proper place, and I would later check off that I had read the entry.

CB: Was this approach successful?

YB: Absolutely. The children felt heard (which is what they wanted most), they learned to communicate in creative, nonviolent ways and their tattling decreased. The class climate grew much more peaceful. Also, I could address the issue at the most convenient time for me. They never complained about the process.

CB: Do you think the United Nations could adopt a Tattle Book?

YB: I believe the United Nations would benefit from more brainstorming and more communication.

CB: I'll contact our UN Ambassador right away.

World Tattle Book

Sample Entries:

Dear Secretary-General,

Israel has been relocating their new residences on our property in the West Bank. This really bothers us. Also, they built a tall, stinky wall that cuts off many of our people from each other.

Sincerely, Palestine

Dear Secretary-General,

Palestine keeps bothering us with attacks. Please tell them to stop. They make us distrust them. Tell them we'll let them have their own nation if they'll stop the bombs and stuff.

Sincerely, Israel

5—Mahatma Gandhi on creative redemption (from the film *Gandhi*)

Nahari: I'm going to hell! I killed a child! I smashed his head against a wall.

Gandhi: Why?

Nahari: Because they killed my son! The Muslims killed my son!

Gandhi: I know a way out of hell. Find a child, a child whose mother and father have been killed, and raise him as your own. Only be sure that he is a Muslim and that you raise him as one.

6—Four paths toward lasting peace

The official Adventist church document[2] titled "A Seventh-day Adventist Call for Peace" proclaims:

> While it is inevitable that nations and people will try to defend themselves by responding in a military way to violence and terror—which sometimes results in short-term success—lasting answers to deep problems of division in society cannot be achieved by using violent means. . . . From both a Christian and a practical perspective, any lasting peace involves at least four ingredients: dialogue, justice, forgiveness and reconciliation.

7—Thursday, April 26, 31 AD

Each appears distracted, too busy to notice, but all know.[3] Mindless chatter can't hide their gnawing unease. At a feast, it's customary for a servant to wash the feet of the guests, and while the pitcher of water, the basin and the towel are in place, no servant appears. The disciples manifest an engaged unconcern, seemingly unaware that anything needs to be done.

Jesus waits, watching. He longs to tell them things that will ease their imminent pain and confusion, but they are not ready, for jealousy and discontent dance feverishly in their eyes. They are still surmising who will be the greatest in the kingdom of heaven. Earlier, James and John had asked to sit on either side of Jesus' throne, now all of them are livid with resentment. John reclines on the left side of Jesus, Judas on the right side. How can Jesus show them that humility constitutes true greatness? How can He kindle their love for one another?

Slowly the Master rises from the table, lays aside His outer garment and wraps the towel around His waist. With shocked interest the disciples look on. Without a word, Jesus pours water into the basin and begins washing the disciples' feet. The abashed disciples look away and look within.

Jesus reaches Judas. He bends down to His knees, lifts one of Judas' filthy feet, bathes it thoroughly, the basin water darkening, and rubs the warm skin dry with the towel. Then the other foot. Gently, around the toes of His betrayer.

With a thrill of sympathy, Judas experiences the love this Man holds for him and is tempted to confess his plans. But he will not humble himself. His pride is too fierce. Hardening his resolve, he views this act as the cinching piece of evidence that Jesus could never be a ruler. *A king would never debase himself like this. This kingdom is a fraud.* He will never wash another's feet. It is beneath him.

When Peter's turn comes, he exclaims, "Master, are You going to wash my feet?" Jesus' meekness is tearing Peter apart.

Jesus replies, "You don't understand what I'm doing, but later you will understand."

"No," Peter asserts. "You will never wash my feet."

Jesus looks into Peter's eyes. "Unless I wash you, you have no part with Me."

"Then, Lord, not just my feet," responds Peter, "but also my hands and head."

Jesus stifles a smile. "One who has already washed," He says, "needs only to wash his feet." After washing each disciple's feet, Jesus comments, "Now you are clean." His gaze travels around the circle until He stops at Judas. "Though not every one of you."

Two weapons for a conqueror: a basin and a towel.

8—A Different Prayer (Franciscan blessing)

May God bless you with discomfort
At easy answers, half-truths, and superficial relationships
So that you may live deep within your heart.

May God bless you with anger
At injustice, oppression and exploitation of people,
So that you may work for justice, freedom and peace.

May God bless you with tears
To shed for those who suffer pain, rejection, hunger and war,
So that you may reach out your hand to comfort them and
To turn their pain into joy.

And may God bless you with enough foolishness
To believe that you can make a difference in the world,
So that you can do what others claim cannot be done
To bring justice and kindness to all our children and the poor.

Amen.

—Chris Blake is a custodian at Union College in Lincoln, Nebraska, US, where he cleans up student thinking and language. He has written many books and hundreds of published articles. Chris is also the astoundingly youthful grandfather of Campbell and Judah Blake.

1. Charles Colson, *Kingdoms in Conflict: An insider's challenging view of politics, power, and the pulpit*, Morrow and Zondervan, 1987, pages 325–7.

2. Dated January 10, 2006, <adventist.org/beliefs/statements/main-stat52.html>.

3. This section is taken largely from Chris Blake, *Searching for a God to Love*, Pacific Press, 2008, pages 153–4.

THE ART OF LIFE

Creativity and Living

Nathan Brown

A few months ago, I took the opportunity to visit the travelling exhibition of the finalists of the Archibald Prize, one of Australia's best-known and most prestigious art prizes awarded each year for the best portrait painting. The criteria for the competition encourages artists to paint portraits of Australians who have publicly contributed to the arts, letters, science or politics, and part of the popularity of this annual competition and exhibition is that many of the subjects of the paintings are well known, meaning the artist's portrayal of their subject is open to assessment and judgment by even the most amateur art critic.

As such an amateur, viewing the 41 paintings selected as finalists, I was surprised at the number of self-portraits in the exhibition. In one of the gallery's rooms, I paused and counted that nine of the 19 paintings—including the prize winner and runner-up—were self-portraits. I was disappointed, not only because I was deprived of the "celebrity spotting" offered by the other paintings but also because, as a survey of this kind of art and creativity, it seemed too self-centred and self-serving. I later discovered that I was not the only "critic" who had noticed and questioned this trend.

Of course, there are pragmatic reasons for this. The entry conditions for the Archibald Prize require that the portrait be "painted from life"—that the artist gets to know their subject personally and has them participate in at least one live sitting. Arranging time and place for such sittings can be difficult and potentially expensive, when considering the busy-ness of most prominent people and travel costs. So it is understandable why many artists choose to paint themselves or each other.

While convenience is not always the best criteria for worthwhile art, there is a measure of truth reflected in such an act of creative self-representation. There is a sense in which all art is about the artist. As William Zinsser comments about writing—but his statement could be equally applied to all acts of creativity—"Writing is an act of ego, and you might as well admit it."[1] Zinsser later makes the distinction between ego and egotism—the first, necessary for creativity, the second, a drag on it—and, despite its well-established place in the traditions of art, where individual examples of self-portraiture fit within this distinction often seems open to question.

But there is also a deeper truth, perhaps not intended by some of the artists but hinted at in some of the other self-representations I viewed that afternoon, that the artist's life is an important work of creativity in its own right. And this is even more true in the faithful life of the creative Christian.

In *Art and the Bible*, creative Christian thinker Francis Schaeffer put it like this: "No work of art is more important than the Christian's own life, and every Christian is called upon to be an artist in this sense. He may have no gift of writing. No gift of composing or singing, but each man has the gift of creativity in terms of how he lives his life. In this sense, the Christian's life is to be a thing of truth and also a thing of beauty in the midst of a lost and despairing world."[2]

Living creativity

One of the recurring tasks of this collection of perspectives has been to reflect on the meaning of creativity. But the call to faithful creativity gives this term the widest possible meaning: creativity is primarily a way of living life. It is never only on the page, canvas, musical instrument or stage of whatever kind. It is first about the home, the community, the workplace, the school, the office, the church and the street. Wherever we have a choice how we live, respond and react, we can choose creativity or not.

Our most important acts of creativity might never be awarded, framed, published, performed, sold or even recognised. Large or small, they make a difference in the lives of those with whom we have influence. At times, this may call for artistic creativity within our skills and abilities but, perhaps more often, it might be about simply showing up and doing our part—but doing it well, doing it thoughtfully, doing it creatively.

Jesus was quoting from Deuteronomy when he explained the greatest commandment as loving God (**see Mark 12:30**), so this command was first given in the context of the larger laws that encompassed all of life, worship, annual festivals, care for health, care for others, care for land and animals, even what we eat. As suggested by the second "great" commandment—love for others as ourselves—loving is not so much a fuzzy feeling but active living. So loving God is not about our feeling so much as our faithfulness, loving and living with passion, engagement, energy, purpose and creativity, living "with all our heart, all our soul, all our mind, and all our strength" (**see Mark 12:30**).

Truth and beauty

Such creative living will be focused on the most important values, including truth and beauty. But our first instinct might suggest that beauty does not belong among the cardinal values of faithfulness, demonstrating our need for a larger and deeper understanding of beauty. True beauty is not the province of salons, fashion or gossip magazines—the "beauty" industry—rather it is the appreciation, sharing and creation of what is true, good and pleasing in so many ways.

In the beginning, God created a world that He described as "very good" **(see Genesis 1:31)**, expressing a contented, justified and healthy pride in not just the function but also the beauty of all He had created. This beauty is a recurring cause for praising God and something God points to in responding to questions about the true nature of life in our world **(see Job 38–40)**. In God's explanations, beauty is an important factor in a proper understanding of His creation and our lives.

We can be tempted to view faithful living as a succession of grim and dour tasks but that is not the world God created or the way of living Jesus taught: "He has surrounded you with beauty to teach you that you are not placed on earth merely to delve for self, to dig and build, to toil and spin, but to make life bright and joyous and beautiful with the love of Christ—like the flowers, to gladden other lives by the ministry of love." Again, this is a call to faithful and beautiful creativity.

Resisting despair

However, we cannot and should not try to deny that we live in a "lost and despairing world." So much around us is broken. So many people are hurt. Violence and power grab the headlines. The problems and tragedies seem overwhelming. We can succumb to compassion fatigue and the paralysis of repeated pain. We are tempted to despair.

Paul responds: "Don't let evil conquer you, but conquer evil by doing good" **(Romans 12:21)**. This is a call to faithful creativity and imagination. Art in all its forms can confront the brokenness and despair around us and within us, as well as creating beauty as an act of profound resistance and hope in the face of seeming hopelessness. We reject the voices that tell us that what we see and feel are all there is and all that can be. Instead, we offer alternative and hopeful acts of imagination that begin to transform the world around us today, as well as pointing to our ultimate hopes about what our world will be and how our Creator will re-create.

> We offer alternative and hopeful acts of imagination that begin to transform the world around us today.

And, as we have seen, this is not only about art but about the faithful art of living well. We resist despair in our choices, actions, engagement, love and creativity, always seeking to overcome evil by doing good, by creating beauty, by practising hope.

Collaboration with others

One of the romanticised images of art and creativity is that of the lonely artist working feverishly in a cluttered studio or remote location, but the art of the creative faithful life is best lived in collaboration. The tasks of creativity are difficult, requiring our best efforts and a healthy balance of ego and empathy. It is more difficult still when practiced as resistance against evil and despair.

The Christian's life as a thing of truth and beauty—our great call to creativity—needs a community of collaboration and support. In the context of the hope we have, the writer of Hebrews urges, "Let us think of ways to motivate one another to acts of love and good works" (**Hebrews 10:24**). We are not expected to do this on our own. We should be able to draw on the resources of a creative and faithful community.

We must also be prepared to contribute to such a creative collective, encouraging others in their creative living and contributing to a community environment in which creative and counter-cultural lives and projects are supported and welcomed. When others fear and attack acts of creativity or when truth is devalued or beauty dismissed as worthless or unnecessary, we will use our voices and influence to create safety and support for those whose work has been criticised and to encourage them to still greater "acts of love and good works."

Collaboration with our Creator

But even this creative role, together with all the other creative calls on our lives, is built on a deeper and greater collaboration with the Creator Himself. The call to live our lives as our greatest work of art is daunting—until we recognise that even this work is one of collaboration with the Great Artist: "For we are God's masterpiece. He has created us anew in Christ Jesus, so we can do the good things he planned for us long ago" (**Ephesians 2:10**).

The art of our lives is primarily God's work, made possible by our collaboration with Him. Our best lives, our best creativity, are based on the grace, hope and love He offers us. The most profound truth and beauty we can imagine are found in His acts of creativity and re-creativity. Our invitation—and our most significant creative act—is to choose collaboration with the kingdom-building creativity of God in our lives and in our world.

Remarkably, our creativity is one of the ways He is at work in our world. Our most authentic and faithful creativity—in all its forms: life, relationships, good works, art, imagination and so much more—spring from our Creator, as do we ourselves, as His masterpieces of creativity. And when we acknowledge this inspiration and this source, the self-portraits our lives create become less acts of ego than acts of worship.

—Nathan Brown is book editor at Signs Publishing Company, based near Melbourne, Australia. He is an editor of this book and a co-convener of the Manifest Creative Arts Festival.

1. William Zinsser, *On Writing Well (30th Anniversary Edition): The Classic Guide to Writing Nonfiction*, Harper Perennial, 2006, page 23.
2. Francis Schaeffer, *Art and the Bible (IVP Classics)*, Intervarsity Press, 2006, page 94.
3. Ellen White, *Thoughts from the Mount of Blessing*, page 97.

About the editors

Nathan Brown is author of six books, including *I Hope*, *Nemesis Train* (a novel) and *7 Gründe für ein Leben mit Gott* (yes, that's German). He has received a number of awards for writing and continues to write regularly for various publications around the world—including writing monthly short stories. He also preaches occasionally and reads quite a bit, some of which is connected to his continuing university studies. Nathan and his wife Angela live in a small community near Melbourne, Australia, with a large garden, a large dog and a small dog, among other animals.

Joanna Darby is an artist, educator and preacher living in Newcastle, Australia, with her husband and two small sons. She received the Gabe Reynaud Award at the inaugural Manifest Creative Arts Festival in 2011, recognising excellence in using the creative arts for ministry. Her work has appeared in galleries in Newcastle, Port Macquarie and Sydney and can be found in private collections in Australia, New Zealand, Canada and the United Kingdom—though most days she spends more time pretending to be a sea turtle and playing trains than in the studio. Joanna is passionate about God's Word—reading it, studying it and preaching it. She is currently pursuing further study at Avondale College, where she also lectures and demonstrates occasionally in the School of Humanities and Creative Arts. Connect with her art at <www.joannadarby.com> or like "Jo Darby—ministry" and "Joanna Darby (artist)" on Facebook.

Nathan and Joanna work together on various events, topics and projects. They are co-conveners of the Manifest Creative Arts Festival and have a shared interest in the church's call to speak and act for justice and the end of poverty and oppression in our world, which has seen them collaborate on projects including the resource website <www.LivingJustice.com.au>.